WHAT IT MEANS TO BE A BAPTIST

Seven Distinctives

WHAT IT MEANS TO BE A BAPTIST

Seven Distinctives

MICHAEL W. McDILL

ACADEMIC

BENNINGTON, VT

For Becky

Table of Contents

Introduction

C an we all get along? This was the question posed by Rodney King, the unmanageably intoxicated man who was beaten by policemen after a high-speed car chase and ensuing struggle in California in 1991. In response to the race riots in Los Angeles after the officers were acquitted, King uttered his plaintiff call for unity as he emerged from the hospital in a wheelchair: "Can we all get along?" This has become the cry of our times. You've seen the "Coexist" bumper stickers, telling all of us who are "religious" to get along. The premise seems to be that religions are causing most of the rancor and violence in the world. If we would just be like the peace-loving secularist, everything would be smooth sailing for the world community. In America we now have red states and blue states representing differing political ideologies. The map is divided, and so we feel that genuine unity is elusive. We can't seem to get along in any area of life.

The same type of question is sometimes heard in Christian circles. Why can't Christians get along? What is the big deal about things like baptism, and how and whom we should baptize? It seems so petty. Can't like-minded believers coexist? Can't we primarily emphasize what we agree on? One answer to that, in part, is that we do actually get along fairly well and celebrate what we share as Christians.[1] But the other part of the answer is where this book comes in. There are principles of biblical truth at stake, which cannot be swept under an ecumenical rug. The viewpoint from within the Christian sheepfold put forth here will be that of the Baptist. You might be thinking: "Oh, here we go with some guy

---

1   See C. S. Lewis, *Mere Christianity.*

thinking he and his group are the only ones who know the truth." Well, can we talk about the truth? Are we to surrender truth for the sake of a shallow unity? You might even find an appeal to something sure and plain could be refreshing. Before you come to a conclusion, let me ask you to set aside any quick judgments. Baptists have never claimed to have a corner on the market of truth, instead consistently pointing inquirers to Scripture. The request here is for a hearing. This seems fair. Determine for yourself whether the case made is based on solid thinking.

One of the principal reasons that Baptists insist on their views is that one's understanding of salvation is affected by his or her view of the church. Who's in the church? How do we *know* who's in and who's out? These questions necessarily affect one's conception of salvation. How do I know that I am delivered from sin and death and the tyranny of the self, and can look forward to a final and conclusive deliverance ushering into eternal life? That is kind of an important question. And believe it or not, your view of church makes a difference in how you answer that question. So as you track the ideas here, you will notice the connection between *soteriology* (the study of salvation) and *ecclesiology* (the study of the church) in Baptist thought.

For example, if a denomination baptizes babies, a worrying question is introduced when it comes to salvation: how and when does the baby have faith? The New Testament is full of assertions emphasizing the necessity of faith (on the part of the person who is delivered from sin and death by God through Christ). He or she receives this salvation by simply believing. This is a conscious and personal decision. It is a *changing of the mind* of which infants and very small children do not appear capable. The potential for someone to think that he or she is right with God because of a baptism in infancy and yet never to have personally believed and professed Christ leads the Baptist to take a firm stand on a biblical view of baptism. A true understanding of salvation is at stake. But not every Christian group sees it this way.[2]

---

2   As an example of the confusion which comes from a glossing of Scripture with traditional theology concerning these matters, take the Tenth Presbyterian Church in Philadelphia. The following is an explanation of infant baptism from their website: "Infant baptism is based upon the continuity

between New Covenant baptism and the Old Covenant rite of circumcision. A considerable amount of Scripture upholds this continuity. In Romans 4:11, the apostle Paul notes that circumcision was the seal of 'the righteousness of faith.' In Colossians 2:11, 12, Paul points to the same spiritual reality (separation from the sinful nature) by means of both circumcision and baptism. Furthermore, the privileges of the New Covenant are hardly less than those of the Old Covenant. The inclusion of children in the covenant is not rescinded under the New Covenant, but is directly affirmed in Jeremiah 31:33 and in Acts 2:38-39. Finally, Gal. 3:27-29, one of the key texts on baptism, relates baptism to circumcision by rejoicing that not only men but women may receive the covenant sign, not merely Jews but Greeks, etc. By baptizing infant children of believers, we take seriously the promise at the core of God's covenant: 'I will be your God and the God of your children after you' (Genesis 17:7; Exodus 19:5, 6; Deuteronomy 7:6, 14:2; Jeremiah 31:33). We take seriously Jesus' words regarding the little children, as found in Matthew 19:13, 14: 'Then little children were brought to Jesus for him to place his hands on them and pray for them. But the disciples rebuked those who brought them. Jesus said, "Let the little children come to me, and do not hinder them, for the kingdom of heaven belongs to such as these." When he had placed his hands on them, he went on from there.' This is not just a story about how Jesus was nice to little children. These are the covenant, circumcised children of Israel (at least the boys were circumcised). And here is the Messiah, the Lord of the Covenant, laying His hands on them for blessing and praying for them to the Father. What an encouragement this is for us to bring our children to receive the blessing of the covenant sign of our Lord. Along similar lines, we note that children of believers are accountable as members of the covenant. In Ephesians 6:1, 4 and Colossians 3:20, 21, the apostle Paul commands children to obey their parents 'in the Lord'. Parents, he says, are to bring their children up 'in the training and instruction of the Lord'. Here we find that the children of believers are treated as Christians, to receive the benefits and obligations thereof. Furthermore, in 1 Corinthians 7;14, in a passage discussing marriage and divorce, Paul remarks that children of a believing parent are 'holy'. Paul is not saying that these children are automatically saved or that they automatically come to faith in Christ; however, he is saying that such children are set apart in God's sight. Finally, we take note of the household baptisms seen in the New Testament (Acts 16:15, 33, 34; 1 Corinthians 1:16). Of only twelve actual baptisms recorded in the New Testament, three of them are household baptisms. Scripture does not tell us that infants were baptized in these occasions, nor

What it Means to Be a Baptist

The denominational label "Baptist" may not mean much to the general population in our postmodern, post-colonial, post-gender, posthuman and, it would seem, for our purposes, post-denominational society. This is not overly disturbing as one examines history, however. Many important events and figures of great consequence have come upon the scene and scarcely been noticed at first. Key historical figures have been scoffed at or ignored early on, only to be lauded for extraordinary foresight belatedly. Winston Churchill comes to mind. One man asked if anything good could come out of a little village called Nazareth. Likewise, simply gauging the current popularity of an idea may not tell us much in the end. Martin Luther, for instance, apparently "rediscovered" a truth which had been staring at anyone with access to the New Testament for a millennium or more when he was confronted with the history-changing phrase "the just shall live by faith." Living, as we do, in a "post-truth" culture does not banish truth from existence. To casually encounter it, however, on the streets of Boston, New York, Los Angeles, or San Francisco is probably unlikely in our current cultural climate.

---

does it say that all who were baptized believed. Indeed, the clear inference from these household baptisms is that those under the headship of the head of the house received a benefit from his/her belief. That benefit was baptism, and a public identification with the church. It is because of this biblical data that our church, along with the whole of the Reformed tradition, baptizes infants of believing adults." (https://www.tenth.org/resource-library/articles/christian-baptism). From a Baptist point of view, it is telling that in the conclusion of the full explanation of Christian Baptism, it is noted that someone joining the Tenth Presbyterian church is "required simply to affirm your faith in the Lord Jesus Christ and your willingness to accept the authority of this church. You are not required to assent to the Westminster Standards nor to the above teachings regarding baptism." Contrast this non-committal stance regarding baptism for those joining this Presbyterian church with the Baptist argument put forth here in the introduction to the book that what a Christian believes about baptism emphatically affects beliefs about the church and, more crucially, potentially fuddles the clarity of the biblical message of personal salvation by faith alone. The idea that children of believers, in some vague fashion, based on conflating the old and new covenants, are in some way part of the church, and therefore ambiguously saved, surely muddies the waters of *sola fide*.

Not only did Luther reintroduce the theological concept "faith alone" to the world, he also, in effect, wedged open a channel for the flood of denominations that became the norm for the modern western world in the centuries to follow. Despite (or perhaps because of) the deluge of new church groups which poured upon the scene of history after the Reformation, the question of how to define the church still hovers in the atmosphere of our times and causes confusion and discomfort for those who claim the name Christian. Throughout the Middle Ages, the church was seen as the gatekeeper of salvation. Since Cyprian famously declared, "Outside the church there is no salvation" in the third century, the accepted idea was that *one had to be **in the church** to be saved.*[3] Although Protestants seized upon a new theology of salvation founded upon faith, it could be argued that they failed to clarify or debunk the idea that salvation is received *through the church.* Exhibit A in this argument would be infant baptism. A baby who is baptized is a member of the church and thus, being inside the church so to speak, is granted salvation. The Roman Catholic church is the model for this notion, but the Protestant reformers also embraced church membership via paedobaptism. Inseparable from the practice of infant baptism is the idea that entry into the church is, in some sense, entry into salvation. The great reformers not only retained infant baptism, bequeathed to them by the Roman Catholic church, but also embraced the medieval devotion to the state-supported church. To be born and baptized in Lutheran or any other Protestant territory was to receive salvation and also to be registered as a citizen. The question arises: are these biblical ideas?

Baptists, on the other hand, have always believed that *one must be saved to be in the church.* This is directly contrary to the medieval ecclesiology *(one must be in the church to be saved)* borrowed by the majority of the Protestants of the sixteenth century. Believer's baptism is the baptizing of those who have made a conscious decision to follow Christ

---

3   The Latin phrase *extra Ecclesiam nulla salus* is translated "outside the Church there is no salvation." This statement comes from a private letter (LXXII.21) of Cyprian, bishop of Carthage, in the 3rd century. The letter was written regarding a controversy over whether it was necessary to baptize subjects who had previously been baptized by heretics.

and, according to His word, have received salvation. Baptism is thus the public and symbolic expression of having already accepted redemption, reconciliation, and rebirth by faith in the promise of God accomplished by Christ's death, burial, and resurrection. The result is that to be in the church, one must be saved by faith. The church, then, is simply composed of those who are saved through Christ and publicly demonstrate this relationship through baptism. Baptists name this arrangement, which they claim is derived from Scripture, a *believers' church* or a regenerate church.

Clearly, this is the biblical definition of church communicated in the New Testament. Without a commitment to believer's baptism, the scriptural concept of a church of believers is not possible. Any mixture of infant baptism into the formula introduces unscriptural ecclesiology and with it the questionable notion that salvation is through the church instead of through faith in Christ alone. The human religious inclination is to trust in the institution and its rites rather than in Christ. The New Testament idea of church is that it is made up of those who have already trusted Him and are His disciples. Faith in Christ, therefore, is the groundwork for the establishment of the organic edifice He founded called the church (as Peter likened the church to a building made up of living stones). The temporal institution or organization, which is only the outward human structure, should never be the object of faith. To take the institutional approach is to veer badly from scriptural truth and introduce considerable confusion into people's minds as to the way of salvation.

In light of the importance of these issues, the theme of this book will be *Baptist beliefs*. How are they unique? How can they be distinguished from other Christian denominations? As we confront these questions, we will access historical and biblical evidence in an attempt to answer them. Church history helps us go back and see how we got here and understand why Christians may seem so intransigent about their differences. The Bible will be our guide as we look at what the New Testament says concerning church and salvation. I will argue that the Baptist perspective on these things is the simplest, and the closest to the biblical view. That is why the name Baptist really has meaning for those who claim it. Are you a Baptist? Perhaps this book will help you understand more thoroughly the principles that go with the name. If you are not a Baptist, then hopefully you will gain a clearer understanding of what Baptists believe. We will explore seven crucial principles that make Baptists distinct: biblical authority, believer's baptism, a believers' church, congregational rule, cooperation for missions, the priesthood of every believer, and religious liberty.

Chapter 1

Biblical Authority

"By what authority do you do these things?" Jesus was asked this question by those who were skeptical of Him. He employed an effective strategy: He answered a question with a question. He asked His skeptics by what authority John the Baptist baptized: heaven's or men's. They could not return an answer.[4] The question of authority is crucial in all times in all circumstances, whether we are aware of it or not. By what authority? We all constantly make decisions and come to conclusions based on some kind of authority. Many claim authority in matters of faith, but what person, institution, or entity can impose genuine accountability upon us? It is rather like the following scenario (before my kids grew up and left home): My daughter instructs my son to take out the trash. My son will inevitably reply, "Who says?" If the response is "Dad," then he will say, "oh." That little "oh" is very telling. He respects the authority of his Dad. He considers his sister to have no authority at all that would require acknowledgment. But the trash gets taken out because of Dad's authority.

Christians, broadly speaking, have a great respect for the Bible. It represents an authority as sacred scripture. Baptists see the scriptures as the *only* authority for Christians. They have generally not added any institution, creed, pontiff, power structure, judicial body, or any other ancient writing to the list of authorities by which the Christian life and church are informed. In fact, there is just the one authority on the list: the Bible, consisting of the Old and New Testaments. It's like

---

4   See Luke 20.

1

telling my wife she's my favorite wife. She's my only wife, and that's actually a more exclusive claim than merely a favorite. My wife doesn't mind being the only one on my list, so there seems to be a place for this sort of exclusivity. Baptists have even been accused of placing the Bible on too high a pedestal. This does not bother them much because the standard Baptist view has been to see the Bible as the very words of God Himself.

The conventional wisdom in our world today is that any claim to truth is questionable, on par with my daughter commanding her brother by her own authority. The approved slogan of the times is that truth is relative. The world family has many dissonant voices claiming to be speaking with authority, but no one really has any. "Take out the trash." "Who says?" "I do!" "*Whatever.*" Everything is relative, and all statements are only a matter of opinion. According to this postmodern view, there is no father figure to whom we may appeal. Or is there? That is just what the Bible claims: that there *is* a Father-Creator who holds ultimate authority by His very nature, so that whatever He says is true. The Bible claims to be those very words of the Father inscripturated and preserved so that we might know, directly from our Creator, what He has to say to us. This is the historic Baptist view. It is *not* a popular view. Modern people see this view as comparable to one of the many children in the "world family" claiming to be a parent when there *are* no parents. To say that you have the truth is seen as utter arrogance in our time. But Baptists correct this misunderstanding by pointing out that Christians who believe the Bible is God's very word to us are *not* claiming to *be* God; they are simply claiming to believe that God has spoken. And if God has really spoken, then by virtue of His nature and authority as God, the creator and author of all, people really need to listen closely to what He says. An example of the importance of listening to God is recorded in the gospel of Matthew: "While Peter was still speaking, the shadow of a bright cloud passed over them. From the cloud a voice said, 'This is my own dear Son, and I am pleased with him. Listen to what he says!'"[5]

---

5   Matthew 17:5 (CEV). Notice that God actually *interrupted* Peter while he was still talking to remind him to listen to Jesus.

BAPTISTS' HISTORICALLY HIGH VIEW OF SCRIPTURE

Since the early seventeenth century, Baptists have held a very high view of Scripture. Of course, not all modern Baptists honor this heritage, some tending to rely more on the current science or culture, but many still affirm Scripture as a sure word from God. This legacy goes back to some of the very first English Baptists, Thomas Helwys and John Smyth. These two were instrumental in Baptist beginnings in England from 1609, and were the leaders of the earliest Baptists, called General Baptists by historians because of a belief in a general atonement. In a book entitled *Baptists and the Bible*, L. Russ Bush and Tom Nettles trace the legacy of Baptists trusting the Bible as the one authority which is infallible and without error, believing it to be God's very words. A reviewer of *Baptists and the Bible* gives the substance of Bush and Nettles' research:

> Beginning with John Smyth and Thomas Helwys, Bush and Nettles demonstrate that the inerrancy of Scripture was a foundational doctrine of the earliest Baptists . . . . Additionally, General and Particular Baptists, although differing in their understanding of soteriology, both held to a high view of Scripture. This theological framework pervaded their confessions and sparked the modern mission movement through Andrew Fuller, William Carey, and Adoniram Judson. . . . Bush and Nettles provide strong support to their arguments that Baptists have a long legacy of believing that Scripture is inspired by God, infallible in its original presentation, and sufficient for all matters of life and doctrine.[6]

Helwys himself said: "The scriptures of the Old and New Testament are written for our instruction (2 Timothy 3:16) and . . . we should search them for they testify of CHRIST (John 5:39). Therefore they are to be

---

6   Keith Collier, Southwestern Baptist Theological Seminary, *Baptist Theology* website: http://www.baptisttheology.org/BaptistsandtheBible.cfm.

used with all reverence, as containing the Holy Word of GOD, which only is our direction in all things whatsoever."[7]

To illustrate that this legacy continued among Baptists, we might consult a statement of faith from about 200 years after the first English Baptists. One of the most widely used confessions of faith among Baptists in America was the *New Hampshire Confession*. It was issued in 1833 by the Baptist convention of, you guessed it, New Hampshire. Concerning the Bible, it says:

> We believe that the Holy Bible was written by men divinely inspired, and is a perfect treasure of heavenly instruction for it has God for its author, salvation for its end and truth without any mixture of error for its matter; that it reveals the principles by which God will judge us; and therefore is and shall remain to the end of the world, the true center of Christian Union and the supreme standard by which all human conduct, creeds and opinions should be tried.[8]

Notice that the idea here is that biblical authority trumps all other sources as far as truth is concerned. This statement equates the Bible

---

7   Thomas Helwys, *A Declaration of Faith of English People Remaining at Amsterdam in Holland*, 1611, article 23.

8   W. J. McGlothlin, *Baptist Confessions of Faith* (Philadelphia: American Baptist Publication Society, 1911), 301-302. The *New Hampshire Confession of Faith* can be found in various primary resource volumes and is available, as are most published documents one hundred years old or more (being in the public domain), on the internet. A profound idea found in this statement that could easily be skimmed over and missed is that unity is founded on scripture truth, so that scripture is "the true center of Christian Union." Unity must be based on truth in the end, or it will not last, and in retrospect will be seen to have been shallow and perhaps even cynical. Unity for unity's sake may sometimes appear effective if fighting a common enemy, but even then the unity is based on a shared truth: the enemy is evil or the enemy must be defeated. Baptists have generally built unity around shared principles of truth rather than a hierarchical organization or a desire to be unified in and of itself.

with the words of God and therefore as eternal and inerrant. These ideas are largely consistent in Baptist history, from Smyth and Helwys to New Hampshire Baptists to many Baptists today. Baptists, then, have traditionally maintained a firm and profound regard for Scripture and its authority.

A Contrast: Early Protestant Ulrich Zwingli

It may help further to highlight the strength of this Baptist belief in Scriptural authority by way of a contrast. We may be able to show a marked difference between the original English Baptists and early Protestants when it comes to Biblical authority. Thus, it will be instructive to take a look at one of the original Protestant Reformers, Ulrich Zwingli of Zurich, Switzerland. Early in the sixteenth century, Zwingli led a Bible study composed of some younger students, his protégés.[9] They were all Christian *humanists*. In other words, they were interested in ancient sources of truth and wisdom rather than simply relying upon the traditional medieval cultural and intellectual constructs of their age. Thus, this Bible study in Zurich was intent on exploring the original Greek New Testament rather than the conventional Latin translation of the Roman Catholic church, called the *Vulgate*. This new edition of the Greek New Testament had recently been published by another Christian humanist named Desiderius Erasmus of Rotterdam in the Netherlands.

Zwingli led his students to look at the New Testament with fresh eyes, not constrained by officially sanctioned Catholic dogma. When the issue of baptism arose, Zwingli admitted that the New Testament asserted believer's baptism and never described any infant being baptized. His pupils took this biblical view of baptism very seriously

---

9   This account is from the 1520s, around eighty years *before* the early English Baptists, Smyth and Helwys, initiated believer's baptism and inaugurated the first General Baptist church in Holland [the Netherlands] in 1609. This 1609 date is generally viewed by historians as the beginning of the Baptist denomination.

and eventually became known as *Anabaptists*. This was an evangelical group during the time of the Reformation which held many of the same convictions that Baptists have held through the centuries. They called themselves *brethren* and thus are known to historians as the Swiss Brethren. These "brethren" sought to follow scripture and, in accordance with their recent New Testament studies, began to advocate adult baptism for believers only and to claim that infant baptism was illegitimate.[10] In response, there were official debates on the subject in Zurich, called disputations, and eventually these former students of Zwingli were outlawed.

Zwingli had decided the best way to advance his reform was by working with the city council of Zurich. Thus, his reform was a total cultural and governmental program, bearing upon every aspect of the lives of the citizens of this Swiss canton. Despite his earlier position during the Bible study days, which had demonstrated believer's baptism to be properly derived from the New Testament, Zwingli became a champion of infant baptism due to this magisterial (state-supported) approach to reform.[11] Zwingli's reform went forward, then, with the power of the state behind it, and thus the power to punish those with contrary reforming ideas. One of Zwingli's former Bible students was put to death for advocating *rebaptism*, as the leaders of the city called it (thus the name Anabaptist, meaning 'one who baptizes again'). On January 5, 1527, Felix Manz was tied up with rope and thrown into the river

---

10 Historian Kenneth Scott Latourette, a Baptist, wrote: "They were called Anabaptists because they insisted that the baptism of infants was not true baptism, that only believers should be baptized, and that if an individual had been baptized in infancy, after he had the experience of being justified by faith he should be re-baptized." Kenneth Scott Latourette, *Christianity Through the Ages* (New York: Harper & Row, 1965), 102.

11 Baptist theologian E. Y. Mullins writes: "Zwingli's clear mind perceived distinctly that the Reformers' principle of faith necessarily excluded infant baptism and so taught in his earlier career. Under pressure of ancient custom, however, and for expediency's sake he finally decided to retain it, and sought to find Scripture warrant for it." Edgar Young Mullins, *The Axioms of Religion*, (Philadelphia: American Baptist Publication Society, 1908), 108.

Limmat, drowned for nothing other than his baptismal theology. "Just two days before his drowning, Zwingli wrote to a fellow Reformer: 'The Anabaptist, who should already have been sent to the devil, disturbs the peace of the pious people. But I believe, the axe [execution] will settle it.'"[12] Manz's execution by drowning was derisively named the 'third baptism' by Protestant leaders in Zurich.[13]

This seems an inauspicious beginning for what came to be known as the Reformed tradition in the Protestant Reformation. The Bible does not sanction either infant baptism or execution for those who deny

---

12   Insertion added. Ruth A. Tucker, *Parade of Faith: A Biographical History of the Christian Church* (Grand Rapids: Zondervan, 2011), 267. The following is Tucker's description of the martyrdom of Manz in full: "In March of 1526 . . . the Zurich city council had enacted a law making believers' baptism (re-baptism) a capital offence punishable by drowning. Manz would become the first Anabaptist martyred for this offence. Insisting that he was not seeking to prevent Reformers from baptizing infants, he argued that his only motive was 'to bring together those who were willing to accept Christ, obey the Word, and follow in His footsteps, to unite with these by baptism, and to leave the rest in their present conviction.' But Zwingli and the city council were determined to make Manz's death a deterrent. Just two days before his drowning, Zwingli wrote to a fellow Reformer: 'The Anabaptist, who should already have been sent to the devil, disturbs the peace of the pious people. But I believe, the axe will settle it.' But Manz would not be axed to death. Rather, officials executed him by his own baptismal prescription—immersion of an adult believer. His death is ridiculed as the third baptism: infant, believers, and drowning—'He who dips shall be dipped!' The story is chilling. Bullinger describes the scene: On a bitterly cold Saturday afternoon in January of 1527, 'Manz was taken out of the Wellenberg prison and led to the fish market there by the Limmat [River]. There his death sentence was read. He was taken to the butcher shop, and then forced into a boat, in which the executioner and a pastor were standing.' A crowd of onlookers, including his mother and brother, had accompanied him. Offered an opportunity to recant, he publicly proclaims his faith, encouraged by his family and other supporters. He is then rowed some distance from shore, where he is pushed into the icy water, declaring his faith in Christ until the water engulfs him."

13   See William R. Estep, *The Anabaptist Story*, for the full narrative pertaining to the Swiss Brethren.

it. Thus, we must look to other sources to find the authority to which Zwingli turned in order to act in this manner in Zurich. An editor of Zwingli's *Selected Works* in English, Samuel Macauley Jackson, comments on Zwingli's change of heart concerning baptism:

> It is doubtless true that in his earlier addresses from the pulpit he exposed the unbiblical character of the church doctrine upon the general subject of baptism, and probable that he inclined towards ruling out infant baptism, as lacking biblical support. . . . Zwingli found himself criticised severely in Zurich when his remarks upon infant baptism were repeated. To those who were brought up to regard baptism as necessary to salvation it was a great shock to be told that the ceremony had no validity. To those who believed that the rite of baptism was the Christian obligation in lieu of circumcision, and just as binding, to hear that there was grave doubt whether it should be so considered was to knock the underpinning from their faith. When Zwingli found that opposition to the popular belief and practice upon this point meant that he would be exposed not only to clerical and lay adverse criticism, but probably would lose him his influence with the city magistrates, who were all friends of the Old faith [infant baptism] on this doctrine, he devoted a great deal of attention to it, with the result that he convinced himself that as to the subjects of baptism he had been wrong, and henceforth he took the orthodox [infant baptism] side.[14]

---

14 Insertions added. Samuel Macauley Jackson, ed., *Selected Works of Huldriech Zwingli, (1484-1531) The Reformer of German Switzerland*, (Philadelphia: University of Philadelphia, 1901), 123-124. Jackson, who was a Presbyterian minister, goes on to describe Zwingli's treatment of his former students who became Anabaptists, whom Jackson calls 'Baptists': "The Confession of the . . . Baptists is in very simple language, showing a very honest and God-fearing mind, and is in itself a triumphant refutation of the charges of fanaticism and immorality which Zwingli brings against them. In fact in this paper Zwingli shows himself up in a very bad light. This is no place in which to describe the *outrageous* treatment which the Baptist party received in Zurich and elsewhere through Switzerland. The writer feels the freer to use such a term because he is

Michael W. McDill

The fact that Zwingli's reform was tied to the city council, and that church and state were not separated in Zurich, would seem to shed light on Zwingli's motivation for supporting infant baptism. Whereas when early on he had floated the idea that infant baptism was improper he had appealed to biblical authority, now as a staunch supporter of infant baptism, his reasons would appear to be more political. In contrast to the persecuting career of Zwingli, the early Baptist leader Thomas Helwys was among the persecuted in his own time, thrown into prison for his beliefs in 1612. He had the audacity to challenge the King of England's authority over church and faith and sent King James a personal note to that effect, written on a copy of his recent essay on religious liberty.

---

not himself a Baptist, but he comes to the subject merely as a historical student. He considers that the part which Zwingli played in this wretched business is a serious blot upon his reputation, and reveals a defect in his character. The Baptists were pursued relentlessly; drowning, beheading, burning at the stake, confiscation of property, exile, fines and other forms of social obloquy were employed to suppress them and prevent their increase. The fact shows plainly that the persecuting spirit in the times of the Reformation was just as rife among Protestants as among Roman Catholics, and that the devil was abroad in the hearts of those who considered themselves on both sides as the true servants of the Lord Jesus Christ, whose tenderness and love must have been greatly tried by these wicked doings of his friends. Peace came at last to Switzerland--the peace of the grave-yard and of the sea which gives not up its dead. The orthodox party congratulated themselves upon having got rid of the pestilential heresy of adult baptism, yet the student of history as he looks upon the large, flourishing and world-wide Baptist church of to-day asks himself which side really won the battle for the right of private judgment and liberty of action, the side of the persecutor or the side of the persecuted?" Emphasis added. Samuel Macauley Jackson, ed., *Selected Works of Huldriech Zwingli*, 125. As Jackson points out, Zwingli was not the only one to oppress the Anabaptists (and others who disagreed with the official Protestant-state position). Calvin secured the execution by burning of Miguel Servetus in Geneva (among others who were punished in various ways there) and even Luther, the great spark of the Reformation, was also guilty of quashing opposition to his own state-supported reform: "'Here I stand, so help me God, I can no other,' cried Luther, though he refused to allow Anabaptists, whom he regarded as anti-social heretics, to appeal to their consciences against Lutheranism." Christopher Hill, *The Century of Revolution* (New York: Norton, 1961), 93.

James reacted negatively, seeing religious liberty as a threat to his authority, and locked Helwys away, where he languished and died as an outlaw because he was willing to stand for his beliefs no matter what political pressure he faced.[15]

Baptists, like the Anabaptists before them, have desired to uphold the Scripture as the final authority, especially for the Christian life and the life of the church. This view of the Bible eliminates baptism for anyone except for believers. It also eliminates any definition of church which includes government interference or coercion. This touches on another issue which will be treated in a later chapter concerning Religious Liberty,[16] but for now, the distinction between a Baptist view of Scripture and the early Protestant outworking of reform in Zurich, in spite of a claim by

---

15   The book Helwys wrote on religious liberty was entitled *A Short Description of the Mistery of Iniquity*: "Thomas Helwys wrote the book at a time when men bent the knee and spoke of the 'divine right of kings.' To question the power of church or rule of king was to risk prison and death; but *Helwys had the backing of the scriptures* and a courage from God, and the rights that he proclaimed were the rights of the common man. He denied that kings had divine authority over the souls of men or could in any way shape their worship. Helwys, the founder of the first Baptist church in England, ignored all threat to his personal liberty, and even risk of his life, so that he might proclaim the freedom of his soul and the same freedom for every man." Emphasis added. James Saxon Childers, ed., *A Way Home: The Baptists Tell Their Story* (Atlanta: Tupper and Love, 1964), 4.

16   It might be said that biblical authority and religious liberty are connected in a more crucial way than it may seem at first glance. Christians who believe that the Bible is the only authority will be vigilant to exclude all other authorities when it comes to truth about God and therefore about eternity *and* temporality. This exclusion would apply especially to any governmental or any other traditional or man-made authority. To watch any authority other than Scripture dominating or assisting churches is to forfeit Christian liberty. To ensure liberty for the Christian, as he or she acknowledges God's word as the ultimate authority, the Baptist has traditionally urged states to ensure liberty of conscience for all. This is not simply enlightened self-interest but has been considered by Baptists as a biblical principle, since Jesus and the apostles never forced folks to believe, but always invited them to repent.

Zwingli to hold Scripture as the highest authority,[17] illustrates the exceptional nature of the Baptist (and Anabaptist) perspective. This perspective designates Scripture as the lone authority for the Christian, excluding all others as constructs of men and thus not fully trustworthy.

One of the themes of the Reformation was *Sola Scriptura*, which in Latin means "scripture alone." What were those in the Reformation excluding with this statement? Primarily they were thinking of the Pope, a man-made authority. How can Baptists today claim that this is a uniquely Baptist distinctive? Baptists would argue that although many Protestant traditions claim to give Scripture alone authority for belief and practice, Baptists have consistently upheld this great Reformation watchword by following the New Testament faithfully with affirmations of believer's baptism and a believers' church. This endorsement of Scripture's authority as all-sufficient was well expressed by a Baptist scholar back in 1900 and still holds true for many Baptists today:

> To believe as Baptists do and stand aloof from other Christians as Baptists have to do in much of their religious life, would be criminal if they are not bound by loyalty to God so to believe and so to stand. Baptists, however, are sure that the Word of God is the only infallible and all-sufficient rule of faith and practice, and that nothing should be taught for doctrine which is not contained therein; and that all that is taught therein must be believed; and that all that is commanded therein ought to be obeyed *as commanded*. This is their first and most fundamental principle as individuals and as a denomination. If this principle is not their distinctive and differentiating principle, the *emphasis* they place upon it *is*. Other denominations claim to believe that the Bible is their rule of

---

17   Baptist historian Robert A. Baker comments on Zwingli's commitment to Scripture and his change concerning baptism: "Zwingli claimed that the Scriptures were his only authority. However, because it would have played havoc with his state support to deny the efficacy of infant baptism, he specifically repudiated the Anabaptists and clung to infant baptism; otherwise he would have 'unchurched' all of his political supporters." Robert A. Baker, *The Baptist March in History* (Nashville: Convention Press, 1958), 35-36.

faith and practice, but some of these do not pretend to make it their *all-sufficient* or only rule. They make a place alongside of the Bible for the traditions of the fathers. And it may, I think, well be questioned if any other religious denomination stands as firm and inflexible as Baptists do upon this article of faith concerning the Bible.[18]

In other words, not only do Baptists claim that Scripture is the only authority, they have actually followed through, preserving the pattern of the New Testament in how to baptize and how to view the makeup of the church. Somebody who claims "Sola Scriptura! That's what we're all about!" and then is found baptizing babies seems to have a problem with consistency. But this is the way many traditional Protestant groups function. So that's why Baptists say that Scriptural authority is one of our distinctive beliefs. After looking at a Protestant example (Zwingli) contrasted with Baptist belief in relation to biblical authority, let's look at Catholicism next. The Roman Catholic Church regards its own tradition as on par with Scripture, and thus equal in authority. This is problematic because traditions of men, which are flawed by definition, have been appealed to by Roman Catholics and set forth as truth.

Another Contrast: Catholicism

The Roman Catholic Church represents another contrast by which to distinguish the Baptist stance on Biblical authority alone. The modern

---

18   Franklin Howard Kerfoot, "Why the Baptist Doctrine," in J. M. Frost, ed., *Baptist Why and Why Not: Twenty-Five Papers by Twenty-Five Writers And A Declaration of Faith* (Nashville: Sunday School Board of the Southern Baptist Convention, 1900), 353-354. Kerfoot continues: "This being true, the answer that any intelligent Baptist has to give to the question, 'Why the Baptist doctrine?' must be, as already intimated, 'Because this is the teaching of the Word of God.' Of course he may be mistaken in his interpretation of the Word, but he can only go by his own understanding of it. And whatever he thinks God's Word teaches, that he must hold and practice. Not to do so would be to him disloyalty and disobedience to God. There can be no compromises with men or with churches where he thinks he has a plain teaching from God." Kerfoot, "Why the Baptist Doctrine," 354.

Catholic church affirms the customs and beliefs of the church which have been added over the centuries, like barnacles on the hull of the great institutional ship. If the ship is listing, it is because it has added the authority of human words and traditions through the years, and ultimately has proclaimed these to be equal with the Bible.[19] In fact, the Roman church claims that the Scriptures' authority comes from the church itself. The *Catholic Encyclopedia* has this to say concerning Scriptural authority in an entry under the word 'tradition':

> The word tradition in the ecclesiastical sense . . . refers sometimes to the thing (doctrine, account, or custom) transmitted from one generation to another; sometimes to the organ or mode of the transmission . . . . At first there was question only of traditions claiming a Divine origin, but subsequently there arose questions of oral as distinct from written tradition, in the sense that a given doctrine or institution is not directly dependent on Holy Scripture as its source but only on the oral teaching of Christ or the Apostles. Finally with regard to the organ of tradition it must be an official organ, a magisterium, or teaching authority. Now in this respect there are several points of controversy between Catholics and every body of Protestants. Is all revealed truth consigned to Holy Scripture? or can it, must it, be admitted that Christ gave to His Apostles to be transmitted to His Church, that the Apostles received either from the very lips of Jesus or from inspiration or Revelation, Divine instructions which they transmitted to the Church and which were not committed to the inspired writings? Must it be admitted that Christ instituted His Church as the official and authentic organ to transmit and explain in virtue of Divine authority the Revelation made to men? The Protestant principle is: The Bible and nothing but the Bible; the Bible, according to them, is the sole theological source; there are no revealed truths save the truths contained in the Bible; according to them the Bible is the sole rule of

---

19   Listing is a nautical term meaning leaning to one side and in danger of capsizing.

faith: by it and by it alone should all dogmatic questions be solved; it is the only binding authority. Catholics, on the other hand, hold that there may be, that there is in fact, and that there must of necessity be certain revealed truths apart from those contained in the Bible; they hold furthermore that Jesus Christ has established in fact, and that to adapt the means to the end He should have established, a living organ as much to transmit Scripture and written Revelation as to place revealed truth within reach of everyone always and everywhere. Such are in this respect the two main points of controversy between Catholics and so-called orthodox Protestants (as distinguished from liberal Protestants, who admit neither supernatural Revelation nor the authority of the Bible). The other differences are connected with these or follow from them, as also the differences between different Protestant sects--according as they are more or less faithful to the Protestant principle, they recede from or approach the Catholic position.[20]

Baptists through the centuries, for the most part, have seen themselves as representatives of a 'protestant sect' of the 'more faithful' kind regarding the orthodox Protestant view of Scripture, so much so that some Baptists have claimed no connection with Protestantism.[21] As we have seen already, Baptists have often taken the Protestant 'sola Scriptura' (Scripture alone) motto to the extreme, even in the estimation of many Protestants, especially in the matter of believer's baptism (thus the name Baptist: I can sense it all coming together in your mind).[22]

---

20   *Catholic Encyclopedia* online, (www.newadvent.org/cathen/15006b.htm)

21   This question of Protestant origins when it comes to Baptist history is not the subject of this book and is a complicated and debated issue. Suffice it to say that the author sees both Protestant *and* other forms of influence (namely Anabaptist) as decisive in shaping Baptist origins.

22   Presbyterians, Lutherans, Anglicans, Methodists, Congregationalists, Reformed, and other Protestant groups all have been baptizing infants from the beginning (though some Protestant churches and traditions do follow the New Testament pattern for baptism). This introduces a confusion into their theology when it comes to salvation, since an adherent of one of these groups

Since Catholics claim that Christ handed down other 'truths' (separate from the New Testament) to the apostles, who then handed them down to others so that somehow they are still with us today, it makes sense that an institutional authority (the Roman Catholic Magisterium) must preside over what may be legitimate or not in these supposedly surplus apostolic traditions.[23] The problem is that a modern group of men decide these issues. Based on what? What, then, is the authority to end all arguments to which the Magisterium turns? By definition, the Catholic Church itself, represented by the Magisterium, serves as this ultimate authority. So we are left with an elite group of Catholic men with all the authority, even over Scripture. In contrast, Jesus appealed constantly to the Scriptures. He was actually the enemy of the Jewish 'magisterium' of His day, the Sanhedrin.[24] Regarding church tradition as authoritative, as is the Roman Catholic approach, makes Catholic dogma dependent on human beings,

---

can easily conclude that he is right with God as a 'Christian' through baptism and miss the simple biblical necessity of faith.

23   The Magisterium of the Roman Catholic Church is the church's authority or office, made up of the Pope and the bishops, to give authentic interpretation of the Word of God, whether in its written form or in the form of Church Tradition.

24   The comparison between magisterium and Sanhedrin was also made by a Catholic television website in a news article: "25-May-2011 -- Catholic World News Brief – *US Jewish-Catholic Dialogue Examines Religious Authority*: Representatives of the United States Conference of Catholic Bishops' Committee for Ecumenical and Interreligious Affairs and the National Council of Synagogues met on May 17 to discuss 'Sources of Authority in Catholicism and Judaism.' 'One of the obvious differences between our two faith communities is that while no one rabbi or religious body can speak for all Jews, the Church has a "Magisterium" made of bishops in communion with the pope, whose interpretation and application of the word of God can be binding on all Catholic believers,' said USCCB official Father James Massa. Rabbi Avram Reisner, professor of ethics at the University of Maryland, noted that only between 200 B.C. and A.D. 70 did Judaism have a body analogous to the Magisterium: the Sanhedrin. He asked, 'Is it any coincidence that the Christian community emerges from Judaism precisely at the time when such a body of authoritative teachers is in place for the parent religion?'" EWTN Global Catholic Network online, (www.ewtn.com/vnews/getstory.asp?number=113507).

who are faulty at best. Thus, the claim that the Roman Catholic institution is the final authority strikes Baptists as unreliable and, compared with the affirmation of the authority of the Scriptures by Jesus Himself, unbiblical.

This Roman institutional approach to religious authority can be observed in a formal and official statement of the Church:

> Thus it comes about that the Church does not draw her certainty about all revealed truths from the holy Scriptures alone. Hence both Scripture and tradition must be accepted and honored with equal feelings of devotion and reverence.[25]

If the Church itself, its tradition, is on a par with Scripture, and the church is seen as the source of Scripture, then it follows that salvation is also from the church. This is exactly what the Roman Church claimed for itself in the twentieth century church council known as Vatican II:

> This holy council first of all turns its attention to the Catholic faithful. Basing itself on Scripture *and* Tradition, it

---

25   *Dei Verbum*, II, 9, in Austin P. Flannery. *Documents of Vatican II* (1975), 755. It is obvious to the outsider that Catholic tradition and Scripture do not always agree. But the tension here between Scripture and tradition is not lost on certain Catholic theologians either. Raymond Brown saw this tension as something of a crisis even in 1975, especially in light of biblical criticism: "I do not mean that the voice of Scripture, critically studied, is the only voice that the Church has to live with and respond to. The voice of Tradition (i.e., church experience and thought in the centuries after the first) has also to have its say. But I do not think that the voice of subsequent Tradition should drown out the voice of Scripture, the tradition of the first century. Nor do I think we should be allowed to gloss over the tensions between the two on the dubious principle that the Spirit always says the same thing. Only when each has had its say, resonant with all the sharpness of the tensions between them, can the Church of our times face its crises with the fullness of Christian experience brought to bear. Scripture is not the master of the Church; but when it is allowed to speak freely, it can serve as the nagging conscience of the Church." Raymond E. Brown, *Biblical Reflections on Crises Facing the Church* (New York: Paulist Press, 1975), vii-viii. From a Baptist point of view, relegating the Scripture to a 'nagging conscience' status is another example of the dangerously troubling nature of the Catholic approach to biblical authority.

teaches that the Church, a pilgrim now on earth, is *neces-sary for salvation*: the one Christ is the Mediator and the way of salvation; He is present to us in His Body which is the Church. He Himself explicitly asserted the necessity of faith and Baptism (cf. Mk. 16:16; Jn. 3:5), and thereby affirmed at the same time the necessity of the Church which men enter through Baptism as through a door. Hence they *could not be saved* who, knowing that the Catholic Church was founded as necessary by God through Christ, would refuse to enter it or remain in it.[26]

It is clear from this statement that the Catholic Church claims to be the only way of salvation. Although the attempt is made to base this assertion on the teaching of Christ in Scripture, it is a tortured logic which includes the necessity of baptism in the Roman church for salvation. This conclusion can only be reached via a syllogism which includes the premise that the Roman church is the 'true' church by reason of apostolic succession. This specific claim is not accepted by all Christians (especially the ancient Eastern Orthodox) and is certainly not contained in Scripture. The Bible states that Christ is the *head* of the church, not the church itself, which is His body. This confusion, and the direct identification of Christ, who said *He* was the only way (John 14:6), with the Roman Church through the centuries, with all of its inquisitions and corruptions, is quite a pill to swallow. Baptists claim no authority other than Scripture in seeking the answers to two crucial human questions: how may I be delivered from evil and death (salvation in Christ alone) and where do I belong while on this earth (with the people of God, the Church). The Bible's answers are much simpler than any religious tradition, and yet deeper and more profound, since they are all focused on Christ Himself and His finished work.

The Catholic approach amounts to institutional magic. If only someone is in the church, as Noah was in the ark, then that person is saved. The church offers its seven sacraments as dispensers of the medicine of salvation, which only the church can confer, by special ceremo-

---

26 Emphasis added. *Lumen Gentium*, 2,14, in Austin P. Flannery. *Documents of Vatican II* (1975), 365-366.

nial incantations of the proper word formulas.[27] Babies are baptized into the church so that the Catholic is *safe* as soon as possible after birth. All of these additions to the Scriptural text have the effect of substituting the Roman rites for what Christ offers: Himself. The Bible speaks clearly of a genuine and direct relationship with God Himself, as a result of the atoning work of His Son, enlivened through the actual presence of the Holy Spirit in the here and now, so that, as Jesus said, one is born again. This wonderful reality is appropriated by faith, not by the brewing in Rome of a mystical-institutional ceremonial 'potion'. The simple, direct approach to God by faith in Christ, Baptists believe to be the Scriptural truth. No mediator intercedes between God and man except Christ, our High Priest and the Lamb of God, who promises the Spirit to those who believe. Thus, no pope, priest, cardinal, magisterium, bishop, deacon, or any other modern man or institution can stand in the gap and offer salvation to a soul.[28] That's why the New Testament called Jesus of Nazareth *the* Messiah, the anointed *one*.

So why is all of this talk about religious authority so important? Well, the question comes to this: Who will tell me the truth about deliverance from evil and death? There are differing claims of authority as

---

27   Only in the 20th century did the Church officially sanction the saying of the mass in the vernacular (common language) rather than in Latin. For centuries, folks knew that unless the proper Latin words were spoken in the mass—*Hoc est corpus meum* etc.—then the salvific effects were void for the communicant. These words must be said by the proper person, an ordained clergyman of the Roman Church. It was and is also believed that the bread and wine became the literal body and blood of Jesus Christ. This is known as transubstantiation, which is Catholic dogma to this day.

28   The theological issue of mediation is at the heart of another key Baptist principle: the priesthood of the believer. Every believer is a priest with immediate access to God Himself through Christ. Christ is the great High Priest and mediator, having given Himself as the sacrifice to open the way back to fellowship with God, doing away with sin and death. No merely human mediator is needed or allowed according to the New Testament (see especially the book of Hebrews). When a priest is required for delivery of salvation benefits doled out by the church, as in Roman Catholicism, this is sometimes called sacerdotalism. Baptists believe this to be dangerously unbiblical. This issue will be covered more fully in a later chapter.

to the way of salvation. The book that claims to be the word of God is at odds with the Roman Catholic institution, which claims to speak for God. A definite choice must be made here, and Baptists have chosen the Bible. In addition, no government or state coercion or influence may alter such a stance for the Baptist, remembering what the apostles said to the Sanhedrin after having been imprisoned: "We must obey God rather than men."[29] The temptation with religion (human approaches to God) is for the institution or religious way to offer a sense of control to the initiate. Just pull the authorized spiritual levers and you will receive divine bene-fits. This is a man-made way to God. From Roman Catholicism to Islam to Buddhism to Voodoo to the New Age, the allure is that of power to command personal supernatural benefit (salvation), but in the end, it is the adherent who is controlled (by rules, institutions, or spirits). The bib-lical way of *faith* represents a sharp contrast. It is simple, childlike trust in God, a *surrendering* of control to a heavenly Father who offers grace and forgiveness, reconciliation and love. This way is the way of God Himself, who by His own authority made salvation possible through His own Son.

A MODERN EXAMPLE OF SCRIPTURAL AUTHORITY FROM THE BAPTIST FAITH AND MESSAGE

One of the most controversial topics in recent years among Christians has been whether women should be placed in positions of leadership in the church, such as pastors or deacons. To do so is culturally acceptable and approved. But what does the Bible say? In simply asking this ques-tion, Baptists appear very hidebound and boorish to many modern eccle-siastical and secular people. Here again many Baptists, along with other evangelicals, come to the issue appealing to the authority of Scripture. Southern Baptists present a statement in their confession of faith, known as *The Baptist Faith and Message*, which addresses this issue: "While both men and women are gifted for service in the church, the office of pastor

---

29   See Acts 5.

is limited to men as qualified by Scripture."[30] This is one sentence, but it represents a plunge against the tide of contemporary conventional sentiments when it comes to women in the church. In many cases, this Southern Baptist view will generate a shrill censure, and perhaps a derisive label for the group as sort of neanderthal cave-men (and women?) by those who claim to be 'offended' by this statement on ecclesiology.

Now, why would Southern Baptists desire to take such an unpopular stance when updating their confession of faith? The answer is a sim-

---

30   *The Baptist Faith and Message: A Statement Adopted by the Southern Baptist Convention*, 2000, article 6. Paige Patterson, former president of Southwestern Baptist Theological Seminary in Ft Worth Texas, expands further on this issue concerning the place of women in the church and biblical authority from a Southern Baptist perspective: "No legitimate question exists with reference to either the adequacy or the acceptability of a woman serving in some teaching roles. Apollos profited not only from the instruction of Aquila but also from that of Priscilla (Acts 18:26). Women are expressly commissioned to teach younger women (Titus 2:4), and Timothy, as a child and presumably even as a young man, was taught by his maternal mentors–Lois and Eunice (2 Timothy 1:5; 3:14). Neither should there remain any uncertainty about the opportunity extended to women to participate in public prayer or prophecy (1 Corinthians 11:2-16). Any suggestion of an ontological inferiority of women cannot survive the first declaration of Adam, 'This is now bone of my bones and flesh of my flesh' (Genesis 2:23), or the statement, 'In the image of God created he him, male and female created he them' (Genesis 1:27). Yet Clark Pinnock observed: '. . . I have come to believe that a case for feminism that appeals to the canon of Scripture as it stands can only hesitantly be made and that a communication of it to evangelicals will have difficulty shaking off the impression of hermeneutical ventriloquism. . . . If it is the Bible you want, feminism is in trouble; if it is feminism you want, the Bible stands in the way.' Why would a theologian of Pinnock's stature and egalitarian sympathies arrive at such conclusions in light of the acknowledged truths stated above? The answer is that for many evangelicals, the Bible is intractably hierarchical. It teaches definite role assignments, together with their corresponding mandates, opportunities, and limitations. Great scholarly efforts have been made to prove this, but–as with other crucial truths–it seems obvious to average readers." Paige Patterson, "The Meaning of Authority in the Local Church," in *Recovering Biblical Manhood and Womanhood: A Response to Evangelical Feminism*, ed. John Piper and Wayne Grudem (Wheaton: Crossway, 1991), 258.

ple one. They believe that the Bible calls for the officers of the church to be men. There really is no other reason. The authority of the Scripture must override any hope for popularity. Baptists see the apostle Paul's admonition to the Corinthians to avoid "going beyond what is written" as an indispensable principle, and therefore resist yielding to a leisurely drift toward societal conformity and going with the flow of conventional culture.[31] Some, echoing the contemporary politically correct thought grid, might accuse Baptists of being 'patriarchal' or even misogynists or 'male chauvinist pigs,' but this would be to misinterpret the intention, which is not to subjugate women in any way. It is simply to order the church according to the New Testament.

In another article from the same confessional document, there is an affirmation of the equality of women as of the same value as men. This part of the statement deals with the family: "The husband and wife are of equal worth before God, since both are created in God's image."[32]

---

31 1 Corinthians 4:6. Speaking of the drift of culture, several modern writers have claimed that our culture is now post-Christian. Gabriel Vahanian, writing in 1961 in a critique of modern culture and current-day Christianity, wrote: "We live in a post-Christian era because Christianity has sunk into religiosity. No longer can this type of Christianity vitally define itself in terms of Biblical faith. Instead, it acquires the attributes of moralism, or those of a psychological and emotional welfare-state. We live in a post-Christian era because modern culture is gradually losing the marks of that Christianity which brought it into being and shaped it. . . . And we live in a post-Christian era because tolerance has become religious syncretism, an amalgam of beliefs and attitudes without content or backbone. Indeed, faith, hope, and love have nothing to do with these substitutes, no more than God with an idol, or my authentic self with the masks I am wearing." Gabriel Vahanian, *The Death of God: The Culture of Our Post-Christian Era* (New York: George Braziller, 1961), 228-229. This appears to be an insightful synopsis of contemporary western culture and its relation to Christianity. Christianity is seen in our time as primarily just another world religion. In spite of the tolerance and syncretism in vogue, anyone who claims exclusivity for Christianity based on Scripture is seen as a dangerous 'fundamentalist,' shouted down and marginalized, even demonized. One thing may be said about Baptists and their insistence on Biblical authority from the point of view of Vahanian's analysis: they surely display the presence of a backbone.

32 *The Baptist Faith and Message,* 2000, article 18.

What it Means to Be a Baptist

This is a clear affirmation of the essential equality of men and women from a biblical point of view. Men and women are of equal value in God's sight, both being made in His image, though they operate in discernable roles in the family and church, which are inherent in their respective genders (having been created male and female by God).[33] Southern Baptist theologian Paige Patterson understands the Scripture as making "a sharp distinction between essence and office." In this distinction we find the greatest example is Jesus Christ Himself. Patterson asserts that in the great Christological passage in the Apostle Paul's letter to the Philippians, it should be understood "that Jesus is equal with His Father in essence but subordinate in His office. Such a paradigm properly applied should remove the stigma from role assignments in the domestic, civil, or ecclesiastical arenas."[34] These views, which simultaneously uphold the authority of the Bible, the sanctity of the family, and the great value of *all* people in God's sight, are scoffed at in our time, but this particular group of modern Baptists adhere closely to them, primarily because they believe that the Bible is God's word. If temporary cultural norms were the guide for Baptists rather than the Bible, we would necessarily have to reject Christ's own words when He said, "heaven and earth will pass away, but My words will never pass away."[35]

There are a couple of important matters to note when it comes to this example of the Southern Baptist confession of faith, *The Baptist Faith and Message.*[36] The first is that this is a confession and not a creed.

---

33   We find that mankind is made in God's image and specifically in two designated and designed genders, which are historically bound together by the narrative of creation and in relation to God Himself: "So God created man in his own image, in the image of God created he him; male and female created he them." Genesis 1:27 (KJV).

34   Paige Patterson, "The Meaning of Authority in the Local Church," in *Recovering Biblical Manhood and Womanhood: A Response to Evangelical Feminism*, ed. John Piper and Wayne Grudem (Wheaton: Crossway, 1991), 259.

35   Matthew 24:35.

36   Three editions of *The Baptist Faith and Message* have been issued over the years: in 1925, 1963, and 2000. The first statement from 1925 was heavily influenced by The New Hampshire Confession of Faith, 1833, and the subsequent editions are updates of the first.

It is not binding upon folks in Southern Baptist churches, but is simply an attempt to express the Baptist faith in session as messengers convene together. It becomes a useful and important guide, but is not an authoritarian creed. Along with that, it is to be understood that this is an attempt to interpret Scripture to the best of our ability as a group of Baptists (I say 'our' since I am a Southern Baptist), to express our understanding of what the Bible says about key articles of the faith. This does not amount to "Thus sayeth the Lord," because the status of being a mouthpiece for God Himself is reserved for sacred Scripture. The second matter of note is that this confession is not meant to be foisted upon other denominations and religions as if every other expression of faith is in error and must be overcome. It is not an aggressive maneuver designed to shoot down other groups. Again, it is simply an expression of faith issuing from a group calling themselves Baptists trying to explain why they take that name, identifying the principles of the faith which are believed to be derived from Scripture.[37] It is published in accordance with a strong belief that God has spoken and can be understood.[38] It is intended for the Baptist body itself as an endeavor to state clearly a self-definition in the form of a set of convictions based on the Bible. The other primary intention is to publish Baptist beliefs for those outside who may desire to know how the Baptist faith is defined. Looking back at the first Baptist confessions in the seventeenth century, Leon Mc-Beth outlines this double purpose: "Their aim was obviously twofold: to those without, they explained, defended, and clarified the Baptist faith. To those within the Baptist fold, the confessions educated, unified, and confirmed the faithful."[39]

---

37 Baptist theologian David Dockery provides the following simple definition: "A confession of faith by a group or a denomination helps to define and to defend their basic beliefs and identity. Baptists, since the seventeenth century, have been a confessional people." David S. Dockery, *Southern Baptist Consensus and Renewal: A Biblical, Historical, and Theological Proposal* (Nashville: B&H Publishing, 2008), 223.

38 This characteristic of the understandability or clarity of Scripture is sometimes called its *perspicuity*.

39 H. Leon McBeth, *The Baptist Heritage* (Nashville: Broadman Press, 1987), 68.

A BIBLICAL AND CHRISTOLOGICAL ARGUMENT FOR BIBLICAL AUTHORITY

Why do Baptists take up such a seemingly extreme position regarding the authority of Scripture alone? Well, some of the logic behind this view of the Bible is that the Scriptures claim this great authority themselves. The Old Testament prophets legitimized their proclamations by prefacing them with "Thus sayeth the Lord" (to use a little KJV lingo). The test for a prophet, according to Scripture, was one hundred percent accuracy. If any of the prophet's predictions were proven wrong, then he was designated a 'false' prophet, one who did *not* speak for God.[40] This is a very high standard,

---

40 Many people say that they believe in Scripture as their unique authority but are inconsistent (Nobody's perfectly consistent, but you want to be as consistent as you can). For instance, Quakers and Spiritualists historically depended on personal revelation in addition to Scripture. Sometimes we might observe that certain modern Charismatic groups use this same spiritualist approach to authority. In some of the Charismatic churches of today, for example, a member might tell you, "The Lord told me to do this or that." What are they claiming? Are they claiming authority? Indeed, they are. And what authority are they claiming? "The Lord told ME." That's quite a statement, isn't it? The Lord told you? Really? Again, we note the test of a prophet in the Old Testament: if he was wrong one time, then he was a false prophet. So, how many times does it take to be a false prophet? Even if it's one out of a hundred times that you are wrong, you are still false (See Deuteronomy 18: 9-22). So, this constitutes a warning against running around telling people the Lord gave you a special, extra-biblical message, because it's a serious matter to make that claim. A lot of people do, though, and say, "Well, I've got the Holy Spirit, and he's talking right to me and has given me a personal revelation." Or they will often say, "He has given me a revelation for you, and God's calling you to this or that." We want to be careful of that. Can God speak to us personally? I would say so. What do we want to do with that? Just assume our own impressions and insights have the stamp of approval of God Himself? No, like the noble Bereans, whom the Apostle Paul commended, we check everything with Scripture! Here's the big question that most people never talk about in church (maybe every once in a while): If they talk in terms of "God told me this, God told me that"–*How do you know it's God?* Isn't that a good question? We just always assume that if it's some kind of special, sentimental message, that it must be God. How do we

which the Scripture sets for itself. Another piece of this logic is that Jesus Himself treated the Scriptures, the Old Testament in His case, as the very words of God. Those who say that an exclusively high view of the authority of scripture compromises the Lordship of Christ seem to miss the fact that Christ Himself treated the Scriptures as the authority which ended all argument.[41] He often said to the Pharisees or Sadducees, "Have you never read the Scriptures?" appealing to the Old Testament as the final authority derived from its status as God's word.[42]

This kind of uncompromising appeal is seen in Jesus demonstrating to the Sadducees the truth of life after death when He quoted God's statement to Moses, "I *am* the God of Abraham, Isaac and Jacob."[43] Jesus noted that God is the God of the living, not of the dead. The whole weight of His argument lay on one small verb and its tense. He also said that not one jot or tittle of God's word would pass away or be invalidated.[44] This is equivalent to us saying today that even the crossing of the t's and the dotting of the i's of Scripture is valid for all time. This is a very high view, equating the Scriptures with God speaking, and therefore we also hear Jesus say things like, "the Scriptures cannot be broken." [45] Jesus also said that His own words

---

know if things are from God? We check with His Word. "Heaven and Earth will pass away, but my words will never pass away," Jesus said (equating himself with God and God's word). We might want to pause before going around saying "Brother, I have a special word of knowledge for you" in light of God's exclusive (and always reliable) authority in His word. Jesus went around saying, "Have you not read the Scriptures?" So this is important. A Spiritualist approach is dangerous, I believe, because of the authority that the Bible claims for itself. It is a grave and solemn matter to claim to speak for God!

41   For a recent treatment of this controversy over Scripture and Christ among Southern Baptists, see Paige Patterson, *Christ or the Bible?*

42   Matthew 21:42.

43   Emphasis added. Matthew 22:32.

44   Matthew 5:18

45   Baptist leader B. H. Carroll spoke of the Scripture as unbreakable: "Now we come to an important point. When these inspired declarations were written, they were absolutely infallible. Take these Scriptures: John 10:35, *'The scripture cannot be broken;'* Matthew 5:18, *'Till heaven and earth shall pass away, one jot or tittle shall in no wise pass away from the law, till all things be accomplished;'* Acts 1:16, *'It was needful that the scripture should be fulfilled.'* That is one of the most

would never pass away, which is an assertion of His own Deity.[46] So, to contend for the Lordship of Christ as having more authority than Scripture, as some do, and thereby to deny Christ's own view of Scripture, seems rather misguided. Jesus saw Scripture as indestructibly authoritative (since it is from God Himself). Jesus the Messiah claimed to *be* God, and therefore His authority is attached to the Scriptures already.[47] Setting Christ against Scripture is therefore illogical and vacuous. If a Christian has less esteem for Scripture than for Christ, then he is claiming to be smarter than his Lord (as if Jesus didn't know there were so-called 'errors' in the Old Testament, as some claim, for instance), or is at odds with Him regarding Scripture's authority. Either way, there is a problem.

Thus, the authority of Scripture comes ultimately from the character of God Himself. It is not a separate authority but linked with the heavenly person Himself. Scripture has God for its Author. It is inspired

---

important points in connection with inspiration, viz.: that the inspired word is irrefragable, infallible; that all the powers of the world cannot break one *'thus saith the Lord.'*" B. H. Carroll, "Inspiration of The Scriptures As Believed By Baptists" in *Inspiration of the Bible: A Discussion of the Origin, the Authenticity and the Sanctity of the Oracles of God*, ed. J. B. Cranfill.

46   Luke 21:33.

47   A clearer connection between Word and Christ cannot be found than in the apostle John's Gospel with its opening statements: "In the beginning was the Word, and the Word was with God, and the Word was God. He was with God in the beginning. All things were created through Him, and apart from Him not one thing was created that has been created. Life was in Him, and that life was the light of men. That light shines in the darkness, yet the darkness did not overcome it. There was a man named John who was sent from God. He came as a witness to testify about the light, so that all might believe through him. He was not the light, but he came to testify about the light. The true light, who gives light to everyone, was coming into the world. He was in the world, and the world was created through Him, yet the world did not recognize Him. He came to His own, and His own people did not receive Him. But to all who did receive Him, He gave them the right to be children of God, to those who believe in His name, who were born, not of blood, or of the will of the flesh, or of the will of man, but of God. The Word became flesh and took up residence among us. We observed His glory, the glory as the One and Only Son from the Father, full of grace and truth." John 1:1-14 (HCSB)

by God Himself, "God-breathed" according to 2 Tim 3:16, and therefore inerrant and infallible because God Himself, the source of Scripture, is inerrant and infallible. This idea concerning inspiration logically extends to the whole of Scripture and to every word. The Bible tells us that God never lies, and Jesus Himself claimed to be "the Truth" (another of His claims to deity). Consequently, if what God says is true, and the Bible claims to be the words of God, then the Scriptures are true and indestructible, as Jesus claimed. If God has spoken, then these are the most important words that can ever be heard. They have been written down over some fifteen hundred years and yet exhibit an astounding unity, and a central theme focused on Christ. They attest to God's desire to relate to mankind in love and of His fulfilling that plan through His Son Jesus Christ, the mediator between God and men, issuing forth in a multitude who are called God's people.

Both the Old and New Testaments orbit around this essential message of love fulfilled in the central Person of history, the man from Nazareth, the Messiah, who takes away the sins of the world. The Bible calls this the gospel for a reason. It really is the good news announced by God Himself, and achieved by God the Son Himself, to reconcile us to God our creator and Father, even though we had become His enemies through our rebellion and sin. If the Bible contains error, then this message is suspect, and we must look elsewhere for a trustworthy authority. If the Bible contains error, then the good news loses its luster and fails to have its maximum impact, because we are not sure of a genuine word from God. As the apostle John wrote, "I have written these things to you who believe in the name of the Son of God, so that you may know that you have eternal life."[48]

Conclusion

As we have seen, the concepts of truth and authority are crucially important. A lot of people today question whether truth can even be known. Maybe some of the friends you grew up with think this way. But these same people will still make statements and claims *as if they are true*. For in-

---

48   1 John 5:13 (HCSB).

stance, someone in our current culture might say, "there is no truth." This person probably does not realize that this is a self-defeating (or self-refuting) statement. The statement "there is no truth" is self-refuting because it's a statement that *represents a claim of truth*, an absolute statement about truth itself. So there seems to be at least one absolute truth statement for this person, and that is "there is no truth." We might ask, "By what authority do you make this claim?" Do you see the problem here? You have refuted your own statement (there is no truth) by stating it *as an absolute truth*. Someone else might say, "everyone has their own truth." But this is also self-refuting. You have said "everyone," therefore making an absolute (universal) statement. But if everyone has their own truth (truth being relative in this scenario), then how can you make the *absolute* truth statement that "everyone has their own truth?" The question becomes: does that statement apply to everyone? Yes, you have claimed that it does. But to be true, the statement by its own definition would only be applicable to the one saying it (because the statement is their own personal truth), and thus would not really apply to anyone else and, therefore, the statement is meaningless. The statement, though, is actually absolute, so it must be shared by everyone and thus claims greater authority than each person's "truth," and so refutes itself.

No matter what we do, we can't seem to get away from truth, and, therefore, the issue of authority. There is still an innate desire to figure out what's right, to determine what I can know for sure in this world, about the purpose of my own life, about the purpose of existence in general. This can be a confusing pursuit, so that we are forced to appeal to some authority or other to try to sort out what we believe. Everybody, even if they say there is no truth, will appeal to some kind of authority. This is interesting and very telling. For instance, someone might say, "there's no God because Stephen Hawking said so."[49] The assumption is that he must know because

---

49 The famous English cosmologist stated the following (see if you note several glaring inconsistencies even in this small sample of his beliefs): "We are each free to believe what we want, and it's my view that the simplest explanation is that there is no God. No one created the universe and no one directs our fate. This leads me to a profound realisation: there is probably no heaven and afterlife either. I think belief in an afterlife is just wishful thinking. There is no reliable evidence for it, and it flies in the face of everything we

he's the "greatest theoretical physicist in the world." He's a scientist! We can see here that appealing to authority is natural to us, and even practiced by people who doubt the veracity of truth itself, especially of an ultimate authority like God. So, what authority will you personally appeal to in your own life? Baptists have always answered: Scripture. Scriptural authority for Baptists is not just for being a Christian or how we do church, but for everything: What is the true nature of humankind? Is there a standard for right and wrong? How should you conduct yourself in life? How should you build your family? How should you conduct business? How should you think about politics or government? The Bible is the scriptural authority for every part of life.

Early Baptist leader, and founder of Rhode Island, Roger Williams spoke of the unassailable, irreplaceable nature of the truth of the Bible in contrast with any other authority or any council of elders, even the most learned: "Scripture *only* must be heard: yea one Scripture in the mouth of one simple Mechannick before the whole Councel. By that only do I desire to stand or fall in triall or judgement: *For all flesh is grasse, and the beautie of flesh* (the most wisest, holiest, learnedst) *is but the flowre or beautie of grasse, only the word of Jehovah standeth fast for ever.*"[50] In order to possess genuine confidence in a God-willed and God-achieved salvation from sin and death, we must have a sure word from God, an unchangeable *truth* which "standeth fast." Baptists have always believed that we have this word in the Bible. Moreover, there is a connection between biblical authority, salvation, and baptism. If the New Testament tells us that baptism follows faith, then we have good authority by which to operate as churches. Amazingly, we also

---

know in science. I think that when we die we return to dust. But there's a sense in which we live on, in our influence, and in our genes that we pass on to our children. We have this one life to appreciate the grand design of the universe, and for that I am extremely grateful." Stephen Hawking, *Brief Answers to the Big Questions* (New York: Random House, 2018), 38. Who is he extremely grateful to? Also, if there is no one directing our fate, why does he use the words 'grand design' in reference to the universe? Are we genuinely free to believe what we want if everything is determined by the laws of nature? This seems a rather superficial philosophy for one so vaunted as an intellectual giant of our age.

50   Emphasis added. Roger Williams, *The Complete Writings of Roger Williams*, Vol. 1 (New York: Russell & Russell, 1963), 323.

find that this safeguards salvation by faith alone, since faith always comes first, and baptism follows as a sign of that faith. Faith is so important because it represents the principle which involves trusting *God's* power and actions for salvation and not anything I (or any other mere man) can accomplish. Put these two together, Scriptural authority and salvation truth, and you have a strong endorsement from the Bible itself for a Baptist view, that is, baptism for believers only, which is the subject of the next chapter.

Chapter 2

Believer's Baptism

For Baptists, the principle of believer's baptism emerges naturally from a commitment to biblical authority. There is no indication in Scripture (much less any command) that anyone except the believer is to be baptized. Believers are those who have already received salvation by faith and are therefore already regenerate (born again by the Holy Spirit). This doctrine of believer's baptism, then, has been regarded as pivotal by Baptists through the centuries because it serves to connect soteriology with ecclesiology in Baptist theology.[51] In other words, to gain salvation, one simply believes in Christ. Then, to exhibit that belief incontrovertibly and identify with other believers, one is baptized. Those who are in the

---

51 Some may be tempted to think that today the controversy over baptism is all a thing of the past or is not applicable for Christians now, since all has been settled over time. A modern Baptist theologian, however, declares that in our time, "the debate involves virtually the same issues." He goes on: "The debate between infant baptism and believer's baptism at the end of the twentieth century is, despite the advances of modern biblical scholarship, surprisingly alike the sixteenth-century debates between the magisterial Reformers and the Anabaptists on the European Continent or the seventeenth-century debates between Anglicans, Puritans, and Separatists on the one hand and the English Baptists on the other hand. Except for the Qumran documents and more knowledge about Jewish proselyte baptism, the debate involves virtually the same issues. Partisans make particular use of Old Testament material, New Testament material, and data from the patristic era." James Leo Garrett, Jr., *Systematic Theology: Biblical, Historical, and Evangelical,* Vol. 2, 2nd ed. (North Richland Hills, TX: Bibal Press, 2001), ch. 73, V, A.

church, therefore, are merely believers who have chosen to be baptized. Being in the church doesn't save you. You're in the church because you've already been saved by faith and publicly demonstrated that belief by baptism. Thus, we see that what we believe about the church affects what we believe about salvation (and vice versa). Salvation is by faith, and the church is made up of those who have been baptized as a public sign of the decision of faith already made by the individual believer. Consequently, the lynchpin for remaining biblical respecting salvation and church, from the Baptist viewpoint, is believer's baptism.

THE NEW TESTAMENT ORDER FOR BAPTISM

For Baptists, baptism is only for those who have made a conscious decision to follow Christ. In the last chapter, and in the last words, of the gospel of Matthew, Jesus instructed His disciples to baptize other new disciples. They were to make disciples: those who followed the teachings of Jesus. These fresh disciples were to identify themselves as Jesus' followers through baptism. The unique claims of Jesus are here demonstrated in the naming of the Trinity in the baptismal ordinance: the Father, the Son, and the Holy Spirit.[52] Jesus is identified not as simply another teacher, but as the Son of God. One who trusts that this is true and

---

52 Baptist theologian J. L. Dagg emphasized the importance of the trinity in baptism, pointing to Jesus' divinity: "In the formula of Christian baptism it is clearly exhibited. We are baptized into one name, because God is one; but that is the name of the Father, and of the Son, and of the Holy Ghost, because it belongs alike to each of these divine persons. Here, this doctrine meets us, at our very entrance on the profession of the Christian religion. If Christ was not God, he was justly condemned to death, and his religion is false; and the Holy Spirit, the Comforter whom he promised, is as little entitled to regard as he was. If Christ and the Holy Spirit are not God, the form of baptism should be rejected, as of a piece with the false religion into which it introduces us. No man can consistently receive Christian baptism, without believing the doctrine of the Trinity." John Leadley Dagg, *Manual of Theology* (Charleston: Southern Baptist Publication Society, 1859), 247-248.

decides to identify himself with Jesus and His teaching, in an ongoing commitment to follow Him, is a disciple.

All of this is evident and straightforward as we look at what is known as 'the great commission' of Matthew twenty-eight. There is, then, a definite and logical biblical order here assigned to baptism from the mouth of Christ Himself. Furthermore, baptism is not to signify citizenship in Christendom, as baby baptism does (which is reflected in the idea of 'christening'),[53] but is a sign of discipleship, joining others (i.e. a church) who have made the same deliberate faith commitment to be a follower of Jesus Christ.[54] A venerable Baptist professor put it this way:

---

53   James Leo Garrett writes concerning what I have called 'Christendom' above (the idea of a Christian state-church), as it is associated with infant baptism, that "infant baptism, it has often been alleged, has led to the primarily European phenomenon of the *Volkskirche* or *Staatskirche* (state church) with its great masses of non-worshiping, non-practicing church members who in effect have repudiated their baptism." James Leo Garrett, Jr., *Systematic Theology: Biblical, Historical, and Evangelical*, Vol. 2, 2nd ed. (North Richland Hills, TX: Bibal Press, 2001), ch.73, V, A2. In other words, Garrett is suggesting that infant baptism leads to nominal Christianity, as is seen throughout Europe today.

54   John Calvin (who was, of course, from the Protestant Reformed tradition) is a good example of a theologian who is able to exegete clearly the Scripture with regard to believer's baptism, as here in Matthew 28, and *still* go on to support infant baptism. See if you are convinced by his arguments in support of pedobaptism: "Christ enjoins that those who have submitted to the gospel, and professed to be his disciples, shall be *baptized*; partly that their *baptism* may be a pledge of eternal life before God:, and partly that it may be an outward sign of faith before men. For we know that God testifies to us the grace of adoption by this sign, because he engrafts us into the body of his Son, so as to reckon us among his flock; and, therefore, not only our spiritual washing, by which he reconciles us to himself, but likewise our new righteousness, are represented by it. But as God, by this seal confirms to us his grace, so all who present themselves for *baptism* do, as it were, by their own signature, ratify their faith. . . . But as Christ enjoins them to *teach* before *baptizing*, and desires that none but *believers* shall be admitted to *baptism*, it would appear that *baptism* is not properly administered unless when it is preceded by faith. On this pretense, the *Anabaptists* have stormed greatly against infant baptism. But the reply is not difficult, if we attend to the reason of the command. Christ orders them to convey to *all nations* the message of eternal salvation, and confirms it by adding the seal of baptism. Now it was proper that *faith* in the word should be placed before

What it Means to Be a Baptist

In the New Testament we have no account of any being members of churches except such as were considered to be truly regenerated believers and had actually submitted to the rite of baptism. Now the Baptist churches insist as one of their fundamental principles that only truly regenerated believers in Christ, after having been properly baptized on profession of their faith in the Lord, should be received as members of the church.[55]

---

baptism, since the Gentiles were altogether alienated from God, and had nothing in common with the chosen people; for otherwise it would have been a false figure, which offered forgiveness and the gift of the Spirit to unbelievers, who were not yet members of Christ. But we know that by *faith* those who were formerly despised are united to the people of God. It is now asked, on what condition does God adopt as children those who formerly were aliens? It cannot, indeed, be denied that, when he has once received them into his favor, he continues to bestow it on their children and their children's children. By the coming of Christ God manifested himself as a Father equally to the Gentiles and to the Jews; and, therefore, that promise, which was formerly given to the Jews, must now be in force towards the Gentiles, I will be thy God, and the God of thy seed after thee, (Gen.17:7) Thus we see that they who entered by faith into the Church of God are reckoned, along with their posterity, among the members of Christ, and, at the same time, called to the inheritance of salvation. And yet this does not involve the separation of *baptism* from faith and doctrine; because, though infants are not yet of such an age as to be capable of receiving the grace of God by faith, still God, when addressing their parents, includes them also. I maintain, therefore, that it is not rash to administer baptism to infants, to which God invites them, when he promises that *he will be their God.*" John Calvin, *Calvin's Commentaries, Matthew*, 324. Historian Henry Vedder summarizes well the Baptist view in contradiction to Calvin: "Baptists hold that the baptism of any but believers is contrary to the whole spirit of Christianity, and that it totally subverts the principle on which the Church of Christ was founded. Judaism had been based upon natural descent, upon the law of the flesh, but Jesus came to teach and establish the utterly new law of the spirit. 'Except a man be born from above, he cannot see the kingdom of God. . . . That which is born of the flesh is flesh, that which is born of the Spirit is spirit.' To be a Christian is to enter into a new and spiritual relation to God, through faith in his Son." Henry C. Vedder, *The Baptists* (New York: Baker & Taylor, 1903), 11.

55   Edwin Charles Dargan, *Ecclesiology: A Study of the Churches*, 2nd ed. (Louisville: Charles T. Dearing, 1905), 167.

If one is to have anything at all to do with Christianity, there seems to be no good reason to add to or take away from this simple order. Deciding to follow Christ, believing that He truly is the Son of God, and therefore has the power and has already accomplished what is needed in order for me to be forgiven of sin and reconciled to God, I publicly confess this and witness to my sincerity through baptism in His name.[56] Any other formula for salvation or baptism or church is misleading and therefore rejected by Baptists.

If the Bible calls for each individual to respond to God by accepting the truth of the gospel for himself, then infant baptism may grievously misdirect those involved in it, whether Catholic or Protestant.[57] Salvation is not because of baptism but because of faith. Faith is by necessity a personal decision, corresponding to the call for repentance in Scripture. Baptist theologian H. Wheeler Robinson wrote that believer's baptism "emphasizes, as no other interpretation of the rite can ever do, the significance, the necessity, and the *individuality of conversion*."[58] The choice to trust Christ for salvation

---

56   Concerning confession (or profession) of faith and baptism, George Eldon Ladd, a Baptist New Testament scholar, wrote: "In the early church profession of faith in Christ and baptism were practically simultaneous events. Baptism in water, along with confession of Christ, was the outward sign of faith." George Eldon Ladd, *A Theology of the New Testament*, rev. ed. (Grand Rapids: Eerdmans, 1993), 326 n. 16.

57   Baptist Biblical Theologian Augustus Strong wrote the following decisive charges against pedobaptism: "The evil effects of infant baptism are a strong argument against it: First,—in forestalling the voluntary act of the child baptized, and thus practically preventing his personal obedience to Christ's commands. Secondly,—in inducing superstitious confidence in an outward rite as possessed of regenerating efficacy. Thirdly,—in obscuring and corrupting Christian truth with regard to the sufficiency of Scripture, the connection of the ordinances, and the inconsistency of an impenitent life with church-membership. Fourthly,—in destroying the church as a spiritual body, by merging it in the nation and the world. Fifthly,— in putting into the place of Christ's command a commandment of men, and so admitting the essential principle of all heresy, schism, and false religion." Augustus Hopkins Strong, *Outlines of Systematic Theology*, (Philadelphia: Griffith & Rowland Press, 1908), 251.

58   Emphasis added. H. Wheeler Robinson, *Baptist Principles* (4th ed.; London: Carey Kingsgate Press, 1960; 1st publ. 1938), 17. On this matter of the

cannot be made by someone else on one's behalf. It must be made personally. The nature of the theological case outlined in the Bible is such that each
person is estranged from God because of conscious decisions to sin. Therefore, each person is given a way to restore a relationship with God through
the sacrifice of Christ. He died for the sins of the whole world so that each

---

individuality of accountability to God, Baptist scholar, and founder of Southwestern Baptist Theological Seminary, B. H. Carroll writes an eloquent and uncompromising declamation in his book *Baptists and Their Doctrines* under the heading
'Individuality': "This New Testament law [NT as final authority for believers] of
Christianity segregates the individual from his own family, from society with all
its customs and requirements, from race and nationality, from caste, however
exclusive, from all government control or intimidations, from all the bonds of
friendship, though dear as the tie between David and Jonathan or Damon and
Pythias, then isolates him of every artificial distinction arising from wealth or
poverty or social status, and then shuts him up in an exclusive circle alone with
God, who is no respecter of persons, and there demands of his naked and solitary
personality a voluntary surrender of his will to God's will and an immediate obedience to all it demands. There are no sponsors, or proxies. Enforced or insincere
obedience counts nothing at all. The sole responsibility of decision and actions
rests directly on the individual soul. Each one must give account of himself to
God. This is the first principle of New Testament law—to bring each naked soul
face to face with God. When that first Baptist voice [John] broke the silence of
four hundred years it startled the world with its appeal to individuality: 'Think
not to say within yourselves, we have Abraham to our father. Behold, the axe is
laid at the root of the trees, and every tree that bringeth not forth good fruit is
hewn down and cast into the fire.' Do thou repent. Do thou confess thy sins. Do
thou be baptized. It was the first step of Christianity, and what a colossal stride!
Family ties count nothing. Greek culture nothing. Roman citizenship nothing.
Circumcision nothing. O soul, thou art alone before God! The multitude shall not
swallow thee up. 'If thou shalt be wise, thou shalt be wise for thyself; but if thou
scornest, thou alone shalt bear it.' [Proverbs 9:12] . . . Well did our Lord know that
there could be no evangelization of the world if ancestors, families, customs, government, commerce and priests could stand between the individual soul and God.
Thy relation to God is paramount. His law takes precedence of all and swallows
up all. In giving emphasis to this doctrine of individuality our Baptist fathers have
suffered martyrdom at the hands of the heathen, the Romanist, the Greek, and
the Protestant alike." Insertions added. B. H. Carroll, *Baptists and Their Doctrines:
Sermons on Distinctive Baptist Principles* (Nashville: Broadman Press, 1913), 15-17

individual can now be called to repentance, to turn from self and sin to the grace of God in Christ. This is essentially the definition of faith. Faith is saying no to my way and saying yes to Him who said, "I am the way." It is a personal matter between the individual and God. It cannot be decided by a community or a parent or any other intermediary.

Trusting God personally by trusting Christ individually is the key to biblical salvation. The individual relates to God personally through Christ. The New Testament never recommends trusting any other mediator, representative, or even parent, no matter what institutionally-sanctioned claims are made. Christ shed His own blood for us as our High Priest. He is the mediator of that once-and-for-all sacrifice which is of highest value, the life of the Son of God Himself. He is also a mediator who continues His role eternally as "our great High Priest who has passed through the heavens," and, because of the resurrection, offers life in exchange for sin and death, which He took upon Himself on the cross.[59] Because of all this, He is unassailably trustworthy, and thus the Bible calls us to trust Him and no one else. "For there is one God, and one mediator between God and men, the man Christ Jesus; Who gave himself a ransom for all, to be testified in due time."[60]

So, we see one of the chief failings of infant baptism: the practice necessarily inserts a proxy for the baby, another mediator whose faith or office represents the baby. This is not biblical and is the reason Baptists stand so staunchly upon the principle of *believer's* baptism. A decision for faith in Christ must take place or there is no salvation. Baptism symbolizes this faith and all that it represents as far as what God has accomplished for the individual. It is a command of Christ which the believer gladly obeys, since it identifies him with his Lord and Savior. It represents him saying to the church and the world: this Jesus is *my* Lord and *my* Savior, and I am His follower and servant. All the riches of this new relationship and new life are received by faith and are because of God's grace. These riches may all be missed if a person is taught the false doctrine that he or she has salvation conferred because of the mediation of the Roman church or a Protestant clergyman, a parent, godparent, priest, or any other official, in the rite of baptism.

---

59   See the book of Hebrews.

60   1 Timothy 2:5-6, KJV.

What it Means to Be a Baptist

An important Baptist thinker, E. Y. Mullins, wrote in this same vein, stressing "how intensely personal and individual is Christian faith. The element of proxy, or substitutionary faith, is alien to the gospel. Hence the baptism of infants upon the alleged faith of parents or sponsors is foreign to New Testament teaching. Personal faith is the only kind of faith recognized in the New Testament."[61] Baptist Historian Henry Vedder concisely expressed the Baptist view:

> Religion thus becomes, according to Christ's teaching, a
> matter between each human soul and God. There is no need

---

61 Edgar Young Mullins, *The Christian Religion in Its Doctrinal Expression* (Philadelphia: Roger Williams Press, 1917), 375-376. The idea of faith being personal and individual is sometimes called soul-competency by Baptists, although this term may be linked with other aspects of Baptist belief such as religious liberty and the priesthood of the believer. It is explained (in this personal faith sense) further by professor Mullins: "Observe then that the idea of the competency of the soul in religion excludes at once all human interference, such as episcopacy and infant baptism, and every form of religion by proxy. Religion is a personal matter between the soul and God." Edgar Young Mullins, *The Axioms of Religion*, 54. This Baptist idea of soul-competency is in stark contrast with what the Catechism of the Catholic Church says concerning faith and baptism: "For all the baptized, children or adults, faith must grow after Baptism. For this reason the Church celebrates each year at the Easter Vigil the renewal of baptismal promises. Preparation for Baptism leads only to the threshold of new life. Baptism is the source of that new life in Christ from which the entire Christian life springs forth. For the grace of Baptism to unfold, the parents' help is important. So too is the role of the godfather and godmother, who must be firm believers, able and ready to help the newly baptized child or adult on the road of Christian life. Their task is a truly ecclesial function (officium). The whole ecclesial community bears some responsibility for the development and safeguarding of the grace given at Baptism." *Catechism of the Catholic Church*, online, art. 1254-1255 (www.vatican.va/archive/ENG0015/__P3K.HTM). Contrast this nebulous idea of faith and baptism from Catholicism with a simple statement from a Baptist scholar: "We Baptists love our children, and rather than finding false security in the deceptive practice of paedobaptism, we instruct our children about who Jesus Christ is and what He has done for us." Malcolm Yarnell, *Calvinism: A Cause for Rejoicing, A Cause for Concern*, paper from "Building Bridges: Southern Baptists and Calvinism" 27 November 2008, Ridgecrest Conference Center, North Carolina.

of priestly mediation, there is no possibility of regeneration by a magical "sacrament." To baptize one who has not believed is, in the eye of a Baptist, an empty form, but as the act of one who sees in it more than that, it is something worse: it is an impertinent interference with the personal rights of another soul, it is to nullify the fundamental principle of the gospel of Christ.[62]

Salvation is accomplished only by God. This is the clear message of the New Testament: Christ and Him crucified. This is God's plan, and we must not add to it. These enormously important salvation truths are obscured when we introduce any baptism other than for believers. This is why Baptists embrace their name and refuse to blanch when others mock and fuss at a perceived hidebound narrowness. In spite of this perception, great numbers of Baptists are determined to continue to display a simple, fixed tenacity, holding on to what they deem to be biblical truth. The potential for dilution of the simple truth of salvation by faith *alone* is what is at stake. Considering this issue and the confusion introduced with baby baptism, we now turn to the example of Martin Luther.

AN EXAMPLE OF THE THEOLOGICAL CONFUSION IN INFANT BAPTISM: MARTIN LUTHER

Contrary to the Baptist idea that the decision of faith *precedes* baptism, the idea that faith is merely a gift, practically indistinguishable from grace, led the great Protestant Reformer Martin Luther to affirm infant baptism. Roger Olson states that, "Luther and Zwingli both defended infant baptism on the ground that faith is a gift of God and not a contingent, free decision. Their monergistic views of salvation form at least a part of their foundations for this practice."[63] Luther said that if

62   Henry C. Vedder, *The Baptists* (New York: Baker & Taylor, 1903), 12.
63   Roger E. Olson, *The Story of Christian Theology: Twenty Centuries of Tradition and Reform* (Downers Grove: InterVarsity Press, 1999), 421.

faith is a gift, then there is no difficulty for God to give the gift to an infant.[64] Thus faith, in this view, appears to be a mysterious power fur-

---

64   See, Martin Luther, *Table Talk*, trans. William Hazlitt (London: Fount, 1995), 181, where he writes: "The Anabaptists pretend that children, not as yet having reason, ought not to receive baptism. I answer: That reason in no way contributes to faith. Nay in that children are destitute of reason, they are all the more fit and proper recipients of baptism. For reason is the greatest enemy that faith has: it never comes to the aid of spiritual things but— more frequently than not—struggles against the Divine Word, treating with contempt all that emanates from God. If God can communicate the Holy Ghost to a grown person, he can, *a fortiori* communicate it to young children. Faith comes of the Word of God, when this is heard; little children hear the Word of God when they receive baptism, and therewith they receive also faith." To use the logical construct *a fortiori* (meaning 'with more or greater reason') after discounting the role of reason in these matters appears contradictory. In addition, one of Luther's arguments for infant baptism is that the person can come to faith later if faith was not present at the time of baptism (since we can never be sure if anyone really has faith: an argument he uses to accuse the Anabaptists of making baptism a work, since they are trying to be "sure" of faith by baptizing believers which, of course, was not the point for the Anabaptists). He actually undermines his refutation of a personal decision in matters of faith with this argument: "So here again the Anabaptists are urging on to a work, so that when the people are baptized they may have confidence that everything is right and complete. In reality they pay little attention to faith, but only seem to praise it. For, as we have already said, were they to be sure beforehand of faith, they would never again baptize anyone. [In other words, Luther is arguing that the Anabaptists must be sure that belief is present before they baptize, since they claim that the Scripture says "whoever believes" is baptized. Confession is not enough for Luther. This appears to be a specious argument considering that Jesus Himself commanded us to baptize new followers.] If they did not rely on works but earnestly sought for faith, they would not dare to rebaptize. The unchanging Word of God, once spoken in the first baptism, ever remains standing, so that afterwards they can come to faith in it, *if they will,* and the water with which they were baptized they can afterwards receive in faith, *if they will.*" Emphasis Added. Martin Luther, *Concerning Rebaptism in Martin Luther's Basic Theological Writings,* ed. Timothy Lull (Minneapolis: Fortress Press, 1989), 361. Note the obvious language referring to the human will in these statements concerning the faith of one already baptized as an infant. Accordingly, Luther seems to be implying that there is free choice in this case, which is not exhibited

nished to infants at baptism. In contrast to Luther's view, Baptist New Testament scholar George R. Beasley-Murray writes that, "in the New Testament it is everywhere assumed that faith proceeds to baptism and that baptism is for faith" and thus "faith *comes* to baptism; the idea of baptism creating faith is not on the horizon."[65] Yet, confounding his theology further, Luther also admits that one may receive baptism *without* faith. This undermines the effectiveness of infant baptism, as those who continue in sin and unbelief even though baptized as babies

---

by the baby in infant baptism. He also undermines his own confidence in infant baptism by the striking admission that one baptized as a baby may not possess faith later on, which contradicts the doctrine Luther is best known for, *sola fide*, faith alone is needed for salvation. Also note that 'faith in it' refers to the baptism ceremony, 'the water,' and thus the concept of baptismal regeneration appears here for Luther. Contrary to Luther's accusation of the Anabaptists, the doctrine of baptismal regeneration makes a work of baptism much more than did the Anabaptists. If baptism does the work in the infant, then faith in Christ alone is set aside to a great degree. See the *Large Catechism* where Luther writes, "But as our would-be wise, new spirits assert that faith alone saves, and that works and external things avail nothing, we answer: It is true, indeed, that nothing in us is of any avail but faith, as we shall hear still further. But these blind guides are unwilling to see this, namely, that faith must have something which it believes, that is, of which it takes hold, and upon which it stands and rests. Thus faith clings to the water, and believes that it is Baptism, in which there is pure salvation and life; not through the water . . . but through the fact that it is embodied in the Word and institution of God, and the name of God inheres in it. Now, if I believe this, what else is it than believing in God as in Him who has given and planted His Word into this ordinance, and proposes to us this external thing wherein we may apprehend such a treasure?" The Anabaptists saw baptism as only an outward confirmation, a sign, of the inward conversion of faith which was already achieved and entirely based on Christ's work revealed in His Word by the Holy Spirit. Luther continues: "Even if they contradict the Word a hundred times, it still remains the Word spoken in the first baptism. Its power does not derive from the fact that it is repeated many times or is spoken anew, but from the fact that it was commanded once to be spoken." This statement seems to leave no room for the markedly biblical idea of confession of faith *of the believer* as being associated with salvation. Insertions and emphases added. Luther, *Concerning Rebaptism*, ed. Lull, 361.

65   George R. Beasley-Murray, *Baptism in the New Testament* (Grand Rapids: Eerdmans, 1973), 272, 274.

clearly illustrate. Therefore, faith alone effects salvation, weakening Luther's affirmation of baptismal regeneration.[66] So, proponents of infant baptism seem to go back and forth with contrasting ideas about faith and baptism, with no consistent baptismal theology. Luther later altered his idea that faith is a gift to infants and based the baptism of infants on the faith of the parents, which contradicts the idea of faith as a mysterious gift which babies can somehow receive.

These conflicting notions concerning faith and baptism make evident the practical problem in Luther's theology, which flows from his decision to retain belief in his own Roman Catholic baptism, and therefore infant baptism as a Lutheran practice, as legitimate and salvific. William Estep remarks on this:

> Luther's battle cry, "Justification by faith," became his plumb line for interpreting the Bible. However, due to the persistent Roman Catholic appendages of his theology, he was never able to give this truth consistent expression. Consequently, in Lutheranism there has always been an irreconcilable contradiction between the theology of justification by faith and the theological support of infant baptism.[67]

This mixture of faith and baby baptism muddies the waters of a clear and biblical definition of faith. Faith cannot be given through a rite of the church. It is a personal commitment on the part of the believer and is focused on the object of faith alone, that is, Christ and His finished work. W. J. McGlothlin concurs. He writes of Luther, "He retained the baptism which he had received in the Catholic church including infant baptism and the doctrine of baptismal regeneration. This was a radical contradiction of his doctrine of justification, but he does not seem to have felt the inconsistency."[68]

---

66   See Luther, *Concerning Rebaptism*, ed. Lull.

67   William Roscoe Estep, *The Anabaptist Story: An Introduction to Sixteenth-Century Anabaptism*, 3d ed (Grand Rapids: Eerdmans, 1975), 196–197.

68   W. J. McGlothlin, *The Course of Christian History* (New York: Macmillan, 1926), 112. Here we see the inherent problem of assurance for the believer in Luther's theology. Since assurance cannot be based on simple faith in the effectual work of Christ followed by confession and baptism, because of

There is a confusion in affirming infant baptism relating not only to the concept of salvation by faith alone but also to a correspondent concern: assurance. How can one be sure of salvation? This is to ask almost the same question as the initial query, which is: how can one be saved? But the assurance question applies subjectively to the professed believer in the work of Christ. How can I have a sense of assurance about what I have believed? Doubts assail us at times, and we seem to be thrown back on our own devices. We may be overwhelmed again by our own unworthiness and succumb to grief concerning assurance. Where do we turn when we are deluged by these waves of uncertainty? Well, Scripture tells us plainly to look to the promise of God Himself and to the evidence, so brightly luminous in His Son, that He is a keeper of promises without equal. This character trait of God is spoken of in the Old Testament in Numbers 23:19: "God is not a man who lies, or a son of man who changes His mind. Does He speak and not act, or promise and not fulfill?"[69]

Assurance *by faith* views the fulfillment of the promise through Christ for salvation as sure because God has already accomplished it all for our sakes: "Blessed be the God and Father of our Lord Jesus Christ, which according to his abundant mercy hath begotten us again unto a lively hope by the resurrection of Jesus Christ from the dead, to an inheritance incorruptible, and undefiled, and that fadeth not away, reserved in heaven for you, who are kept by the power of God through faith unto salvation ready to be revealed in the last time."[70] Note also the strong promise of Jesus Himself:

> "I am the bread of life," Jesus told them. "No one who comes to Me will ever be hungry, and no one who believes in Me will ever be thirsty again. But as I told you, you've seen Me, and yet you do not believe. Everyone the Father gives Me will

---

double predestination and because faith is simply a gift (with no decision, or personal choice to surrender, possible on the part of the Christian because of the bondage of the will), Luther indicates that the reality of infant baptism, in his time a Roman Catholic baptism, becomes the basis of assurance in the life of the believer, even though he admits that faith alone justifies and baptism is bereft of its potency without faith.

69   (HCSB)

70   1 Peter 1:3-5 (KJV)

come to Me, and the one who comes to Me I will never cast out. For I have come down from heaven, not to do My will, but the will of Him who sent Me. This is the will of Him who sent Me: that I should lose none of those He has given Me but should raise them up on the last day. For this is the will of My Father: that everyone who sees the Son and believes in Him may have eternal life, and I will raise him up on the last day."[71]

When we look again at God's promises for assurance, just as in salvation, our doubt is broken, not by confidence in our own good works or experience or any other human thing, but by God Himself and His fulfilled Word in Christ. As the apostle Paul wrote to the Corinthians, "For every one of God's promises is 'Yes' in Him."[72] So the foundation of the Christian gospel is the promise of salvation for any who believe, from a God who does not lie and does not fail. This is also the rock of assurance on which we rest and trust, as Paul told the Corinthians, "because you stand by faith,"[73] and therefore we find our salvation not only gracious and joyful, but also sure!

This simple assurance of faith, all confidence placed in God Himself and His promise, is thrown into confusion with infant baptism, since conscious faith comes after baptism. What, then, is baptism in this case? The temptation is to swerve toward the concept of baptismal regeneration and to see baptism itself as having power to save. Martin Luther, unfortunately, represents one who embraced this misconception. He writes in his *Large Catechism*:

> Therefore, expressed in the simplest form, the power, the effect, the benefit, the fruit and the purpose of Baptism is to save. No one is baptized that he may become a prince, but, as the words declare, that he may be saved. But to be saved, we know very well, is to be delivered from sin, death, and Satan, and to enter into Christ's kingdom and live forever with Him.[74]

---

71   John 6:35-40 (HCSB).

72   2 Corinthians 1:20a (HCSB).

73   2 Corinthians 1:24b (HCSB).

74   Martin Luther, *Luther's Large Catechism*, trans. John Nicholas Lenker (Minneapolis: The Luther Press, 1908), 162.

This understanding of baptism as necessary to salvation[75] appears to have affected the advice Luther gave when the question of assurance arose:

> Thus we must regard Baptism and make it profitable to ourselves, that when our sins and conscience oppress us, we strengthen ourselves and take comfort and say: Nevertheless *I am baptized*; but if *I am baptized*, it is promised me that I shall be saved and have eternal life, both in soul and body. For that is the reason why these two things are done in Baptism namely, that the body, which can apprehend nothing but the water, is sprinkled, and, in addition, the word is spoken for the soul to apprehend. Now, since both, the water and the Word, are one Baptism, therefore body and soul must be saved and live forever: the soul through the Word which it believes, but the body because it is united with the soul and also apprehends Baptism as it is able to apprehend it. We have, therefore, no greater jewel in body and soul, for by it we are made holy and are saved, which no other kind of life, no work upon earth, can attain.[76]

If one is to appeal to his baptism as a baby for assurance, this of necessity conflicts with salvation and assurance by *faith alone*. Luther and his Reformation are famous for this great Protestant theological motto. Baptists believe this to be biblical and are passionate bearers of this reformation banner, believing that faith alone for salvation is biblical truth. Sadly, we find the great sixteenth century reformer himself affirming baptismal regeneration for infants, corresponding to assurance of salvation for Lutherans. Baptists believe that the biblical doctrine of believer's baptism safeguards the wonderful certainty gained by those who perceive God's work in Christ *alone* as effective for salvation. If

---

75   Luther writes boldly, referring of course to infant baptism: "I, likewise, boast that baptism is no human plaything, but is instituted by God himself; and, moreover, it is solemnly and strictly commanded that we be baptized or we shall not be saved." Luther, *Luther's Large Catechism*, 159.

76   Emphasis added. Luther, *The Large Catechism*, trans. F. Bente and W. H. T. Dau in *The Master Christian Library*, version 8 [CD-Rom] (Rio, WI: Ages Software, 2000), 89.

What it Means to Be a Baptist

God alone accomplishes my salvation, then faith alone is the proper biblical response to His proffered grace. This emphasis is just what we find in the pages of the New Testament. The witness and sign of this truth, then, is *believer's* baptism, ordained by Christ Himself.

Some early Protestants, along with their modern enthusiasts, based their affirmation of infant baptism on the Old Testament practice of circumcision. Baptists through the ages have seen this as a grotesque mistake, and a basic hermeneutical blunder when reading the Old Testament. One of the Baptist arguments *against* infant Baptism is that Baptism is *not* related to circumcision. They would argue that in the New Testament the pattern changes. There is no more circumcision. Remember how Paul writes in all his epistles that we are free from all that? He did have Timothy circumcised so that he could be accepted in Jerusalem, on the principle of "becoming all things to all men," but he didn't do that as a prerequisite for salvation. So, in Acts 15, the Jerusalem council sent the letter to all the Christians in Antioch who were Gentiles, and they said: avoid sexual immorality and idol worship, don't eat blood or animals that have been strangled. Other than that, neither circumcision nor any other Old Testament law is necessary. So, the whole church at Antioch received the letter and rejoiced! Notice that the letter didn't say you have to be circumcised. It is no longer a mark of being a person of God. As Jesus said to the woman at the well, "A day will come when people will worship in spirit and in truth," with no need for all sorts of physical signs and rule-keeping.

So it is not the position of your body, or cleansing of your body, or any religious rules that matter. And there were a lot of rules in the Old Testament. All those rules pointed to the finality of God's grace and salvation in the coming Messiah; that He would clean us up, and that His blood would save us. The Old Testament helps us understand our own inability to be righteous and our need for a savior. It's very important theologically to understand these things. In the New Testament there is no circumcision, nor any equivalent such as baby baptism, only faith. Baptists have consistently argued through the centuries that since you don't find circumcision in the New Testament, then you shouldn't baptize babies, nor use the Old Testament as your example, citing circumcision. Not only is circumcision gone in the New Testament, but no babies are baptized there either! Historically for Baptists, this was one of the arguments against infant baptism: that baptism in the New Testament is not related to circumcision. The denominations who still, to this day, baptize babies *do* use this argument: "well it's just like circumcision, people coming into the community of God, becoming part of it." But how do you become part of the community of the people of God, the church, according to the New Testament? By faith alone. Baptism is the sign that someone is already saved, and thus belongs in the church, not the means of entering into that salvation.

THE BIBLICAL MODE FOR BAPTISM: IMMERSION

The candidate or subject of baptism is one who already possesses salvation, having been delivered from sin and death by Christ and renewed through the Holy Spirit and reconciled to the Father. These great gifts are offered to any who will believe. For Baptists, baptism demonstrates and confesses these all-important truths in the life of the believer. Therefore, another controversy regarding baptism is the mode. There are three traditional modes: immersion, affusion, and aspersion. In other words, how should one be baptized: by dunking, pouring, or sprinkling? Baptists believe in dunking. In fact, the very word in the Greek New Testament βαπτίζω (*baptizo*) literally means to immerse.[77] Augustus Strong confirms that "every passage where the word occurs in the New Testament either requires or allows the meaning 'immerse.'"[78] Again,

---

77 Augustus Strong, who was greatly influential among Baptists through his systematic theology texts, writes: "The prevailing usage of any word determines the sense it bears, when found in a command of Christ. We have seen, not only that the prevailing usage of the Greek language determines the meaning of the word 'baptize' to be 'immerse,' but that this is its fundamental, constant, and only meaning. The original command to baptize is therefore a command to immerse." Augustus Hopkins Strong, *Systematic Theology: A Compendium and Commonplace-Book*, Vol. 3 (Philadelphia: Griffith & Rowland Press, 1909), 938.

78 Augustus Hopkins Strong, *Outlines of Systematic Theology*, 245.

we witness the importance of biblical authority for Baptists, as Henry Vedder writes, "Because they accept the Scriptures and not tradition as authority, Baptists practice immersion only as baptism."[79] Not only do we have scriptural support for this practice in the word 'baptize' and in that Jesus *came up out of the water* at His baptism by John the Baptist,[80] but also there are very important theological concerns which impel us to insist on immersion. These doctrinal considerations tie together the candidate (believer) and the mode (immersion) regarding proper New Testament baptism.

Immersion pictures clearly the believer's identity, through faith,

---

Strong writes further concerning the Greek word βαπτίζω: "The absence of any use of the word in the passive voice with 'water' as its subject confirms our conclusion that its meaning is 'to immerse.' Water is never said to be baptized upon a man. . . . ."Strong, *Outlines of Systematic Theology*, 245.

79   Henry C. Vedder, *The Baptists*, 12. A contemporary Baptist pastor expressed his affirmation of immersion this way: "The word baptism means immersion. Martin Luther said, 'The word means to put entirely under the water until it closes over you.' Some may say, if it is a symbol and only a symbol, why is it important to be immersed? Well, no New Testament scholar will deny that all the New Testament baptisms followed a decision to accept Christ and were by total immersion. They say, 'Why, for convenience sake, is not a symbol of the symbol all right?' Well, I'll not judge that except just to let the scripture stand on its own. I don't see how any other form of baptism can represent the death, burial and resurrection of our Lord Christ." Frank Pollard, *The Preaching Pastor* (2003), 81-82.

80   See Matthew 3:16 and Mark 1:10. The same language is used in the account of the baptism of the Ethiopian eunuch in Acts 8:39, which also says that Philip and the Ethiopian both *went down into the water*. If one is pouring or sprinkling for baptism, going down into the water is not necessary. This would seem to be good evidence that immersion was the practice of the New Testament. There are perfectly useful Greek words for pour (*katacheo*) and sprinkle (*rhantizo*) which could have been used in the New Testament. Baptism means to dip, plunge, or dunk; to immerse. Also, the apostle John writes in John 3:23, "John also was baptizing in Aenon near Salim, because there was plenty of water there." (CSB) Why would John the Baptist need plenty of water to baptize unless he was practicing immersion? Each person was being immersed, going down into the water, dipped under by John, and coming back out.

with Jesus Christ; that is, being crucified, buried, and then rising again with Him. The person being baptized is lowered down under the water, signifying death and burial, the payment for sin. He or she is then lifted back out of the water, signifying resurrection and eternal life. Baptist scholar Walter T. Conner described the significance of immersion in this way:

> Every time a penitent sinner goes down into the water to be baptized he is preaching the gospel of salvation through a crucified and risen Redeemer. He thereby confesses himself a sinner and Christ as his Savior. Therefore, the form of baptism is important. Somebody says it is only a form, so why stickle for a form. It is a form, but we must remember that it is a form with a meaning, and the meaning lies in the form. Therefore, if the form be changed the meaning is destroyed. There is no Christian baptism then apart from immersion, which pictures a burial and a resurrection.[81]

In baptism, the believer is dramatizing his own reception of the work of Christ, finished once and for all for his or her sake in His death, burial, and resurrection, in order to garner for the sinner overwhelming spiritual riches: death to the self, and therefore freedom from the self, who was put away at the cross; sacrifice for sins by the shed blood, achieving a new right status with God who gives forgiveness; new eternal life given with the Holy Spirit which is proved by the power of God in raising Jesus from the dead. Surely, we can perceive that these great salvation certainties, which are accessed solely by faith, are attested clearly in no other mode of baptism except immersion.

So, for the Baptist, not only is infant baptism to be rejected on the grounds that it obscures the clear New Testament truth of salvation by faith alone, but also any mode other than immersion (again, the Greek word for immersion is *baptizo*) is rejected because it blurs the plain truth which baptism depicts in identifying the believer with Christ's death, burial, and resurrection. This is expressed in the Apostle Paul's letter to

---

81   Walter T. Conner, "The Essentials of Christian Unity," *Southwestern Journal of Theology* 51, no.1 (Fall 2008): 29.

the Romans, in which he explains that baptism signifies the unity of the believer with Christ:

> Or are you unaware that all of us who were baptized into Christ Jesus were baptized into His death? Therefore we were buried with Him by baptism into death, in order that, just as Christ was raised from the dead by the glory of the Father, so we too may walk in a new way of life. For if we have been joined with Him in the likeness of His death, we will certainly also be in the likeness of His resurrection. For we know that our old self was crucified with Him in order that sin's dominion over the body may be abolished, so that we may no longer be enslaved to sin, since a person who has died is freed from sin's claims. Now if we died with Christ, we believe that we will also live with Him, because we know that Christ, having been raised from the dead, no longer dies. Death no longer rules over Him. For in that He died, He died to sin once for all; but in that He lives, He lives to God. So, you too consider yourselves dead to sin, but alive to God in Christ Jesus.[82]

Paul's association of baptism with the believer's individual faith in the death, burial, and resurrection of Christ, with all of its eternal significance, surely indicates that the deep meaning in the ordinance is only for the *believer*, and only seen clearly as he or she is *immersed*.

E. Y. Mullins notes concerning this passage that Paul presented baptism as emblematic of "spiritual death and resurrection, symbolized by baptism, the initial act of outward obedience. The Christian in his old sinful nature has been crucified, or put to death, with Christ. He has also been raised from the dead into a new spiritual life in Christ. These truths find symbolic expression in the outward act of baptism. (Rom. 6 : 1-14.)"[83] Augustus Strong contends: "Baptism symbolizes the previous entrance of the believer into the communion of Christ's death and resurrection,—or,

---

82   Romans 6:3-11 (HCSB).

83   Edgar Young Mullins, *The Christian Religion in Its Doctrinal Expression*, 427-428.

in other words, regeneration through union with Christ."[84] He concludes: "There are two reasons, therefore, why nothing but immersion will satisfy the design of the ordinance: first,—because nothing else can symbolize the radical nature of the change effected in regeneration—a change from spiritual death to spiritual life; secondly,—because nothing else can set forth the fact that this change is due to the entrance of the soul into communion with the death and resurrection of Christ."[85]

Surely the truth of the gospel is right before our eyes in immersion! When Paul the apostle reiterates the basics of the gospel to the Corinthian church, he gives it in a historical sequence:

> Now brothers, I want to clarify for you the gospel I proclaimed to you; you received it and have taken your stand on it. You are also saved by it, if you hold to the message I proclaimed to you--unless you believed to no purpose. For I passed on to you as most important what I also received: that Christ died for our sins according to the Scriptures, that He was buried, that He was raised on the third day according to the Scriptures, and that He appeared to Cephas, then to the Twelve. Then He appeared to over 500 brothers at one time, most of whom remain to the present, but some have fallen asleep. Then He appeared to James, then to all the apostles. Last of all, as to one abnormally born, He also appeared to me.[86]

---

84   Augustus Hopkins Strong, *Systematic Theology: A Compendium and Commonplace-Book*, Vol. 3, 938. He writes further: "The correlative truth of the believer's death and resurrection, set forth in baptism, implies, first,—confession of sin and humiliation on account of it, as deserving of death; secondly,—declaration of Christ's death for sin, and of the believer's acceptance of Christ's substitutionary work; thirdly,—acknowledgment that the soul has become partaker of Christ's life, and now lives only in and for him. A false mode of administering the ordinance has so obscured the meaning of baptism that it has to multitudes lost all reference to the death of Christ." Augustus Hopkins Strong, *Systematic Theology: A Compendium and Commonplace-Book*, Vol. 3, 943.

85   Ibid., 944.

86   1 Corinthians 15:1-8 (HCSB). When Paul writes that the Corinthians may have believed to no purpose, he is emphasizing the uselessness of belief in a Christ who was not raised from the dead. All of chapter fifteen concerns

Baptism (risking repetitiveness, I will again comment on the word: it is a transliteration of the Greek New Testament term which, literally translated to English, means *immersion*) is the vivid portrayal of this gospel truth for the believer. Jesus the Messiah, God's Son from eternity, is my representative and substitute in real history in His death, burial, and resurrection. In Christ I died, and I was buried, and I was raised again to new life by the power of God. Only baptism of the believer by immersion so beautifully demonstrates this truth and publicly witnesses to the faith of the one baptized. Any other mode is misleading. As Augustus Strong said, "A false mode of administering the ordinance has so obscured the meaning of baptism that it has to multitudes lost all reference to the death of Christ."[87] It is either a wonderful coincidence that this particular tradition does picture Christ's death and resurrection, or it is the biblical design of God for Christ's disciples. Baptists believe it is the latter because, for them, immersion *is* baptism, to use the Pauline phrase, "according to Scriptures."

WHO IS TO BAPTIZE?

One other topic arises concerning baptism: who is allowed to baptize? Some other Christian traditions have a strict rule about this issue. For instance, the Roman Catholic church will ordinarily allow only an authorized priest or bishop of the church to baptize, otherwise the baptism is not seen as valid. This is because baptism is seen as a sacrament, something which conveys grace through the church. Therefore, a duly authorized, ordained representative of the church must administer it, except in

---

this issue. Apparently, some in the Corinthian church were, Sadducee-like, promoting the notion that the resurrection was not necessary. This, of all things, to Paul was ludicrous, and he is correcting this misunderstanding vigorously. To believe in a dead Christ would be no better than any other teacher or guru in all of history who has been given honor. A resurrected Christ is a Jesus with eternal life to give, the Son of God sent from heaven, and therefore we are justified in believing in Him as the only way to God.

87 Augustus Hopkins Strong, *Systematic Theology: A Compendium and Commonplace-Book*, Vol. 3, 943.

cases of necessity. In order of priority, the bishop, then a priest, and then a deacon have authority to baptize in the Roman church. The bishop has preeminence because of the concept of apostolic succession, which is the foundation for the authority the Catholic Church arrogates to itself. The Catholic Catechism teaches:

> The ordinary ministers of Baptism are the bishop and priest and, in the Latin Church, also the deacon. In case of necessity, any person, even someone not baptized, can baptize, if he has the required intention. The intention required is to will to do what the Church does when she baptizes, and to apply the Trinitarian baptismal formula. The Church finds the reason for this possibility in the universal saving will of God and the necessity of Baptism for salvation.[88]

The whole issue becomes rather complicated with hierarchies of 'ordinary' and 'extraordinary' ministers of baptism within Romanism, since baptismal regeneration is taught, and salvation is at stake for the subject of baptism. The extraordinary minister is only authorized in case of necessity where the official, ordinary minister is not available. Garrett sums up the Roman case: "In the Roman Catholic Church, although an ordained priest or bishop normally administers baptism, exceptions in cases of emergency allow for laymen, laywomen, or non-Catholics to administer baptism."[89]

Baptists, on the other hand, view baptism as an ordinance authorized by the command of Christ for the church (thus the word *ordinance*: ordained or ordered, and established, by Jesus Himself) and therefore, whomever the church designates to baptize is the administrator, most often the pastor. Jesus did not baptize often, if at all. In the letter to the Corinthians, Paul says that he, even as an Apostle, did not baptize many. Who the baptizer is does not seem to be as important in the New Testament as the name in Whom one is baptized. Baptists consider the sacramen-

---

88   *Catechism of the Catholic Church*, online, art. 1256 (www.vatican.va/archive/ENG0015/__P3L.HTM).

89   James Leo Garrett, Jr., *Systematic Theology: Biblical, Historical, and Evangelical*, Vol. 2, ch.73, V, D.

tal view of baptism to be an aberration not found in the New Testament. Therefore, there is no saving power in the ordinance, and the question of who administers it is less significant.

There is no succession of bishops in Baptist theology. The local congregation of disciples governs the church, as is demonstrated in the book of Acts. This authority is bestowed by Christ (as in Matthew 28) and applies to the here and now (Christ being a living Lord and Head of the church), and thus no successionist idea is necessary for church authority. The ordinance of baptism is for the church and therefore should generally be done in a church setting so that worship and celebration can be experienced by the congregation of disciples. As baptism is entrance into the church, identifying oneself with a local gathering of Christians, it is administered within that context. Baptizing someone in the ocean on a whim, for instance, with no church gathered (with which the one baptized seeks to identify), would be misleading to a new convert from a Baptist point of view. So, for Baptists, "baptism is normally administered by the congregation with the pastor as baptizer."[90]

A helpful summary of a Baptist position concerning the question of the administrator of the ordinance is found in W. T. Conner's work *Christian Doctrine*:

> A word might be said here about another phase of the ordinance of baptism. Who has the authority to Baptize? Another way of putting the matter is this: Who is responsible for administering the ordinance?
>
> In general three answers are given to this question. One is that the "clergy," or officially recognized ministry, is responsible for the ordinance and has the authority to administer it. But this theory draws a line of distinction between "clergy" and "laity" that is foreign to the New Testament and tends toward sacerdotalism and sacramentalism. The New Testament gives no intimation that there is to be an official

---

90   James Leo Garrett, Jr., *Systematic Theology: Biblical, Historical, and Evangelical*, Vol. 2, ch.73, V, D. Notice the congregation has the authority to administer baptism, not the minister. He is only given that authority by the congregation.

class who by being "ordained" are to have conferred on them the "authority to administer the ordinances" or to perform other ecclesiastical functions that other Christians cannot perform. A pastor or other "ordained minister" or official in administering the ordinances is only acting as a spokesman or representative of the congregation or church and has no other authority than that which comes by virtue of his being such a representative or spokesman.

Another view is that an individual Christian can baptize. But this would lead to all sorts of irregularities and confusion. The other view is that the responsibility for the administration of the ordinance rests with the congregation or church. This we believe to be the correct position. One reason for it is that baptism is generally recognized as the means of publicly confessing Christ and identifying oneself with the congregation or community of believers. This was clearly the case in the New Testament. If this be true, then baptism is a community affair. It is not a purely individual act. But there is a community responsibility with reference to the administration of the ordinance.[91]

---

91 Walter T. Conner, *Christian Doctrine* (Nashville: Broadman Press, 1937), 283-284. Dr. Conner continues with a reply to a possible objection to his view of the administrator of baptism: "It may be objected here that the case of Philip and the eunuch does not agree with our contention, but supports the view that any Christian should be allowed to baptize. It is true that Philip baptized the eunuch. Nor is it necessary to suppose that any church had given him any special authority in the matter. Such a supposition would be a pure assumption with no ascertainable facts to justify it. Where there is no church, we believe any Christian or group of Christians could administer the ordinance. But where there is a church, the whole church is concerned, since baptism is a ceremony by which one publicly and formally identifies himself with the Christian community. What concerns the whole community of Christians the whole community has the right to regulate. Such a matter should not be left indiscriminately to any individual. When Cornelius and his household were converted, Peter consulted the group of Christians that came down with him from Jerusalem. If an individual should administer the ordinance, where there is no church, as in the case of a missionary in unevangelized territory, when the

It has been interesting to me over the years to note how often this question concerning who may baptize has come up as I have taught Baptist history. There seems to be some confusion in our time, which, for me, Dr. Conner's treatment of the question clears away (you may compare my attempt above to deal with this issue and then read the longish quote from *Christian Doctrine* and understand why I included the several paragraphs). He grounded his conclusions in Baptist principles: a believers' church where *all* are saints and priests and therefore the congregation is the final authority. These principles will be the subjects of the next chapters: Believers' Church, Congregational Rule, and the Priesthood of the Believer.

CONCLUSION

It all comes back to the Greek New Testament word *baptizo literally* meaning 'to immerse.' Baptism, then, is a dramatic representation of the believer's identity with Christ in His death, burial, and resurrection through faith. Therefore, it is not for babies or unbelievers. This is a cardinal tenet of the Baptist faith. Baptists have been insisting on this for 400 years, just as the Anabaptists did before them in the sixteenth century. Baptists believe this doctrine of believer's baptism to be derived from the New Testament and thus even more ancient, going all the way back to Christ Himself and the first apostles. It is consistent with the great salvation doctrine "justification by faith alone," and is the only baptism that safeguards the important Reformation watchwords *sola fide, sola scriptura, and sola gratia:* faith alone according to scripture alone by the grace of God in Christ alone. Salvation precedes baptism and church membership and is preceded by faith. This order establishes the distinction between salvation and the church. It dispels the fog of confusion emanating from the conflation of salvation and church membership which occurs when infant baptism and/or salvation via institutional rites are embraced. One who looks to God alone for salvation through His Son is a believer. He or she is then baptized, attesting to

---

baptized person comes to a church asking for recognition and fellowship, the church can recognize the baptism by receiving him into fellowship."

this new bestowal of grace and the new life and new relationship with God that all come only by faith. These are vital truths that do not admit of any infant baptism or any other mode than immersion. Considering Scriptural authority and salvation truth to be non-negotiable, Baptists resolutely affirm believer's baptism by immersion. That's why Baptists are called Baptists.

Chapter 3

Believers' Church

The foundation for Baptist ecclesiology rests on the biblical cornerstone of the theology of believer's baptism. If only regenerate disciples of Christ are baptized, then only born-again, deliberately professing Christians are in the church. It is simple logic. The key word in these irreplaceable precepts is *believer*. Faith is the key to Christianity, as a response to Christ's word and finished work. We respond to God, Who on His own authority claims to offer us eternal salvation in Christ. Faith, then, is trusting God and no one and nothing else. No religious rite or work avails us. Christ finished the work on our behalf in the first century. Thus, baptism is for believers, and the church is composed of believers who have made a conscious decision to trust Christ for salvation and to continue to follow Him trustingly in fellowship with others who have demonstrated the same belief through their own baptism. So, the Baptist answers the question "who is in the church?" very simply: believers who have publicly identified with Christ and other believers through baptism.

BELIEVERS' CHURCH IN HISTORICAL CONTEXT

During the Reformation, western Christianity was divided into three primary forms: the state-Roman church, the state-Protestant church, and the free church. This free church tradition is one which continues today amongst many evangelicals, including Baptists. It was a radical notion in the Reformation period to think that a church consists not of those who happen to live in a designated area, but of believers who come together by choice. This idea is basic to Baptist belief. Those who have believed and are baptized, by their own volition, constitute the church. This is the believers' church, a gathering of disciples who come together for worship, fellowship, and service. Voluntary faith in Christ, then, is the principle by which the church is delineated, not a territorial boundary as in a parish, diocese, or episcopate.

Baptists share this idea of a free, voluntary church with their spiritual forbears, the Anabaptists. One of the strongest beliefs of the Anabaptists was the biblical idea of a changed, holy life for the Christian. This changed life was to be the mark of the believers' church. They differed from the magisterial (state-supported) reformers in being more radical on this point and reintroduced congregational church discipline as a major element in church order. Discipline's purpose was to maintain the purity of the life and doctrine of the gathered. A territorial church, which the Protestant reformers retained from their Catholic heritage, could not maintain the purity of the church by mere biblical church discipline.[92]

---

92 Although Luther stressed Christian works of love in other writings, the necessitarian statements he made, especially in *The Bondage of the Will*, seemed to imply that all things, including Christian obedience, were already determined. This led, in some instances of the evangelical Reform, to a de-emphasis on a holy lifestyle. This problem is connected with the residual Romanist idea of a regional church, the concept of "Christendom," which the Magisterial Reformers retained, along with its attendant sacrament of infant baptism. In contrast to the Magisterial Reformers' idea of the church, the Anabaptist theologian Balthasar Hubmaier wrote: "For baptismal Scriptures do not apply to them [infants] but to those who now believe and confess their faith orally. On this confession Christ built his church, Matt. 16:18. And this is the order: (1) Christ, (2) word, (3) faith, (4) confession, (5) water baptism, (6) church." Balthasar Hubmaier, On *Infant Baptism Against Oecolampad*, in *Balthasar Hubmaier: Theologian of Anabaptism*, ed. Wayne Pipkin and John H. Yoder, Classics of the Radical Reformation (Scottdale: Herald Press, 1989), 286. A voluntary church as opposed to a territorial church, then, was at the heart of Anabaptist theology concerning the composition (baptized believers) and the character (disciples seeking to follow Christ and represent Him in holiness) of the church. This has also been the essential Baptist view through the centuries.

Since those who were baptized as infants had no real choice in coming to Christ, many exhibited no real change of heart or life. Therefore, the state church called in the secular power to maintain order in society and in the church by law, and thus by force. A regenerate church membership was not on the program for Protestant Europe.

Baptists, like the Anabaptists of the sixteenth century, believe that a regenerate church is the only kind of biblical church. Born-again believers make up the church, not each citizen baptized into a state institution. This is why we constantly go back to our roots, to those like the Anabaptists and English Separatists who attempted to subject all of life to the truth of God's word about Christ and His church.[93] Jesus Himself did not come to create a powerful earthly institution, but a movement of His followers, indwelt by the Holy Spirit, which would not be bound by territory or culture. He lived His life as the very thorn in the side of the religious institution of His day. He so enraged the Jewish leaders that they had Him killed. Of course, God had greater things than simple martyrdom in mind for Jesus' death.

Jesus did not start a local chapter of a new organization with a clever name and nifty organizational chart. This kind of organizational plan would appear to be more in line with a self-satisfied, human approach: to organize things to death, until the original purpose of the organization becomes obscured, crushed under the increasing weight of the superficial institutional shell which grows through the years. Instead, Jesus came to do something no one in His day would have predicted: to die for the sake of the people. He was pulled many times in the direction of establishing some sort of kingdom on earth, but always walked away.[94] Jesus said, "My kingdom is not of this world." He had eternal matters in mind, matters that He and His Father had already planned: forgiveness for all through His sacrifice on a cruel cross and

---

93   Kenneth Scott Latourette notes concerning the English Separatists: "Even more radical [than English Puritans] were the Separatists or Independents. They were akin to the Anabaptists and believed in 'gathered' churches, not made up of all the inhabitants of a given area, but only of those who were consciously Christian." Latourette, *Christianity Through the Ages*, 106.

94   "When Jesus saw that they were ready to force him to be their king, he slipped away into the hills by himself." John 6:15 (NLT)

resurrection from the grave, the vanquishing of death, offering new life as a gift. He commanded His apostles to make disciples, teaching them the truth about Him and illustrating that truth with two simple pictures: the Lord's supper and baptism. No hierarchical earthly establishment, especially not one associated with temporal power, was necessary or even relevant.

Emphasizing the inapplicability of worldly organization and power to Christ's church, as is clear in the New Testament, Baptist scholar W. T. Connor wrote:

> Certainly we cannot have any kind of territorial or national or world-wide organization called a church. The New Testament knows nothing about any such organization, nor can we have such an organization which governs the local church and thus destroys its autonomy. The Roman Catholic idea is that the supreme authority on earth in civil as well as in spiritual affairs is a world-wide organization called the church, with the Pope of Rome at its head. The state, according to this idea, is simply one function of the church. On the other hand is the idea of Martin Luther and of the Anglican church that the supreme authority is civil and that the church is simply one function of the state. Either of these ideas destroys the church as a spiritual body and makes impossible the church as a fellowship of Christian believers.[95]

Therefore, the church, which is simply a group of baptized believers, is not bound up with the world or the state, but subversive to it, just as Jesus was in His day. He did not settle easily into a niche anywhere in the Roman imperial, Jewish religious, or Hellenistic philosophical culture, nor did His church. The church's essential goal is not to organize or programize or merely survive, but simply to point people to Christ: the One who can gather them into God's family by His blood and His resurrection. When the church loses its focus on Christ, for whatever reason,

---

95   Walter T. Conner, "The Essentials of Christian Unity," *Southwestern Journal of Theology* 51, no.1 (Fall 2008): 29.

it loses its true nature and no longer functions as those *called out of* the world of sin.[96]

Similarly, during the Reformation, the very entity the Anabaptists opposed was the worldly institutional state church, whether Roman or Protestant. The Protestant magisterial reformers did not move far enough away from the established Roman church in the estimation of the radicals. William R. Estep explains the Anabaptist view, "Like Nehemiah, who returned to rebuild the Temple on the old foundation, they saw themselves as rebuilding the visible church on the original foundation, Jesus Christ."[97] On this basis, the word of God, especially the New Testament, remains the standard by which the church measures itself, because the church, by definition, consists of those who confess the truth of the revelation of God in Christ as witnessed to in the Scriptures. For Baptists, like the earlier Anabaptists, the principles that apply to Christ and His church found in Scripture define the church, not the accumulation of tradition through the centuries, no matter how venerable or entrenched it may be.

Spiritual and theological principles, and not mere institutional procedure, then, are the key to understanding the church. Institutional encrustation can be scraped away by anyone willing to study the New Testament. Baptists must be careful to join with the noble Bereans (who searched the scriptures to check the Apostle Paul's teaching) and continually submit church practices and procedures to an honest reading of the New Testament. The simplicity of the New Testament record is striking. The churches were simply groups of disciples who gathered together in a common locality. There were leaders called overseers, shepherds or elders.[98] There were practical servants called deacons. There was baptism, almost always administered immediately after confession of faith, and there was the Lord's supper, a memorial of Christ for the

---

96   Note that the very meaning of *ecclesia*, the Greek word for church, is basically 'those called out.'

97   Estep, *The Anabaptist Story*, 244.

98   Baptists have most often seen pastor, bishop, and elder as synonymous, in accordance with the use of these names for church leaders in the New Testament. The words indicate different functions and not different persons or offices.

believers, taken as a community. These elements all fit beautifully with a free church conception in that no top-heavy hierarchy is needed. Simple organization is helpful, and we see it develop as we examine the book of Acts, but no state church or earthly power is associated with the believers anywhere in the New Testament. The church is a spiritual entity, and the analogies given in the New Testament – a bride, a building, a body – are all pictures of a spiritual community. As Jesus prayed, "I pray not only for these [His disciples], but also for those who believe in Me through their message. May they all be one, as You, Father, are in Me and I am in You. May they also be one in Us, so the world may believe You sent Me."[99]

BELIEVERS' CHURCH UNITY

The Baptist view of the church, then, has historically been one which is distrustful of heavy institutional, organizational, or hierarchical complexities. The unity of the members of the church is spiritual, based on belief in Christ and on the unique characteristics of discipleship. The physical gathering of believers enhances and expresses these essential spiritual qualities. One Baptist scholar observes that in the New Testament, even when physical unity is not possible, spiritual unity is preserved: "In Acts 9:31, 1 Corinthians 15:9, Galatians 1:13 and Philippians 3:6 the physical unity cannot be maintained, but these scattered members of Christ's body have one characteristic that makes them constitute an *ekklesia*–a spiritual unity."[100] Since Christ is head of this spiritual body, it has a unity which is spiritual and thus permanent. For Baptists, no institution or organization can represent this New Testament spiritual unity in any complete sense. The church is not equal to its leaders or to its organizational structure. It is composed of those who have become unified with Christ and with one another through faith. It is manifested in the world and in time in individual assemblies, but unity comes from timeless solidarity with Christ.

---

99   John 17:21-22 (HCSB).

100   Earl D. Radmacher, *The Nature of the Church* (Portland, Oregon: Western Baptist Press, 1972), 135.

This balance between local, time-bound fellowship and eternal union with the Son of God has sometimes been hard to maintain when some seek to be joined with Christ yet avoid meeting with fellow Christians, and others have seen the local physical assembling of the Church as its only form of unity. Earl Radmacher, who taught at Western Conservative Baptist Seminary, explained the unity of the Church, linking the spiritual (or invisible) and local (or temporal, physical) identities:

> The union with Christ is invisible but the church is always composed of people. Even in Ephesians when Paul deals in universal concepts he had definite people in mind, Jews and Gentiles. It should be stated even more emphatically: the New Testament assumes that every Christian will take the necessary steps to give outward evidence of his relationship to Christ and His Body. The New Testament knows of no believer who does not submit himself for baptism and join the local church.[101]

The Southern Baptist confession of faith, *The Baptist Faith and Message*, also tries to strike the balance between the concepts of the spiritual (sometimes named invisible or universal) church and the local assembled church, defining the church in this way: "A New Testament church of the Lord Jesus Christ is an autonomous local congregation of baptized believers."[102] However, the article concludes with this additional statement: "The New Testament speaks also of the church as the Body of Christ which includes all of the redeemed of all the ages, believers from every tribe, and tongue, and people, and nation."[103]

---

101 Radmacher, *The Nature of the Church*, 190.

102 *The Baptist Faith and Message, 2000*, article 6.

103 Ibid. W. A. Criswell, longtime pastor of First Baptist Church, Dallas, Texas, explains this balance between local and universal church in a discussion of the New Testament Greek word for church, *ekklesia*: "The use of *ekklesia* to designate a physical assembly that is distinctively Christian by virtue of spiritual unity is used in Acts 11:22; 13:1; and 1 Corinthians 1:2. Some cases also depict a figurative, not physical, *ekklesia*. Spiritual unity is stressed and the church is not relegated to one specific locality. Such is the concept of the

What it Means to Be a Baptist

Neither of these ideas, a simple assembly of baptized believers or a spiritual community in Christ (both of which must be maintained in order to remain biblical in our ecclesiology) are essentially institutional or organizational in nature. Certainly, the church is not in any way associated with state government in the New Testament. Thus, the Baptist view of ecclesiology can simply be defined as a *believers' church*: believers who are a spiritual community in Christ and who assemble to worship Him and fulfill His calling as disciples to make other disciples while in this world in the time given them. This simple view, however, was altered with accumulated additions over the centuries of church history and developed into a labyrinthine, institutional behemoth of man-made traditions, rules, and procedures best typified by the medieval Roman Catholic Church.

Pressures from persecution and heresy during the time of the early church tended to cause key thinkers of that period to appeal to the bishop's authority, especially when false theological ideas were a threat. These bishops were seen as the custodians of the gospel as passed along from those who had it straight from Christ: the Apostles. A scholar elaborates on the development of the authority of the bishop in the early church:

> Persecution over the years made the bishop-presbyter's (senior pastor's) role more authoritative as he passed on the apostolic teachings and had custody of the Scriptures, commentaries, liturgical materials, and ecclesiastical correspondence and records. Moreover, the bishop-presbyter's role became more authoritative as the church exercised pastoral discipline over its members who succumbed to moral laxity

---

universal church (Acts 9:31; Gal. 1:13; Phil. 3:6). In Matthew 16:18, Jesus could not have meant a local institution but *ekklesia* in the generic sense. In Hebrews 12:23 the assembly is linked to Christ, the Firstborn among brethren (Rom. 8:29). The members of the assembly are citizens of the heavenly as well as the earthly spheres. *Ekklesia*, therefore, is that body of people spiritually united by the common experience of faith in Jesus Christ (the universal sense, as Matt. 16:18 and 1 Cor. 12:13) and physically united in assemblies at various times and places (the local sense, that is, the churches of the New Testament). W. A. Criswell, *The Doctrine of the Church* (Nashville: Convention Press, 1980), 40-41

or fell into heresies. In this manner, the "monarchial bishops" arose. Ignatius of Antioch (d. AD 117) mentioned this mon-oepiscopacy (only one bishop as the head of a local church). In reflecting upon earlier centuries of the church, fourth-century church father Jerome (c. 342–420) noted, "Ancient presbyters were the same as bishops but gradually all the responsibility was deferred to a single person, that the thickets of heresies might be rooted out." The churches where the apostles had personally labored were especially respected: Jerusalem, Antioch, Smyrna, Corinth, Ephesus, Philippi, Thessalonica, and particularly Rome. These churches were regarded as "mother churches" and the wisdom of their bishop-presbyters as heirs to the apostolic teachings was especially valued.[104]

This idea of succession of authority was one of the factors in the development of the institutional church throughout medieval Europe. This consisted of tracing the authority of bishops from the Apostolic period. Of course, the most important bishop in medieval times became the pope of Rome, who claimed his authority was transferred over the centuries from the Apostle Peter. Apostolic succession, then, appears to have evolved from being a useful argument employed by those fighting off heretical ideas in the first centuries of the church to an institutional administration which claimed authority by tracing a series of bishops back to the Apostles via traditions and legends.

Reformers like Martin Luther saw freedom from the burdensome and corrupt Roman church officialdom as possible in espousing the idea that the true church is composed of the elect down through the ages, both living and dead. Thus, for Luther, grace comes directly from God, not through any succession of functionaries which the church claims for itself. This doctrine of election (with its idea of an immediate connection with God through faith), notably championed by the English pre-reformer John Wycliffe in the fourteenth century, emboldened the reformers of the sixteenth century to break away from Roman Catholic control and reestablish a direct relationship with God through His grace rather than

---

104 L. Ron Taylor, "Presbyterianism," in Steven B. Cowan, ed., *Who Runs the Church?: 4 Views on Church* (Grand Rapids: Zondervan, 2004), 87

through the Roman institution. The Reformation espousal of this universal church concept (all the saints of the ages) did not correct the notion of a territorial church, however. The Protestant movement did not forsake the pattern of the state church, which had prevailed down through Medieval times in Roman Catholic Europe. That change was left to the Radicals of the Reformation, especially the evangelical Anabaptists, who believed that any state church was an abomination. The radical reformers saw in the New Testament a distinctive model for church which was nothing like what they observed in their surroundings in the sixteenth century, either Protestant or Catholic. This New Testament model was that of a *believers' church*, championed likewise by Baptists in the centuries following the Reformation era.[105]

From the very beginning of Baptist history, we find Baptists clearly affirming a believers' church. One of the earliest Baptist leaders, John Smyth, espoused the believers' church view in 1609, when he wrote a short confession fittingly entitled *Short Confession of Faith in XX Articles by John Smyth*. The confession begins with the words, "We believe with the heart and with the mouth confess" and then proceeds to name the twenty articles of belief. In article 12 Smyth describes the church:

> That the church of Christ is a company of the faithful; baptized after confessions of sin and of faith, endowed with the power of Christ.[106]

Note here the very concise, simple definition of the church as a 'company of the faithful.' The faithful are those who have confessed faith in Christ, having also been baptized. Likewise, the church is not a nominally Christian religious group but is made up of regenerate believers, having been 'endowed with the power of Christ.' There is no mixture here of those who have confessed faith and those who will yet confess or have relied upon a

---

105 For the modern derivation of the terms 'believers'church' and 'free church' see William L. Pitts, "The Relation of Baptists to Other Churches," in *The People of God: Essays on the Believers' Church*, ed. Paul A. Basden and David S. Dockery (Nashville: Broadman & Holman, 1991), 236.

106 William L. Lumpkin, ed. *Baptist Confessions of Faith* (Valley Forge: Judson Press, 1969), 101.

proxy to confess on their behalf, as in the Catholic and many Protestant churches. Thus, we can see how important the connection between believer's baptism and a believers' church is for Baptists.

BELIEVERS' CHURCH UNITY
AND THE ORDINANCES

There is also a connection for Baptists between a believers' church and the church ordinance of the Lord's Supper. The idea of the church as a spiritual community, based on faith in Christ alone, excludes any sacramentalism (the belief that the "sacraments" are inherently efficacious and necessary for salvation). Believers meet together to worship, for mutual encouragement and admonition, and to hear a word from Scripture, but there is no sacrament in Baptist life.[107] The idea that physically ingesting wafers of bread somehow imparts salvation is foreign to the New Testament and therefore rejected by Baptist churches. No priest and no special incantation to make the Lord's supper officially efficacious are needed in any way for Baptists. What makes salvation effective is what Christ has already accomplished, once and for all, outside of Jerusalem on a cross, having been executed by Roman authorities in the first century. The bread and cup taken in the ordinance are a memorial of those historical events and are significant for modern believers because Jesus of Nazareth is the Son of God. This the believer acknowledges as *truth* enacted and revealed by God Himself in His Son.

Baptist thinker E. Y. Mullins associates the ordinances with this word of truth from God in a forceful denunciation of sacramental religious interference:

---

107 Historian David Bebbington comments on the use of the word sacrament among Baptists: "The very word 'sacrament,' initially used by many Baptists, was long rejected by almost all of them. They preferred the word 'ordinance' on the grounds that the two events were ordained by Jesus." David W. Bebbington, *Baptists Through the Centuries: A History of A Global People* (Waco, Texas: Baylor University Press, 2010), 179.

What it Means to Be a Baptist

Truth apprehended and obeyed is the way of God's kingdom in making men holy. "Sanctify them through thy truth, thy word is truth," was the prayer of Jesus. To make of ordinances sacraments possessing spiritual efficacy in themselves is to change the nature of faith and to degrade the entire process of sanctification. The *opus operatum*[108] of the Roman Catholic Church involves a theory of the ordinances which is subversive of the spirituality of the kingdom. Ordinances as symbols of truth assist faith and explicate the ideals of the kingdom. Ordinances as sacraments obscure both. Baptism and the Lord's Supper as symbols of truth with the explicit sanction of Christ for perpetual observance, taking their places in the kingdom of truth along with other things and operating upon intelligence and faith after the manner of the word, are one thing; but transformed into channels of grace limiting and restricting God's love in any degree to the human mediators who administer them, they are a reversion to a lower type of religion. The ordinances are vocal with truth, not magical with occult power.[109]

The power of the supper is in reminding believers of God's love for them, demonstrated in His Son, not in a priest or in the elements of the "sacrament." Nor is it in any institutionalized church which may claim to officiously dispense "salvation" through the elements as, for instance, the Roman Catholic Church and Anglican Church claim. Thus, the Lord's supper is a sign to remind us of Christ. It is a picture, in essence a metaphor, of the historical realities of suffering and death endured by Christ on the cross. These realities are commemorated in the simple supper of remembrance in order to confirm and recall Christ's work on behalf of the recipient *by faith*.

In this same way, Baptism is also a sign, for the believer and for the church, that signifies faith in Christ, as we have already discussed

---

108 *Opus operatum* is a Latin phrase meaning literally 'the work wrought,' used to denote the spiritual effect in the performance of a religious rite which accrues from the virtue inherent in it, or by grace imparted to it, irrespective of the administrator. In other words, the rite itself has the power to impart grace. Jesus told us to remember Him, not to place our faith in ecclesiastical rituals.

109 Edgar Young Mullins, *The Axioms of Religion*, 40-41.

in a previous chapter. These two simple ordinances, then, channel the believer's faith toward the person of Christ, not to any priest, institution, or sacrament. To summarize concerning the two expressions of union with Christ (and therefore with other disciples) in the believers' church: Baptism and the Lord's Supper are *ordinances*;[110] they

---

110 A helpful definition of *ordinance* is: "A ceremony which the Lord commanded that His church should observe and one in which the gospel is portrayed. An ordinance is practiced as a memorial act of obedience rather than as a sacrament. There are two such ordinances: baptism and the Lord's Supper." From *The Believer's Study Bible*, eds. W. A. Criswell, Paige Patterson, glossary. Many Protestants will often throw around the term sacrament as something having an actual, salvific affect on the participant. Baptists say No. Why is this important? Because Jesus said *tetelestai*, "It is finished." That's what our faith is *in*—the fact that He has done it all. That's why it's all grace, and all trust in Him, not in any circus hoop I can jump through that some preacher or priest is there to administer. Jesus has done it all. Once and for all, as the New Testament keeps on saying. The Lord's Supper is therefore viewed as a memorial. That's why in most Baptist churches, you go in and there's a middle aisle, and at the front is the Lord's Supper table. Usually, the words at the front of the table are: "This Do in Remembrance of Me," so that this publicizes to anyone that enters that what we do here in the Supper is a memorial, a remembrance, to remind ourselves that our faith is in what Christ has finished. That He is now the risen Lord that has promised to come back. So, it is not a sacrament; it is not a magical salvation administration that only the priest can give you. It's a memorial, with the bread and the cup being symbolic of the body and blood of Christ. In fact, if you'll humor me, I'll prove to you right now that the bread and cup *have* to be symbolic—*have to be*. When Jesus was there with the disciples at the last supper, and He tore off a piece of bread and said, "this is my body," what were they thinking? Were they automatically thinking, "Wow, He turned that bread into part of His body?" Is that what the disciples were thinking? He was sitting right there—His body was right there. "This is my body." It's a metaphor, from a teacher who used metaphors all through his ministry. "I am the door; I am the shepherd; I am the bread of life," all the way through His teaching. His literal body was right there, and no one saw a chunk of Him being taken out. So, this is a memorial—it is to remind us. That is why Jesus said explicitly, "do this in *remembrance* of me." Now why would I make a big deal of this? Because a lot of Christians don't believe this! It's unbelievable, but true. They believe in their secondary tradition instead of the New Testament, instead of reading it in a straightforward manner. So, the bread and the cup being

are not sacraments, which are represented by Catholic, Orthodox and some Protestant groups as having an actual salvific effect on the participant.[111] Salvation comes through no act or religious rite or priest-

---

symbolic of the body and blood of Christ, these symbols represent the finished work of God in the cross for the believer's salvation, to which nothing is to be added. Very important. *Sola fide, sola gratia.* Nothing is to be added. When we commemorate Christ's sacrifice, we remember His words, "it is finished," and so our faith is directed to our Savior's work and not our own. The *whole point* is to remind myself that it was the Savior's work, and only He could do this for me—I don't contribute anything. I just accept His work for me, and that's called faith. And yet, many churches make of this remembrance supper, with the whole point being to remind me that it's all *Him*, a work. Extraordinary, isn't it? Catholics and Protestants get this idea that somehow going through this motion is partly what saves us, when the whole point is to remind us that Christ has *already* saved us.

111   For example, Augustine's belief in needing baptismal regeneration for guilty infants. The argument runs something like this in summary: " . . . a sinner begets a sinner, so that the guilt of original sin has to be removed in infancy by the reception of baptism . . ." Cited in Henry Bettenson, ed., *The Later Christian Fathers: A Selection from the writings of the Fathers from St. Cyril of Jerusalem to St. Leo the Great* (New York: Oxford University Press, 1972), 198. Augustine based this questionable teaching (infant baptismal regeneration) partly upon the fact that infant baptism was already being practiced in the church during his time:"Hence also that other statement: The Father loves the Son, and has given all things into His hand. He that believes in the Son has everlasting life; while he that believes not the Son shall not see life, but the wrath of God abides on him. John 3:35-36 Now in which of these classes must we place infants—among those who believe in the Son, or among those who believe not the Son? In neither, say some, because, as they are not yet able to believe, so must they not be deemed unbelievers. This, however, *the rule of the Church does not indicate, for it joins baptized infants to the number of the faithful.* Now if they who are baptized are, by virtue of the excellence and administration of so great a sacrament, nevertheless reckoned in the number of the faithful, although by their own heart and mouth they do not literally perform what appertains to the action of faith and confession; surely they who have lacked the sacrament must be classed among those who do not believe in the Son, and therefore, if they shall depart this life without this grace, they will have to encounter what is writ-

ten concerning such—they shall not have life, but the wrath of God abides on them." Emphasis added. Augustine, *On Merits and Remission of Sin, and Infant Baptism*, Translated by Peter Holmes and Robert Ernest Wallis, in *The Collected Words of Augustine of Hippo* (Hastings, East Sussex, UK: Delphi Classics, 2016), ch. 28. Augustine's doctrine of infant baptismal regeneration was founded on, in addition to church practice (for it is not found in the New Testament), his belief that every person born is not only affected or infected with original sin inherited from Adam (and/or Eve as in the case below), but also guilty of that original sin. Augustine expressed these notions in the following: "As a consequence, then, of this disobedience of the flesh and this law of sin and death, *whoever is born of the flesh has need of spiritual regeneration — not only that he may reach the kingdom of God, but also that he may be freed from the damnation of sin.* Hence men are on the one hand born in the flesh liable to sin and death from the first Adam, and on the other hand are born again in baptism associated with the righteousness and eternal life of the second Adam; even as it is written in the book of Ecclesiasticus: Of the woman came the beginning of sin, and through her we all die." Emphasis added. Augustine, *On Merits and Remission of Sin, and Infant Baptism*, ch. 21. The key New Testament passage is Romans 5, which compares Adam as the first man and Christ as the new man. The problem arose, partly, according to James Leo Garrett, because Augustine used an inaccurately translated Latin New Testament: "Augustine of Hippo, who utilized the Old Latin versions of the New Testament that prevailed prior to Jerome's Vulgate, mistakenly read the Greek *eph' hō*, 'because,' as equivalent to the Latin in quo, 'in whom,' and thus misinterpreted the phrase to mean 'in whom all have sinned.' This mistranslation served as biblical 'support' for Augustine's doctrine of peccatum originale, or 'original sin.'" James Leo Garrett, Jr., *Systematic Theology: Biblical, Historical, and Evangelical*, Vol. 1, ch.36, III, A. We find Augustine using this mistaken rendering from the Old Latin version in speaking about the 'seminal identity' of everyone born from Adam's line, in that we all sinned 'in him,' which is the basis for the idea that infants are born guilty of this 'original sin.': "The apostle cries, 'Sin entered the world through one man, and through sin came death, and thus it passed on to all men, for *in him* all sinned'. Hence it cannot reasonably be asserted that Adam's sin harmed those who did not sin; for the Scripture says, 'All Sinned in him'. And those sins are not spoken of as belonging to someone else, as if they did not affect little children: seeing that in Adam all sinned at that time, since all were already united with him by that power to beget them with which his nature was endowed. But those sins are said to be another's in that Adam's descendants were not at that time leading their own lives; however, the life of one man embraces all that was to be in his posterity." Cited in Bettenson, ed., *The Later Christian Fathers*, 198. Just to be clear, Augustine makes a statement about the fact that infants don't have free will in order to commit sin: "Although infants do not possess free will, there is no illogicality in calling their original sin voluntary, since it derives from the misused will of the first man, and is theirs as it were by heredity." Cited in Bettenson, ed., The Later Christian Fathers, 199. Unfortunately, this tedious misapprehension survived for centuries and is still with us in the form of infant baptism, hardened Calvinistic theology, and Catholic sacerdotalism. As Norman Geisler states: "Augustine (354-430) has been given the dubious honor of being the first to teach the damnation of all *unbaptized* infants—essentially, the wrath of God abides on them. He did allow, however, that unbaptized infants who die do not suffer as severely as those who live to adulthood and commit actual sins." Norman Geisler, *Systematic Theology*, vol. 3 (Grand Rapids: Bethany House, 2004), 436. The Southern Baptist New Testament scholar, Walter Conner, unequivocally rejected the idea that infants, or anyone else, is condemned based on Adam's earlier guilt. Commenting on the first chapter of Romans, he wrote: "Paul does not teach here or anywhere else that any man will be condemned purely on the account of Adam's sin." Conner argues that Romans 5 (specifically v. 12) must be interpreted in light of Romans 1, and does so in the following manner: "Paul concluded, then, that all men are under the judgment of God (Rom. 3:19), not on the ground that they have failed to meet the requirements of an ideal and abstract law, of whose requirements they had no specific knowledge, *nor on the ground that they were seminally present in Adam and were responsible for Adam's sin,* nor on the ground that they were held responsible for Adam's sin because Adam represented them in a covenant that God made with Adam. Paul based their condemnation on the facts of experience and history; namely, that they had knowledge of right and wrong–the will of God–revealed through nature and their own inner consciousness, in the case of the Gentiles, and through the Old Testament law, in the case of the Jew, and that in spite of this knowledge they did that which they knew to be wrong. Paul asked men to face the facts of their own experience–facts which they recognized and could not deny–and he pointed out to them that on the basis of these facts they were under the judgment of God." Emphasis added. Walter Thomas Conner, *The*

ly ministrations, but through the finished work of Christ, and faith that He accomplished salvation once and for all on behalf of any who choose to believe in Him (see the priesthood of all believers in a later chapter). The Lord's Supper, therefore, is viewed by Baptists as a *memorial*, with the bread and the cup being symbolic of the body and blood of Christ. These symbols represent the finished work of God in the cross for believers' salvation, to which nothing is to be added. When we commemorate Christ's sacrifice in the Lord's Supper, we remember His words, "It is finished," and so our faith is directed to our Savior's work and not our own. For Baptists, this truth itself is what sanctifies and unifies the saints, not institutional religious rites involving the operations of officious priestly authorities.

Conclusion

Baptists view the church as composed of believers only. These believers have made a conscious decision to become followers of Christ and, as Jesus promised, have received forgiveness and life in Him. This deliberate decision to become a disciple of Christ is a voluntary and free choice, so

---

Cross in the New Testament (Nashville: Broadman Press, 1954), 77-78. The influence of Augustine's wrongheaded interpretation of Romans 5:12, based on a faulty Latin translation, can be seen to this day. An example is in Leland Ryken's *Literary Study Bible* (ESV). In the note for this verse, he states: "In the same way that God once justly imputed Adam's sin to the entire human race (resulting in condemnation and death), so now God freely and graciously imputes the righteousness of Christ to everyone who has faith in him (bringing justification and life)." However, the verse in the ESV itself says nothing about imputing sin to the human race. It says: "Therefore, just as sin came into the world through one man, and death through sin, and so death spread to all men **because all sinned**," which clearly indicates that sin *spread* through the individual sinning of all men and death spread because all sinned. *Because* all sinned, not *in whom* (Adam) all sinned. The guilt and resulting death are due to (*because*) of the sin of each and every person who sinned. No imputation of the guilt and condemnation of Adam's sin is found in a plain and candid reading of this verse.

that the church is a gathered group of believers. A territorial or parish or state church is never sanctioned in the New Testament and is therefore rejected by all Baptists. In a free believers' church, true discipleship is the norm, and the faithful are encouraged by one another as fellow followers of Christ. Rebuke and admonishment are also necessary, and therefore church discipline takes place within the New Testament framework of a voluntary, gathered church. The gathered church is made up of folks who come together on purpose as believers for mutual fellowship, service, and worship. The church is not defined as those in a certain territory or parish who are expected to be "christian" and attend services as in a state church model. Voluntary Christian discipleship is the ideal for the church member, and identification with the Lord Jesus Christ in baptism is the believer's initiation into the church body. The faith confession symbolized in baptism is the sign of solidarity with fellow regenerate Christians in a local church with which the new disciple pursues life with Christ in corporate and spiritual fellowship.

As has been mentioned, this corporate solidarity and fellowship is a *spiritual* (and not a territorial or organizational) one, as is fitting for those in relation, by faith, to the Father, the Son, and the Holy Spirit. The Apostle Peter describes church unity in this way: "And you are the living stones that God is building into his spiritual temple."[112] Baptist scholar John Hammett believes the case for a church made up of regenerate believers as a spiritual body is clear and self-evident in the New Testament:

> The biblical basis for seeing the church as composed exclusively of believers is so strong and obvious that the difficulty is in seeing how this idea was ever obscured. The very idea of the church as the called-out ones presupposes that the members of the church have heard and responded to God's call. The image of the church as the people of God assumes that these are people who belong to God. They are referred to more than sixty times as saints, or holy ones (*hagioi*), or people set aside for devotion to God. They are the ones who believe in Christ and are bound to one another by

112 1 Peter 2:5 (NLT).

the Holy Spirit. The church is the body of Christ, and believers form one body in Christ (Rom. 12:5). A common possession of Christ is the ground of the church's unity. The church shares "one Lord, one faith, one baptism; one God and Father of all, who is over all and through all and in all" (Eph. 4:5-6). It is difficult to see how the church could be described as the body of Christ or the temple of the Spirit if some of the members of the body or some of the living stones in the temple had no connection with Christ or the Spirit. The very distinction in the New Testament between the church and the world indicates that the church differs from the world, and does so because the church is composed of those who believe in Christ, belong to God, and are bound together by the Spirit. The church is obviously composed of believers.[113]

---

113 John S. Hammett, *Biblical Foundations for Baptist Churches: A Contemporary Ecclesiology* 2nd ed. (Grand Rapids: Kregel Academic, 2019), 93.

Chapter 4

Congregational Church Polity

Baptists' affirmation of what we have been calling the Believers' Church features a corollary principle regarding how the church is to be governed. Rather than acknowledging a bishop, a pope, a college of cardinals, a synod, a board of elders, or any other top-down form of human authority over the church, Baptists believe a church is to be governed by the congregation itself. According to the New Testament, the church is made up of believers, and believers are the saints in whom God has placed His Spirit, each saint being able to come directly into God's presence. Therefore, each member of the church has a say in what the church decides to do as a whole. This is especially important theologically, as we find the New Testament insisting that each believer holds the absolute status of a priest before God because of the Spirit's indwelling presence and the High-priestly ministry of Christ.[114] The

---

114 Paige Patterson asserts that the New Testament idea of "congregationalism was quite consistent with the theology of the individual believer-priests, each possessing the permanent indwelling of the Holy Spirit (John 14:17). Governance in the church should develop from a theological understanding of Christ, salvation, and the purpose and nature of the believing community. While important Old Testament concepts are retained in the new order, the church is, nonetheless, a new order. As a part of that new order, the priesthood of the few has been replaced by the priesthood of all true believers, and this alone constitutes a radical departure with extensive ramifications in the life and governance of churches." Paige Patterson, "A Single-Elder Congregationalist's Closing Remarks," in Steven B. Cowan, ed., *Who Runs the Church?: 4 Views on Church* (Grand Rapids: Zondervan, 2004), 280.

Apostle Peter wrote, "But you [believers as a group] are the chosen race, the King's priests, the holy nation, God's own people, chosen to proclaim the wonderful acts of God, who called you out of darkness into his own marvelous light."[115]

In addition, there is no power structure and no individual other than Jesus Christ who can function as the head of the church, because the Scriptures state with bold conclusiveness that He is the head and final authority for the church.[116] Christ Himself asserted ownership over the church as its author and protector, and guaranteed its victory, when He said, "*I will build my church; and the gates of hell shall not prevail against it.*"[117] Therefore, no single living human on earth, nor any elite ecclesiastical hierarchy, should claim the authority that Christ has claimed

---

115   1 Peter 2:9 (Good News Translation).

116   Psalm 118:22, "The stone which the builders rejected Has become the chief corner stone."; Ephesians 1:22, "And He put all things in subjection under His feet, and gave Him as head over all things to the church"; Ephesians 4:12, "for the equipping of the saints for the work of service, to the building up of the body of Christ"; Ephesians 5:23 "For the husband is the head of the wife, as Christ also is the head of the church, He Himself being the Savior of the body."; 1 Corinthians 11:3, "But I want you to understand that Christ is the head of every man, and the man is the head of a woman, and God is the head of Christ."; Colossians 1:18, "He is also head of the body, the church; and He is the beginning, the firstborn from the dead, so that He Himself will come to have first place in everything."; Psalm 68:18, "You have ascended on high, You have led captive Your captives; You have received gifts among men, Even among the rebellious also, that the LORD God may dwell there."; Ephesians 4:8, "Therefore it says, 'When He ascended on high, He led captive a host of captives, and He gave gifts to men..'"; Colossians 2:10, "and in Him you have been made complete, and He is the head over all rule and authority."; (NASB). Acts 20:28, "Pay careful attention to yourselves and to all the flock, in which the Holy Spirit has made you overseers, to care for the church of God, which he obtained with his own blood."; Matthew 28:18-20, "And Jesus came and said to them, "All authority in heaven and on earth has been given to me. Go therefore and make disciples of all nations, baptizing them in the name of the Father and of the Son and of the Holy Spirit, teaching them to observe all that I have commanded you. And behold, I am with you always, to the end of the age." (ESV).

117   Emphasis added. Matthew 16:18 (KJV).

Michael W. McDill

for Himself. Many Christian bodies will affirm Christ as having authority over the church and still appeal to some human person (pope, archbishop, patriarch etc.) or body of elites (synod, council, general conference etc.) as an authority over the local church. This seems to Baptists to be inconsistent logically and, most importantly, biblically.

CONGREGATIONALISM DEFINED

Congregationalism, therefore, is the system of church government in which each local church is autonomous, governing itself through democratic processes, seeking corporately to follow the New Testament's mission and order under the guidance of the Holy Spirit and the Lordship of Christ, with each member's input recognized as being of equal weight.[118] Winston Churchill once characterized democracy as "the worst form of Government, except for all those other forms that have been tried from time to time."[119] Considering the sometimes messy democratic process necessitated by congregational government of the church, the same might be said of congregational polity: it may appear to be the worst, except for the others which have been tried from time to time down through church history.[120] Baptists believe strongly that congregationalism is the biblical model, and therefore the best. A Baptist scholar wrote: "The simplicity of believer-priests functioning in Spir-

---

118 From *The Believer's Study Bible*, eds. W. A. Criswell, Paige Patterson, glossary.

119 Richard M. Langworth, ed., *Churchill By Himself: The Definitive Collection of Quotations* (New York: PublicAffairs, 2008), vii. Langworth adds that Churchill "did not originate that line – and never claimed that he did."

120 *Polity* may be defined as a particular form or system of government. Democratic *process* simply refers to members of the church meeting together and voting on issues, each member having a say in the decisions of the whole body. I remember Dr. Paige Patterson (one of the architects of the conservative resurgence in the Southern Baptist Convention in the late 20th century, and a Churchill-like leader for Southern Baptists, who was my PhD mentor at Southeastern Baptist Seminary), saying something very similar about congregationalism echoing Churchill's witticism concerning democracy.

it-filled cooperation with one another, exercising the gifts of the Spirit under the headship of Christ, is the approach that takes into account not only the evidence of how the New Testament church operated, but also the theology of salvation which makes each believer a priest with access to God through Christ."[121] We find in this statement the important idea, emphasized previously, that one's view of the church affects one's view of salvation, and in this case, we see the reverse is also true.

An expanded example of this affirmation of congregationalism is found in the writings of the Baptist theologian James Leo Garrett, who gives an extended definition in an article affirming congregational rule:

> I propose to define and to defend congregational polity as follows: it is that form of church government in which final human authority rests with the local or particular congregation when it gathers for decision-making. This means that decisions about membership, leadership, doctrine, worship, conduct, missions, finances, property, relationships, and the like are to be made by the gathered congregation except when such decisions have been delegated by the congregation to individual members or to groups of members.
>
> The term "final human authority" suggests that the church is under divine authority, and this is most often described in terms of the lordship of Christ and the leadership of the Holy Spirit. The term "the local or particular congregation" is designed to identify a congregation in distinction from ecclesiastical judicatories or denominational bodies. The term "gathers for decision-making" implies that the whole congregation is responsible for such decision-making and that each member has a voice or vote in such. Consequently, it is the intention under congregational polity that the congregation govern itself under the lordship of Jesus Christ (Christocracy) and with the leadership of the Holy Spirit (pneumatophoria) with no superior or governing eccle-

---

121 Paige Patterson, "A Single-Elder Congregationalist's Response" to "Presbyterianism," in Steven B. Cowan, ed., *Who Runs the Church?: 4 Views on Church* (Grand Rapids: Zondervan, 2004), 110.

siastical bodies (autonomy) and with every member having a voice in its affairs and its decisions (democracy).[122]

It is important to notice the theological underpinnings for this defense of congregationalism. We will unpack some of this theology in the following paragraphs.

CONGREGATIONAL THEOLOGY

Jesus Himself tells us that we must be "born again" or "born from above" as those "born of the spirit." These words occur in the context of John chapter three, Jesus' interview with Nicodemus, in which we find the great gospel summary in verse sixteen: Anyone who believes in Jesus Christ will have everlasting life. In this chapter, speaking with Nicodemus, Jesus associates eternal life with the Holy Spirit, and being "born of the spirit." The very life of God resides in those who believe, through the presence of the Holy Spirit. This great theological certainty concerning salvation also points us in the direction of congregational rule in ecclesiology. Since every believer is born again through the Holy Spirit and is in union with God Himself through that same Spirit, we understand that the church, seen through the lens of the New Testament, is a living body of Christ, and therefore not a typical human institution. It makes sense, then, that these "saints" of the Lord who are ruled spiritually by Christ Himself have a greater status in the church than simply being members of a club under the leadership of some human Grand Poobah, as is ordinarily the case in human organizations.

Each believer is in communion with God Himself in so intimate a way that no other mediator or intervening authority is necessary. Because of faith, God Himself has chosen to take up residence in the believers'

---

122 James Leo Garrett, Jr., "An Affirmation of Congregational Polity," *Journal for Baptist Theology and Ministry* 03:1 (Spring 2005): 38. One of the advantages of this kind of extended definition is that it, in this case, clearly explains exactly what congregationalism is. Another advantage is that you may have been able to learn some cool new 'big words' like pneumatophoria to try out on your friends the next time you're together.

lives, to dwell with them and in them. E. Y. Mullins describes this direct relationship with God as it applies to the authority of the church: "Because the individual deals directly with his Lord and is immediately responsible to him, the spiritual society must needs be a democracy. That is, the church is a community of autonomous individuals under the immediate lordship of Christ held together by a social bond of common interest, due to a common faith and inspired by common tasks and ends, all of which are assigned to him by the common Lord."[123] This relationship with God makes of the believers as a body, as the apostle Peter says, "a royal priesthood." A body of royalty, kings and queens serving as priests can only be ruled by a King of kings, the great High Priest who has passed through the heavens, as Hebrews says, which is precisely the case when it comes to the church. Thus, we as believers are given royal status in the New Testament. Together, Peter says of the church, "you yourselves, as living stones, are being built into a spiritual house for a holy priesthood to offer spiritual sacrifices acceptable to God through Jesus Christ."[124] The apostle John also reports from the scene in heaven surrounding the Lamb of God, which proclaims that the redeemed indeed have been made kings and priests.[125]

In this theological scenario there is no need for any ultimate human authority over the believers. No pope, council, synod, or any other Christian elite is needed theologically, and we find no indispensable earthly leader or ruling organization exerting dominance over the church in the New Testament. As James Leo Garrett put it: "If all believers are to exercise the 'royal

---

123 Edgar Young Mullins, *The Axioms of Religion*, 129.

124 1 Peter 2:5 (HCSB).

125 "Now when He had taken the scroll, the four living creatures and the twenty-four elders fell down before the Lamb, each having a harp, and golden bowls full of incense, which are the prayers of the saints. And they sang a new song, saying:

"You are worthy to take the scroll,

And to open its seals;

For You were slain,

And have redeemed us to God by Your blood

Out of every tribe and tongue and people and nation,

And have made us kings and priests to our God;

And we shall reign on the earth." (Revelation 5:8-10, NKJV)

priesthood' (1 Pet. 2:9) through the offering of spiritual sacrifices, then why should not those same believers, who are priests, together participate in and be responsible for the basic decision–making of the congregation?"[126] In a sense, an eschatological perspective, looking into the future from a biblical point of view, informs our theology of the church in the present when we hear in the book of Revelation: "Blessed and holy are those who share in the first resurrection. The second death has no power over them, but they will be priests of God and of Christ and will reign with him for a thousand years."[127] If this is our destiny, and accordingly our spiritual status in Christ even in the present, then surely each church as a group should rule its own house right now, answering to Christ and His word alone through the ministrations of the indwelling Spirit.

CONGREGATIONALISM IN CONTRAST WITH THE ANGLICAN AND LUTHERAN TRADITIONS

This theological position, acknowledging each church member's status as a priest indwelt by the Holy Spirit, leads us to regard each church as *autonomous*, or self-ruling. As Garrett mentioned above, there is no outside authority over the congregation except Christ. Therefore, each congregation decides its own course under the only legitimate authority which applies, that is, "the head of the church," Jesus Christ, as scripture says.[128] As we look at the biblical and theological reasoning undergirding a belief in congregational rule, it may be instructive to take a glance at some of the Christian organizations who ignore the biblical and consistent theology which views Christ as the only head of the church. For instance, the head of the Anglican Church (Church of England) has been, since 1952, Queen Elizabeth II (and now her son, King Charles III). Since Elizabeth I (daugh-

---

126 James Leo Garrett, Jr., "An Affirmation of Congregational Polity," *Journal for Baptist Theology and Ministry* 03:1 (Spring 2005): 45.

127 Revelation 20:6, NIV.

128 Colossians 1:18 says: "Christ is also the head of the church, which is his body. He is the beginning, supreme over all who rise from the dead. So he is first in everything." (NLT) See also Ephesians 5:23.

ter of Henry VIII) came to the throne in 1558, the sovereign of England has functioned as the head of the Church of England. The hierarchy, from the Queen to the archbishop of Canterbury to other bishops and officials of the Anglican Church, is quite extensive and complicated. Baptists, in contrast, hold that the believers in each church are the earthly human authority for the church.

Another group, the Lutherans, harken back in their traditions to Martin Luther as their founder. Luther's ideas about the spiritual nature of the church are biblical when describing the church as a royal priesthood. Unfortunately, the state-church approach he eventually adopted brought the secular ruler in as an authority in church matters. The *Dictionary of Luther and the Lutheran Tradition* notes the inconsistencies in Luther's views as they progressed over time, especially concerning heresy in the church:

> There is absolutely no place for the sword or force among Christians, because Christ rules them by the Spirit alone. "Heresy is a spiritual matter which you cannot hack to pieces with iron, consume with fire, or drown in water. God's word alone avails here" (On Temporal Authority, LW 45:114). *Later, Luther changed his opinion* in the controversies with the Anabaptists, recommending their execution not only for secular crimes (rebellion) but also for blasphemy.[129]

This change in opinion concerning the church represents a surrender to state intrusion into church affairs, and eventually led to the Lutheran church operating as merely another state-church institution competing with Catholics for territory. Although Baptists are connected as a tributary in the stream of protestant history and theology, they never accepted the state as an authority for the church. A complete rejection of the state or any sort of hierarchy as an authority for their churches led the Baptists to affirm congregational rule from their beginning.

The reason Luther changed his view is that his reform was supported and protected by the Prince of Saxony. This encroachment of

---

129 Emphasis added. Timothy J. Wengert, ed., *Dictionary of Luther and the Lutheran Tradition* (Grand Rapids: Baker Academic, 2017), s.v. "Authority," by Sarah Hinlicky Wilson.

the secular government into the church led Luther to advocate physical punishment for those he deemed to be heretics, especially Anabaptists. This position has no resemblance to the New Testament instructions for discipline, commanded by Jesus Himself in Matthew eighteen, in which the church's ultimate response to unrepentance on the part of a sinning believer was simply to "treat him as a tax collector." Luther's turn from a relatively biblical ecclesiology toward using the power of the state to punish and coerce appears to be a black eye for the Lutheran tradition.[130]

---

130 Reformed historian Leonard Verduin explains the dilemma, and thus the evolution, of Luther's thought on coercion: "We see then that the Reformers had to choose between two alternatives, to continue in the tradition of 'Christian sacralism' [state and church as one unified society] or to go in the tradition of the long rebellion against that concept. The latter alternative was fraught with very great difficulty. It would mean to go it alone, without the help of the princes. This would expose the reformatory movement to almost insuperable danger—for, over against it stood the Catholic order, armed to the teeth with weapons which, as history had shown for a thousand years, it was not loath to use. . . . Luther had a decision to make, a hard decision. Let no one belittle the extremely cruel nature of the dilemma which he and his fellow Reformers faced. Humanly speaking the only thing that offered any hope was to construct a rival Constantinianism, a new territorial Church, which could then offer the older Constantinianism some formidable competition. . . . But Luther also had his other moments, when he was more in accord with the New Testament. . . . 'Heretics must be converted with Scripture and not with fire!' In these early days, in 1523, Luther gave voice to the following: 'The soul's thoughts and reflections are revealed to no one but to God; therefore it is impossible to compel one with physical force to believe this or that. It takes another kind of compulsion to accomplish this; physical force is incapable of it.' . . . There were moments in which Luther cherished the ancient Restitutionist hope of having some day a Church of believers. He spoke sometimes, to his most intimate friends, about this pipe-dream. But each time he was jerked back into the world of reality and its harsh requirement. Then the other alternative beckoned. . . . The Reformation had crystallized in the pattern of neo-Constantinianism; there was nothing left but to turn the guns on those who had deserted the Reform because of it [such as Anabaptists]. Luther assigned to his associate Urbanus Rhegius the task of leading the attack, telling him to write a book against the Schwärmer [zealots, extremists, sentimentalists, dreamers], as he now began to call them. Rhegius complied, with a volume in which lavish praise is heaped

The appeal to state power to punish heretics gave the state and the prince of Saxony authority over the church, which is nowhere espoused in the New Testament. One of the misguided interpretations of church history is to credit the Protestant reformation with the freedom we now enjoy regarding religious matters. The reality is that each protestant group moved toward a state-church approach with the goal of controlling more and more territory for their own unique form of Protestantism. This led to many wars and much bloodshed between (and within) Catholic territories and Protestant territories in the two centuries following the beginning of the Reformation in Wittenberg. Anabaptists and other "heretics" were slaughtered without remorse during this time in all European territories by the local and regional state authorities.

CONGREGATIONALISM IN THE BOOK OF ACTS: CHOOSING DEACONS

In Scripture, we never find the government involved in the church. The New Testament church developed in the Roman empire and grew despite the idolatry and oppression of that society. There is never any suggestion in the New Testament that the design of the church would include state intrusion or any sort of complicated hierarchy within the church. If we look at the book of Acts, which records for us key moments of the development of the earliest church, we find that the congregation is called on to

---

upon Constantine and his successors for the direction they had given. Rhegius endorsed to the hilt the policy of coercing those who stand in the way of sacralism, liquidating [executing] them if need be: 'The truth leaves you no choice; you must agree that the magistracy has the authority to coerce his subjects to the Gospel. And if you say, "Yes, but with admonition and well-chosen words but not by force" then I answer that to get people to the services with fine words and admonitions is the preacher's duty, but to keep them there with recourse to force if need be and to frighten them away from error is the proper function of the rulers . . . . What do you suppose "Compelle intrare" [compel them to come in] means?'" Insertions added. Leonard Verduin, *The Reformers and their Stepchildren*, with a foreword by Franklin H. Littell (Grand Rapids: Eerdmans, 1964), 72–74.

make and approve of organizational and theological decisions. One of the earliest controversies which had to be resolved in the church in Jerusalem was the issue of the care of widows in the congregation. You may recall that the Hellenistic, or Greek-speaking, widows felt that they were not being taken care of with the same close attention that the Hebrew widows were, though both sets were Jewish Christians. The apostles called a meeting of *all the disciples*, which was an assembly of the whole church. This is important to note. It was not a meeting of elders or a special committee or a group considered to be more spiritually mature. Acts says the apostles "summoned the whole company of disciples." That "the whole company of disciples" would correspond with a congregational model is obvious. In this case, it was to sort out a problem among the members of the church.[131]

An attitudinal and procedural lesson is interesting to note here. This first church in Jerusalem had many wonderful things happening, and God was moving. There were miracles done by the Apostles. There was significant growth. But there were also people, and thus the same sort of problems we have in our churches when people feel something is unfair

---

131 "Now in these days when the disciples were increasing in number, a complaint by the Hellenists arose against the Hebrews because their widows were being neglected in the daily distribution. And the twelve summoned *the full number of the disciples* and said, 'It is not right that we should give up preaching the word of God to serve tables. Therefore, *brothers*, pick out from *among you* seven men of good repute, full of the Spirit and of wisdom, whom we will appoint to this duty. But we will devote ourselves to prayer and to the ministry of the word.' *And what they said pleased the whole gathering,* and *they* chose Stephen, a man full of faith and of the Holy Spirit, and Philip, and Prochorus, and Nicanor, and Timon, and Parmenas, and Nicolaus, a proselyte of Antioch. These *they* set before the apostles, and they prayed and laid their hands on them." Acts 6:1-6 (ESV). The Christian Standard Bible renders what the English Standard Version has here in the passage, *summoned the full number of the disciples,* as 'summoned the whole company of disciples'; the NIV says, 'gathered all the disciples together'; the New Living Translation has, 'called a meeting of all the believers'; the KJV has, 'called the multitude of the disciples'; the NASB has, 'summoned the congregation of the disciples'; the Contemporary English Version has 'called the whole group of followers together'; the Good News Translation has, 'called the whole group of believers together.'

and tend to grumble. There is no moral judgement on the people who felt things were unfair in the passage, only a prompt consultation with the whole church and a solution, in this case the introduction of a new officer of the church: the deacon. We shouldn't necessarily think that just because conflicts and people problems arise that somehow, we are out of phase spiritually or someone is at fault. Perhaps the best approach is to find a solution that will be satisfactory to all without finger pointing. This is the approach modeled for us here in Acts. This example seems more sensible and wise than a strategy that would include accusing people of sin or malice (assuming that someone must be at fault if trouble emerges), usually resulting in everything becoming personal and blowing up into open conflict. If a problem arises, finger-pointing and blame is *not* the next step. Coming together to find a solution is.

More importantly, for our purposes, we have here a model for congregational rule. Note what did *not* happen. The Apostles, though they had great shepherding and spiritual authority given them by Christ Himself, did not dictate a solution from on high by appointing deacons by decree, but summoned the whole church to decide what to do. They let the church know that they perceived their primary function in and for the church as preaching the gospel. This likely is also an indication of the area of their primary authority as witnesses of Christ's resurrection and proclaimers of the gospel, as He had directed before His ascension (telling them that they would be His witnesses). There is an inference in the passage that to get involved with the details of the care of widows, and the attendant financial oversight and service which this entailed, would take them away from their primary purpose, "prayer and the ministry of the word." In this we see that the Apostles' primary authority (and priority) lay more in the matters of the preaching of the gospel and God's spiritual work than in practical or organizational matters by reason of their professed urgency to "devote" themselves "to prayer and to the ministry of the word." Thus, they left the authority to choose and appoint the deacons to the whole company of believers.

The Apostles were fulfilling their leadership role in the church by suggesting a solution to the problem: appointing deacons. But the book of Acts makes it clear that the whole church decided it was a good idea, and the proposal was thus ratified and carried out by the authority of the congregation itself. "The proposal pleased the whole company. So they chose Stephen," and the rest of the deacons.[132] Note that the proposal pleased the whole company and *they*, that is the whole company, chose the men who would serve as deacons. The passage goes on to note that *they*, the whole church, had the deacons stand before the Apostles in order to be prayed over by the laying on of hands. This is the same way we ordain men for service in a Baptist church today. It is a spiritual exercise which is ratified and carried out by the whole congregation, just as in the book of Acts.

CONGREGATIONALISM IN THE BOOK OF ACTS: THE JERUSALEM CONFERENCE

Another key passage in the book of Acts regarding congregationalism concerns the controversy known as the Jerusalem conference. This theological debate became rather fierce. Paul the apostle tells us that the idea that salvation was also dependent on the keeping of the law was something he rejected entirely. Over and over in his letters, Paul rejects anything added to salvation in addition to God's grace and a response of faith. He even testifies to his having had to confront the apostle Peter on this. In Paul's great freedom-themed epistle, Galatians, he tells the story:

> But when Cephas [Peter] came to Antioch, I opposed him to his face because he stood condemned. For he regularly ate with the Gentiles before certain men came from James. However, when they came, he withdrew and separated himself, because he feared those from the circumcision party. Then the rest of the Jews joined his hypocrisy, so that even Barnabas was carried away by their hypocrisy. But when I saw that they were deviating from the truth of the gospel, I told Cephas in front of everyone, "If you, who are a Jew, live like a Gentile and not like a Jew, how can you compel Gentiles to live like Jews?" We who are Jews by birth and not "Gentile

---

132 Acts 6:5 (HCSB).

sinners" know that no one is justified by the works of the law but by faith in Jesus Christ. And we have believed in Christ Jesus so that we might be justified by faith in Christ and not by the works of the law, because by the works of the law no human being will be justified.[133]

Paul is saying that the Jews who claimed that salvation required the keeping of the law (thus avoiding Gentile contact) had influenced Peter himself, the lead apostle. What a warning to us today not to add legalistic elements to the gospel! This issue concerning the role of the Jewish law in Christian salvation was so divisive that it finally had to be put to rest at the Jerusalem conference, where the apostles and the church at Jerusalem convened in A.D. 50.

In a sense, the whole book of Acts is thematically centered on this issue. We have the story of Paul's conversion and being sent to the Gentiles. But also in the very next chapter, Peter is sent to Cornelius the Roman centurion, and the Holy Spirit manifests in the speaking of tongues as Cornelius and his family are born again. This confirmed to Peter and the Jewish Christians who had traveled with him that salvation and the very presence of God through the Holy Spirit were for the Gentiles and not just the Jews as God's people. This is all important contextual background that helps to set the stage for our discussion of the Jerusalem conference, but it also serves to remind us of the crucial nature of salvation by faith alone through God's grace alone, the theme not only of the book of Acts but the whole New Testament. In Acts fifteen, both Peter and James stand up and make speeches affirming this gospel doctrine. It may be most helpful to quote the passage at length so that we will get the whole story in its context with the key congregational-related phrases emphasized:

> Some men came down from Judea [to Antioch] and began to teach the brothers: "Unless you are circumcised according to the custom prescribed by Moses, you cannot be saved!" But after Paul and Barnabas had engaged them in serious argument and debate, *the church arranged* for Paul

---

133 Galatians 2:11-16 (HCSB).

and Barnabas and some others of them to go up to the apostles and elders in Jerusalem concerning this controversy. When they had been sent on their way **by the church**, they passed through both Phoenicia and Samaria, explaining in detail the conversion of the Gentiles, and they created great joy among all the brothers.

When they arrived at Jerusalem, **they were welcomed by the church**, the apostles, and the elders, and they reported all that God had done with them. But some of the believers from the party of the Pharisees stood up and said, "It is necessary to circumcise them and to command them to keep the law of Moses!"

Then the apostles and the elders assembled to consider this matter. After there had been much debate, Peter stood up and said to them: "Brothers, you are aware that in the early days God made a choice among you, that by my mouth the Gentiles would hear the gospel message and believe [He is referring to the Cornelius incident here]. And God, who knows the heart, testified to them by giving the Holy Spirit, just as He also did to us. He made no distinction between us and them, cleansing their hearts by faith. Now then, why are you testing God by putting a yoke on the disciples' necks that neither our ancestors nor we have been able to bear? On the contrary, we believe we are saved through the grace of the Lord Jesus in the same way they are."

Then the whole assembly fell silent and listened to Barnabas and Paul describing all the signs and wonders God had done through them among the Gentiles. After they stopped speaking, James responded: "Brothers, listen to me! Simeon [Peter] has reported how God first intervened to take from the Gentiles a people for His name [Again the Cornelius Acts 10 event]. And the words of the prophets agree with this, as it is written:

After these things I will return
and rebuild David's fallen tent.
I will rebuild its ruins

and set it up again,
so the rest of humanity
may seek the Lord—
even all the Gentiles
who are called by My name,
declares the Lord who does these things,
known from long ago.

Therefore, in my judgment, we should not cause difficulties for those among the Gentiles who turn to God, but instead we should write to them to abstain from things polluted by idols, from sexual immorality, from eating anything that has been strangled, and from blood. For since ancient times, Moses has had those who proclaim him in every city, and every Sabbath day he is read aloud in the synagogues."

Then the apostles and the elders, **with the whole church**, decided to select men who were among them and to send them to Antioch with Paul and Barnabas: Judas, called Barsabbas, and Silas, both leading men among the brothers. They wrote this letter to be delivered by them:

From the apostles and the elders, your brothers,

To the brothers among the Gentiles in Antioch, Syria, and Cilicia: [Notice how general this address is. It is not to the elders or leaders but to their brothers in Christ, in other words, the church as a whole.]

Greetings.

Because we have heard that some without our authorization went out from us and troubled you with their words and unsettled your hearts, we have **unanimously** decided to select men and send them to you along with our dearly loved Barnabas and Paul, who have risked their lives for the name of our Lord Jesus Christ. Therefore we have sent Judas and Silas, who will personally report the same things by word of mouth. For it was the Holy Spirit's decision— and ours—to put no greater burden on you than these necessary things: that you abstain from food offered to idols, from blood, from eating anything that has been strangled, and from sexual immorality. You will do well if you keep yourselves from these things.

Farewell.

Then, being sent off, they went down to Antioch, and *after gathering the assembly* [the whole church is indicated here], they delivered the letter. When *they* [the whole assembly, the church at Antioch] read it, *they rejoiced* [again, the whole assembly, the church at Antioch] because of its encouragement. Both Judas and Silas, who were also prophets themselves, encouraged *the brothers* [again, a general reference to the believers in Antioch, thus the church is in view here] and strengthened them with a long message. After spending some time there, they were sent back in peace by *the brothers* to *those who had sent them* [remember, the whole church in Jerusalem is referred to here]. But Paul and Barnabas, along with many others, remained in Antioch teaching and proclaiming the message of the Lord.[134]

As we look at the above passage, our focus will be on the authority of the church for making decisions in the early church, in other words, congregationalism, rather than the passage's main point about salvation by faith alone. We will look at a key phrase here describing the conference in Jerusalem. Acts 15:22 notes that after the apostles and elders conferred, they decided, *along with the whole church*, to send a letter to Antioch confirming their view of salvation by faith, no law-keeping necessary. This is important to note, because in this way the whole congregation is ultimately making the decision about salvation, and it is also them sending messengers to the Antioch (primarily Gentile) Christians to proclaim to them this *faith alone* doctrine. Again, like the case with the deacons, the apostles and elders provide spiritual and theological leadership to find the solution to a controversy, but the whole church, both in Antioch and in Jerusalem, affirm and ratify this momentous decision. This is the pattern we find in the New Testament, and it points us to congregational authority for the church.

---

134 Insertions and emphasis added, Acts 15:1-35 (HCSB).

Congregationalism vs Presbyterianism in View of Church Discipline: Jesus' Instructions in the Gospel of Matthew and Paul's to the Corinthian Church

Those who affirm congregational authority in the church have traditionally also appealed to the scripture passage in which Jesus Himself establishes the congregation, the whole church, as the final authority in matters of discipline. This is the passage in Matthew eighteen when Jesus instructs the disciples in how to proceed should one of their number sin against another. The passage sets forth an orderly process commanded by Christ in which the offended brother first goes to the sinning brother to confront him in an attempt to elicit repentance. If no repentance is forthcoming, the brother is to then take another brother (or two) with him and confront the offender again, and if he refuses to repent, the issue is finally taken before the whole church. Note that Jesus mentions the church twice in this passage:

> If your brother sins against you, go and rebuke him in private. If he listens to you, you have won your brother. But if he won't listen, take one or two more with you, so that by the testimony of two or three witnesses every fact may be established. If he pays no attention to them, tell the *church*. But if he doesn't pay attention even to the *church*, let him be like an unbeliever and a tax collector to you.[135]

Jesus sees the church as a whole as the final authority for dealing with sin in the midst of the brotherhood. This is the last appeal for the offending disciple. He must agree that he has sinned, repent, and be restored. Jesus emphasizes this authority of the church even more strongly in that He refers to the unrepentant brother refusing to listen "even to the church."

---

135 Emphasis added. Matthew 18:15-17 (HCSB).

This emphasizes the authority of the church, representing all the believers in this case, and implies that if the sinner won't even heed the church as an authority, then he should be regarded as someone outside the church, an unbeliever.

It is important to note, when discussing congregationalism as it relates to church discipline, that any other form of church authority rules out this explicit order of discipline given by Jesus in Matthew eighteen. A bishop- or elder-ruled church leaves the final word concerning an erring member not under the purview of the church as a whole but under the ruling judgement of a single bishop or a synod of elders. The latter approach essentially takes the authority away from the church and gives it to specially authorized individuals or councils who are placed over the church. One Baptist scholar makes the point that the elder-rule approach to church polity contradicts Matthew eighteen, and the New Testament in general. After quoting Jesus in Matthew 18:15-20, he comments on the dubious hermeneutic of assuming that a board of elders represents the church as a whole, as in Presbyterianism:

> The passage seems clear, does it not? Yet presbyterians assume that "church" here means the church represented in her elders, not the whole church assembled. Of course, this makes perfect sense on their premises, *but we are now asking exactly about those premises.* Upon what basis do they have the right to assume this? The problem with their theory is there is no basis in the entire New Testament to support it. Rather, in numerous places, the church is clearly distinguished from its elders, or it is clear in some other way that the entire church assembled is in view. (Consider, for example: Acts 5:11; 8:1, 3; 9:31; 11:26; 13:1; 14:23, 27.)
>
> Another proof of the arbitrary character of the notion of the church represented in its elders is found in the only other reference to the church in Matthew. Matthew 16:18 clearly does not have this in mind when it says that Christ will build his church and the gates of hell will not prevail against it. The substance of Matthew 18:15–20 itself is against this interpretation. Surely, it is the whole church that is to hold the offend-

er to be a Gentile [unbeliever]. This strongly suggests that it is the whole church, not just the elders representing the church, that was told of the offense and admonished the offender.[136]

This appears to comprise a rather substantial critique of Presbyterianism when it comes to the issue of church discipline and the key passage in Matthew eighteen. How can Jesus be assumed to be alluding to a board of elders when He advises the disciples to appeal finally to the church in the case of a sinning brother? There is nothing in the context or in the passage itself which points to that interpretation. It would seem this represents a case of Presbyterian eisegesis.[137] The church is not the elders, and the elders are not the church. No matter how long the tradition that says so has been around, Presbyterianism still does not line up with the New Testament.

Another passage which helps place beyond doubt the idea that the church as a whole makes the final determination in the case of church discipline is in First Corinthians chapter five. The apostle Paul is here warning the church at Corinth to acknowledge and discipline a repugnant sin in their midst in an attempt to restore the sinner:

It is widely reported that there is sexual immorality *among you*, and the kind of sexual immorality that is not even tolerated among the Gentiles—a man is living with his father's wife. And you are inflated with pride, instead of filled

---

136 Insertion added. Samuel Waldron, "A Plural-Elder Congregationalist's Response [to Presbyterianism]," in *Who Runs the Church?: 4 Views on Church Government (Counterpoints: Church Life)*, ed. Steven B. Cowan (Grand Rapids: Zondervan, 2004), 118-119. Waldron describes the Presbyterian plan for church discipline: "In a presbyterian system of church government, matters of church membership and church discipline may be decided by the elders alone. They are the church representatively in this matter. No vote of the assembled church membership is necessary. The church membership may be informed. Their support may be sought. The decision of the elders is, however, decisive."

137 Eisegesis is basically interpreting the Bible by putting meaning *into* the text from outside the text, in other words, by the interpreter. This is opposed to exegesis, which is getting meaning *out of* the text, allowing the text to speak for itself in interpretation as far as possible.

with grief so that he who has committed this act might be *removed from your congregation*. For though I am absent in body but present in spirit, I have already decided about the one who has done this thing as though I were present. *When you are assembled* in the name of our Lord Jesus with my spirit and with the power of our Lord Jesus, turn that one over to Satan for the destruction of the flesh, so that his spirit may be saved in the Day of the Lord.[138]

Key phrases indicate clearly the fact that the church itself and not a ruling body of elders, or any other authority, is responsible to deal with discipline. First of all, the phrase "among you" in the first sentence must, in context, refer to the church. The whole point of the passage is to rid the church of this sin, not just a small ruling group within the church.

Next, Paul says the man should "be removed from your congregation," indicating that the congregation as a whole is in view and not some other authority or context. The sinning man is in relation to the congregation itself. This is the problem Paul is addressing: sin in the congregation as a whole, which tends to corrupt the whole church. Thus, the church itself must take responsibility to remove the offense. In the same chapter, Paul uses the analogy of yeast, so often used by Jesus, to illustrate how the sin, if left unchecked, will metastasize and cause the whole body to be diseased: "Your boasting is not good. Don't you know that a little yeast permeates the whole batch of dough? Clean out the old yeast so that you may be a new batch. You are indeed unleavened, for Christ our Passover has been sacrificed. Therefore, let us observe the feast, not with old yeast or with the yeast of malice and evil but with the unleavened bread of sincerity and truth."[139] This not only connects church discipline with the Lord's Supper, as we find in other passages in the New Testament, but primarily, for our purposes, shows how the church itself is admonished to "clean out the old yeast" so that the members may celebrate the feast (Lord's Supper) in holiness. This feast is, of course, a whole church celebration, certainly not for a select ruling group only. Thus, the entire congregation is in view here in Paul's exhortation to deal with the sin in its midst for the sake of the spiritu-

---

138 Emphasis added. 1 Corinthians 5:1-5 (HCSB).
139 1 Corinthians 5:6-8 (HCSB).

al health of the church. The phrase *"your* congregation" in verse two points to the whole church being encouraged to take responsibility.

Next Paul says, "when you are assembled," which is a clear indication of the nature of the congregation itself and how it functions. The church is an assembly, and each member has a voice in deciding how to deal with the issue at hand. Paul says that he has already decided against the sinner and clearly states that the assembly should also "turn that one over to Satan." The decision to do this is the church's, but the power of Christ Himself substantiates the mandate of the assembly according to Paul. A Baptist scholar sums up the implications of the First Corinthians five passage for church polity:

> This passage is plainly given to the whole church at Corinth, the same church addressed in 1 Corinthians 1:2 ("the church of God which is at Corinth, to those who have been sanctified in Christ Jesus, saints by calling, with all who in every place call on the name of our Lord Jesus Christ, their Lord and ours"). *The elders of the church in Corinth are never mentioned in this letter.* Indeed, from the contents of the epistle itself it remains uncertain whether this church even as yet had elders (the term "church," however, is used twenty-three times and each time clearly refers to the entire membership of the church called together). In this particular passage there is every indication that the offender is removed by action of the assembled church.[140]

The presbyterian model in which elders have the final say on issues of discipline is conspicuously absent from this passage as well as from Jesus' instructions in Matthew eighteen. As a Baptist scholar puts it, "Thus, in the two major passages where we would on presbyterian terms expect to find the elders acting as the representatives of the church, we find nothing of the sort and no mention of elders at all. It is the entire church assembled together and acting corporately that enacts church discipline."[141]

---

140 Emphasis added. Samuel Waldron, "A Plural-Elder Congregationalist's Response [to Presbyterianism]," in *Who Runs the Church?: 4 Views on Church* Government, 120.

141 Ibid., 121.

Additionally, congregational authority for church discipline noted in these scriptures appears to harmonize seamlessly with the theological ideas undergirding congregationalism we discussed earlier: the church as a royal priesthood with Christ its only legitimate head. If each member relates to Christ the Head individually through the Holy Spirit, any added human authority is excluded theologically. These ideas dovetail with Christ's instructions to His disciples when He said, "But as for you, do not be called 'Rabbi,' because you have one Teacher, and you are all brothers. Do not call anyone on earth your father, because you have one Father, who is in heaven. And do not be called masters either, because you have one Master, the Messiah."[142] There is a biblical and spiritual egalitarianism in these commands which accords with the idea that each member is a priest who may stand on his own before God through Christ. Therefore, by Christ's authority and the Holy Spirit's guidance, the church as a democratic assembly determines important issues which are brought before the congregation. In Baptist writer W. R. Wright's words, "All great matters are referred to the congregations or churches for settlement."[143] This is plainly the case in the key scriptures touching on discipline. Paul's appeal to the authority of Christ as the congregation assembles is worth repeating here: "When you are assembled in the name of our Lord Jesus with my spirit **and with the power of our Lord Jesus**, turn that one over to Satan for the destruction of the flesh, so that his spirit may be saved in the Day of the Lord."[144]

It is also important to note that the purpose of the discipline Paul challenges the church at Corinth to implement is to restore the sinner to a right relationship with God (and therefore with the church), "so that he may be saved in the Day of the Lord." The ultimate purpose of discipline is to prompt the sinner to repent. This ultimate purpose is also expressed in Paul's second letter to the Corinthians, in which he discusses the church's actions after having disciplined someone, very likely the same man as in the passage we've been discussing: "If anyone has caused pain, he has caused pain not so much to me but to some degree–not to exaggerate–to all of you. The punishment inflicted by the majority is sufficient for that

---

142 Matthew 23:8-10 (HCSB).

143 W. R. White, *Baptist Distinctives* (Nashville, Tennessee: Convention Press, 1946), 38.

144 Emphasis added. 1 Corinthians 5:4-5 (HCSB).

person. As a result, you should instead forgive and comfort him. Otherwise, this one may be overwhelmed by excessive grief. Therefore I urge you to reaffirm your love to him."[145] The ultimate outcome of discipline (the word punishment is used here) is to turn the person back to God and the church, repenting and grieving over his sin in order that the church may turn to him in love.

For our purposes, it is worth pointing out that the "punishment" is "inflicted by the majority," which matches perfectly with the idea that the church, the congregation, has the final word as far as Paul is concerned in disciplining the sinner. Again, this verifies the congregation as the authority for the church, only answerable to Christ Himself. Baptist thinker Mark Dever writes affirming the church as the final authority (as has been noted in reviewing these New Testament passages on discipline, especially Matthew eighteen): "Notice to whom one finally appeals, what court is the final judicatory. It is not a bishop or a presbytery; it is not . . . a synod, or a church committee. It is, we read, 'the church,' the whole local congregation, whose action must be the final court of appeal. In matters of disputes between Christians, the congregation as a whole is the final court held out in Scripture."[146]

OFFICERS OF THE CHURCH

The question we've been asking is, who is in charge of the church? Who runs the church? And the Baptist answer is: the congregation. That's an interesting answer, because you may likely think, "Well, it's the pastor, isn't it? The pastor runs the church." And some pastors operate that way—everything is under their control. But when we look at the New Testament, we find that wasn't the case. It was the church that was always appealed to as the final authority, as Jesus Himself did in Matthew eighteen. So, what does this imply? If the congregation governs the church, then it means the church rules itself. There is no outside ruler. There is no Baptist

---

145 2 Corinthians 2:5-8 (HCSB).

146 Mark Dever, "The Church," in *Understanding the Times: New Testament Studies in the 21st Century,* ed. Andreas J. Kostenberger and Robert W. Yarbrough (Wheaton: Crossway, 2011), 99.

Pope (There is a Baptist named Pope–I know him; he's a pastor, but that's his last name. He always gets a lot of jokes about that. But that's about it.). That means the church is autonomous—which means self-ruled. As a result, the church is what we would call democratic: the congregation (the people of the church) decides things for itself, not a bishop or clergy or board of elders or pope. This often calls for a vote. Again, that's the democratic process.

For instance, when the early church chose a disciple to replace Judas, they had several who qualified, and they drew straws—Peter didn't come in saying, "I am the first Pope; I shall appoint the new apostle!" They didn't do that. The group all decided together. Each church is therefore independent of any higher ruling body or hierarchy—the congregation decides. So, each individual member (a born-again follower of Christ indwelt by the Holy Spirit) has a say, based on the principle that the congregation rules the church. This is all done in the freedom of a love relationship between Christ the Lord and the church. It is through this freedom that each member is encouraged to love one another. As in any relationship in its highest order of mutual love between persons, this is all voluntary. Coercion is never affiliated with Christian love. One Baptist writer summarizes the democratic, relational nature of the church in three essentials:

> (1) *Voluntary membership.*–The church is made up of people who voluntarily enter its fellowship. No one is a member of the church by birth. And no one is to be brought into the church against his will. Each one is to make his own choice. Others may seek to influence him and may help him in making his choice but the decision rests with him.
>
> (2) *Equality of privileges.*–In the church each member has equal rights and privileges with all others. The old and the young, the rich and the poor, the educated and the ignorant–all stand on equal footing. Some, by reason of natural ability and training, will become leaders; but they have no right to lord it over their brethren.
>
> (3) *Self-government.*–The church is a self-governing body. There is no individual or organization above the church which

has any authority over it. Every church, under God, manages its own affairs, without let or hindrance from others. And there is no governing body within the church. Governmental authority rests with the members, but this should always be in accordance with divine authority. All matters of polity or policy are settled by a vote of the congregation in dependence upon the Holy Spirit's guidance.[147]

So, a church ruled by its members must use a voluntary democratic method in order to decide, plan, and organize. Just as we see the church in Acts bring the major issues and their solutions before the whole church, so we are able, because of the love of Christ, to follow the same pattern as Baptist Christians today.

Although they are ruled by the congregation, the churches do have officers, as we find in the New Testament—pastors and deacons.[148] One of the matters the church must decide is who will fill these offices. Of course, the New Testament guides the congregation as to those who are eligible to serve and as to the qualifications and descriptions respecting their offices in the church. Historically, most Baptists have understood the office of pastor to be biblically synonymous with the New Testament concepts bishop and elder. Now, some Protestant groups use these words not as synonyms for the same office but as particular offices in the church. The Presbyterians, for example, divide the ministerial office into distinct positions in the church -- elders and pastors -- and thus they advocate elder rule. Of course, many Baptists believe that elder rule, as in the Reformed/Presbyterian model, is not biblical because of the New Testament's assertion of congregational rule. And what happens with the elder rule idea is that you get the 'elite, spiritual people' ruling the 'regular' church people — "I am wise and mature, and I am more spiritual than you, so I have ruling power in the church." This attitude in leadership would seem to smack of presumptuous spiritual superiority because, according to Scripture, all of the believers in

---

147 J. Clyde Turner, *These Things We Believe* (Nashville: Convention Press, 1959), 121.

148 Walter T. Conner insists that, "pastors and deacons are the only officers of a local church clearly referred to in the New Testament. . ." Walter T. Conner, *Christian Doctrine*, 265.

the church are saints. We all have the same status with Christ. We all have the Holy Spirit, do we not? So, it makes sense that we all rule the church as a congregation, as we find in the New Testament.[149]

The pastor/elder/bishop is a spiritual leader in the church, not an oligarch or dictator. He is of the same status as any other member in the eyes of God, a repentant sinner who has received grace through the Holy Spirit and by the accomplishments of Jesus Christ is saved. Thus, no elder rule is necessary theologically, and Baptists understand the pastor, elder, and bishop appellations as referencing different qualities involving the same officer of the church. If you're not sure that in the New Testament the words pastor (shepherd), bishop (overseer), and elder (someone older) are synonyms, let's look at Acts 20:17-28. This includes a farewell speech from Paul, who is heading to Jerusalem:

> From Miletus he sent to Ephesus and called for the **elders** of the church. And when they had come to him, he said to them: "You know, from the first day that I came to Asia, in what manner I always lived among you, serving the Lord with all humility, with many tears and trials which happened to me by the plotting of the Jews; how I kept back nothing that was helpful, but proclaimed it to you, and taught you publicly and from house to house, testifying to Jews, and also to Greeks, repentance toward God and faith toward our Lord

---

149 Another example, from a Baptist viewpoint, of misreading the New Testament in the area of the officers of the church, would be historic Methodism: "The Methodists disregard the New Testament precedent and practice, and have three orders of ministers, ranking one above the other, the bishop, the elder, and the pastor. The New Testament knows no such gradation. In apostolic times the ministers were, on equality. I could not be a Methodist in the face of such a flagrant disregard of the New Testament teaching and practice. Besides, the Methodists clothe these three orders of the ministry with an authority over the churches which the apostles themselves did not presume to exercise. They utterly disregard the sovereignty of the local churches and invest all government in the bishop, elder, and pastor." R. A. Venable, "Why Baptist and Not Methodist," in J. M. Frost, ed., *Baptist Why and Why Not: Twenty-Five Papers by Twenty-Five Writers And A Declaration of Faith* (Nashville: Sunday School Board of the Southern Baptist Convention, 1900), 121.

Jesus Christ. And see, now I go bound in the spirit to Jerusalem, not knowing the things that will happen to me there, except that the Holy Spirit testifies in every city, saying that chains and tribulations await me. But none of these things move me; nor do I count my life dear to myself, so that I may finish my race with joy, and the ministry which I received from the Lord Jesus, to testify to the gospel of the grace of God. And indeed, now I know that you all, among whom I have gone preaching the kingdom of God, will see my face no more. Therefore I testify to you this day that I am innocent of the blood of all men. For I have not shunned to declare to you the whole counsel of God. Therefore take heed to yourselves and to all the flock, among which the Holy Spirit has made you **overseers**, to **shepherd** the church of God which He purchased with His own blood."[150]

As you will observe, in this single speech, Paul is addressing the elders of the church in Ephesus. He encourages them at the end of the speech to pay attention to themselves and to the church (the flock, which implies a shepherd). He admonishes them to remember that the Holy Spirit has made them overseers (bishops) in order to shepherd (pastor) the church of God, which Jesus, the Son of God, purchased with His blood.

Not only does this passage clearly show that the elders *are* the overseers and pastors, but it does so via a serious Trinitarian exhortation for the Ephesian church leaders, charging them to watch over the church since it is God's church, purchased by the blood of Christ, the

---

150 Emphasis added. Acts 20:17-28 (NKJV). Some of the personal guarantees God gave to Paul seem rather harsh. One, given to Ananias whom God sent to help Paul, was that He would show Paul how much he would have to suffer *for His name's sake* (Acts 9). In this passage in Acts 20, the Holy Spirit says chains and tribulations await him. But we remember that Paul had been a persecutor of the believers, and after his conversion gloried in his weaknesses and distress in order to see God work in His strength. A personal application might be that whatever you suffer on your journey for and with God will be worth it in the end, and is stored up as glory and honor to God, and thus that much more precious to you and to Him.

Holy Spirit having made them overseers by His authority. Thus, the elder/bishop/pastor has a weighty responsibility before God for His flock. Another passage showing the synonymous nature of these three appellations, in the form of a charge to the church leadership, is in Peter's first epistle:

> Therefore, as a fellow *elder* and witness to the sufferings of the Messiah and also a participant in the glory about to be revealed, I exhort the *elders* among you: *Shepherd* God's flock among you, not *overseeing* out of compulsion but freely, according to God's will; not for the money but eagerly; not lording it over those entrusted to you, but being examples to the flock. And when the chief *Shepherd* appears, you will receive the unfading crowning of glory.[151]

Again, we see in this passage the qualities or functions of shepherding (pastor), overseeing (bishop), and exemplary maturity (elder) in one position of leadership in the church, which in this case Peter calls the elder. Peter stresses that this is not an office of lordship but one that answers to the chief Shepherd and is guided by His example of suffering and service. So, we have an exhortation to the pastors which appeals here to Jesus Himself as exemplar and authority, and to the reward of a share in His glory.

It would appear, then, that these three terms represent various duties involving the same position. The Pastor is one who shepherds and cares for the people; the same person is also a Bishop who takes responsibility for the church as spiritual leader and overseer; and he is also an Elder–he has wisdom, offers guidance, and is patient, able to counsel and give biblical direction. All this is undertaken as a serious ministry endeavor under the auspices of Christ and the Holy Spirit. E. Y. Mullins explains:

> The New Testament employs the word bishop and elder to designate the same officer, these terms being descriptive of functions and not of separate officials. The bishop or elder is an officer of the local church, not of any group of churches

---

151 Emphasis added. 1 Peter 5:1-4 (HCSB).

with general jurisdiction. His authority is that of influence and leadership rather than official. He is called of the Holy Spirit to the work and is set apart by ordination for the discharge of special functions and has no authority to lord it over God's heritage. And yet as leader and guide the church owes to him its loyalty and support. His task is particularly that of spiritual leadership, while the deacons are charged rather with the temporal affairs of the church.[152]

So that's how Baptists see it. Why do they see it that way? Because they read the Bible without leaning overmuch on any religious tradition. Therefore, there are two officers in the church: pastors (synonymous with elders and overseers/bishops) and deacons.[153] The authority of these two

---

152 Edgar Young Mullins, *Baptist Beliefs* (Valley Forge: Judson Press, 1925), 67.

153 Walter Thomas Conner outlined the Baptist view of the pastoral office, commenting on the Acts 20 passage: "The most significant officer in the New Testament as connected with a local church was that of pastor. There are three terms used in the New Testament for that office—pastor, elder, and bishop. In Acts 20, in the account of Paul's meeting with the elders of the church at Ephesus, in verse 17, they are called 'elders,' while in verse 28 Paul calls them 'bishops' (AS). The verb translated 'feed' in verse 28 means to tend as a shepherd, act as shepherd. This is the verb corresponding to the noun that is translated 'pastor.' So here in one passage, the same men are called 'elders' and 'bishops' and they are exhorted to 'pastor' the flock. Again, in Titus 1:5, 7, Paul uses the terms 'elders' and 'bishops' to apply to the same office. In 1 Peter 5: 1, 2, Peter addresses the 'elders,' and exhorts them to 'pastor' or 'shepherd' the flock. The duties of the pastors are not defined in detail in the New Testament. Evidently they were intended to exercise general oversight in spiritual matters, teach their people, and guide in all the activities of the church. Their character and spiritual attainments must be such as to qualify them for such leadership (1 Tim. 3: 1ff.; Titus 1: 5ff.; 1 Peter 5: 1ff.)." Walter T. Conner, Christian Doctrine, 264. Another helpful outline on this issue is that of Southern Baptist minister Joseph Judson Taylor: "Paul distinctly identifies elders and bishops, and exhorts them to do the work of a shepherd or pastor (Acts 20: 1 7, 28). He calls the elders of Ephesus, and bids them take heed unto the flock over which the Holy Ghost has made them overseers or bishops, to feed—the Greek is 'act the shep-

offices is granted by the congregation and not derived from some hierarchic ecclesiastical organization, and especially not from any state power.

CONCLUSION

For theological and biblical reasons, Baptists affirm congregational polity and local church autonomy as key for their ecclesiology. There is no indication in the New Testament that an individual or elite group is to rule over the church. Each local church rules itself. Any matters that the church must decide are handled by the believers themselves, who make up the church. They are the saints, the living stones of the spiritual temple God is building. They are born-again, Spirit-indwelt brothers and

---

herd to'—the church of God. Here, then, are elders, who are bishops, doing the work of pastors, the three terms being applied to the same persons at the same time. A similar identification is made in the letter to Titus (1:5-7). Speaking of the ordination of elders in the churches, the apostle passing on to mention their qualifications calls them bishops: 'For a bishop must be blameless.' Elsewhere (Phil. 1:1) he addresses bishops and deacons, as an exhaustive division of Scriptural church officers, bishops representing the preachers, and deacons the non-preaching class, nothing at all being said of a third class. Again in the instructions to Timothy (1, 3:1-13) relative to church officers, mention is made of only two classes, bishops and deacons. If there were another class, it would seem strange for the apostle to ignore them, and give no instructions as to their character and qualifications. The only reasonable conclusion is that there was no such class, but that bishops, pastors and elders were the same persons by different titles. Peter does not use the Greek noun episcopos in speaking of the ministry, but he uses the cognate verb in a way that helps in the solution of this question (1 Pet. 5:1-3). Apostle as he is, he calls himself an elder; he claims no pre-eminence, but exhorts his fellow elders to feed, or act the shepherd to, the flock, taking the oversight, or acting the bishop thereof, not as bosses over God's heritage, but as examples to the flock. The beloved John also calls himself the elder, as he writes unto Gaius and the elect lady. And in the light of these passages the correctness of the Baptist position becomes quite clear." J. J. Taylor, "Why Baptist and Not Episcopalian," in J. M. Frost, ed., *Baptist Why and Why Not: Twenty-Five Papers by Twenty-Five Writers And A Declaration of Faith* (Grand Rapids: Zondervan, 1900), 94-95

sisters who are disciples of the Son of God, their Lord Jesus Christ, and thus operate as priests who may enter into the very presence of the holy God Himself. On these theological grounds, and because of the biblical pattern found in the New Testament, Baptists refuse any outside power, whether secular or religious (or any special elite class within the body of believers), as an authority. Baptists desire to acknowledge Christ alone as the head and Lord of His church.

Chapter 5

Cooperation for Missions

Since the beginning of Baptist life, churches have associated and cooperated to achieve goals together which could not be reached by an individual church. Other reasons Baptist churches came together were for mutual encouragement and accountability and simply for fellowship. The foundation for this ability to cooperate has been the principle that each church is autonomous (self-ruling). And this autonomy is grounded on the belief that every Baptist church is ruled by the members of the church, not by anyone outside the local congregation like a Pope, Bishop or Presbytery, as we saw in the previous chapter. Thus, cooperation and association between churches is not only possible but highly valued in Baptist life. Baptist theologian E. Y. Mullins wrote of the value of cooperation in the context of a basic biblical definition of the church:

> The great majority of the New Testament passages use the word 'church' to indicate a local body composed of believers in Jesus Christ who are associated together for the cultivation of the Christian life, the maintenance of the ordinances and discipline, and for the propagation of the gospel. Jesus Christ is the Lord of the church. It exists in obedience to his command and has no mission on earth save the carrying out of his will. It must not form alliances of any kind with the state so that it surrenders any of its own functions or assumes any of the functions of civil government. Its government is democratic and autonomous. Each church is free and independent. No church or group of churches has any authority over any other church. *Cooperation in Christian work, however, is one of the highest duties*

and privileges of the churches of Jesus Christ. Yet in so doing they do not form or constitute an ecclesiasticism with functions and powers to be authoritatively exercised over the local bodies.[154]

Notice the equilibrium achieved in the above between the free and independent self-governing principle (autonomy) for the church and the ability and privilege of the churches to cooperate without impairment of the crucial congregational safeguard of autonomy. But more to the point, observe the exalted language used. Mullins describes cooperation as "one of the highest duties and privileges of the churches of Jesus Christ," reflecting the high regard this practice of teamwork between churches has retained in Baptist life.

In a hierarchical, top-down system such as the Roman Catholic Church, the idea of "cooperation" could only be used as a euphemism for

---

154 Emphasis added. E. Y. Mullins, *Baptist Beliefs*, 64. Mullins further explains the relationship between any cooperative organization Baptists have produced and the individual churches: "Here we may point out the relation of local Baptist churches to general Baptist bodies, missionary, educational, and so forth. The latter are not composed of churches but of individuals. Churches may use them or not use them, cooperate with them or refuse to cooperate with them. In all such cooperation or refusal to cooperate, however, the church neither assumes authority over the general body, nor submits to the authority of that body. The relation is voluntary on both sides. The church does not create nor is it created by the general body. Where a church is out of harmony with a general body, it cannot legislate the general body into harmony with itself, but it can withdraw if necessary without the consent of the general body. A general body has no power to retain an unwilling church in cooperative relations with it. There is no conflict of jurisdiction between a church and a general body where messengers come from churches into meetings of general bodies. As members of the general body, they vote and act as individual free people in Christ. They may act under influences of the known wishes of their churches in measures that are considered in the general body. This, however, is not ecclesiastical compulsion but spiritual influence. General bodies are themselves autonomous. No Baptist general body has authority over another. They exist in a graded series, but this does not imply legislative or judicial authority. It is for convenience and efficiency. Each body is self-determining as to constitution and bylaws, aims and purposes, territorial limits and methods." Mullins, *Baptist Beliefs*, 65-66.

surrender or obedience to a higher authority in the chain, ascending finally to the Pope.[155] There is either compliance with the authority or there is rebellion or schism. The notion of churches independently cooperating is impossible in actual experience unless congregational rule, the biblical model (as we have discussed) is the norm, as in Baptist life. For instance, the current Pope, Francis, has received criticism from, among others, the Archbishop of New York for his laxity in dealing with the current abuse scandal in the Roman Church.[156] The Bishop, who is over a territory (diocese) and not a single church, cannot simply dissociate from the Roman Church if he so desired and move on, with his authority as bishop intact. That could not even be considered. If he did so, it would constitute a break from the Catholic establishment. If he tried, he would simply be defrocked, and someone else among the hierarchy would be appointed by the Pope to replace him. By contrast, a Baptist church can simply stop associating with any churches or group of churches at any time due to the principle of autonomy entailed in congregational rule.

---

155 Analogous to when the government raises taxes or introduces a new tax and labels it a 'contribution' on the taxpayer's part. The taxpayer really has no choice.

156 The following news item is from the online edition of the *Catholic Herald*, October 6, 2018: "To the surprise of many Catholic commentators, Cardinal Timothy Dolan of New York has emerged as a leading voice in the calls for a full Vatican inquiry into the decades-long cover-up of Theodore McCarrick's sexual misconduct. A consummate insider well regarded by three consecutive popes, Dolan has nevertheless told the press that he is growing 'impatient' waiting for an apostolic visitation – that is, a formal investigation ordered by the Pope. For that reason, he has appointed a former federal judge, Barbara Jones, to review his archdiocese's protocols relating to sexual abuse. Cardinal Dolan was joined in his call for papal intervention by a prominent layman with close ties to the Archdiocese of Washington. John Carr, director of Georgetown University's Initiative for Catholic Social Thought and Public Life, told a panel that the Holy Father 'has been too slow to understand and act on the moral and spiritual consequences of abuse.' Carr went on to say that the 'isolation, institutional protection and lack of connection to anguish of survivors and their families have often led to a lack of empathy, urgency and action' among Church leaders." (https://catholicherald.co.uk/commentandblogs/2018/10/06/even-loyal-bishops-are-dismayed-by-apparent-papal-inaction-on-mccarrick/)

What it Means to Be a Baptist

So, why have Baptists chosen to cooperate through the centuries? Primarily, Baptists have worked together in order to reach folks for Christ. Baptist historian William R. Estep summarized the Baptist principle of cooperation for missions in his book *Why Baptists? A Study of Baptist Faith and Heritage*:

> The ultimate purpose of the church is to bear witness to the saving power of Jesus Christ. In a sense, every Baptist church is a missionary society intent on advancing the cause of Christ by bringing others to a personal relationship with Christ through every means at its command. This is why Baptist churches, even though independent, self-governing (autonomous) congregations, cooperate together in associations, unions, and/or conventions for more effective social action and in missionary witness.[157]

Missions and evangelism have been the focus for cooperation from the local associational level to the national convention and denominational level since the beginning.[158] According to Baptist historian Leon McBeth, the earliest associations were modeled after Oliver Cromwell's Parliamentary army organization:

> In 1651 a General Baptist association convened in the Midlands, probably at Leicester, and may have met even earlier. In 1651 that "association" adopted a confession of faith in the name of thirty affiliated congregations. Within a few years such associations were common among General Baptists.
>
> Apparently the name "association" originated from military practices of the New Model Army. During the Civil

---

157 William R. Estep, *Why Baptists? A Study of Baptist Faith and Heritage* (Dallas: BaptistWay, 1997), 30-31.

158 In W. T. Whitley's *A History of British Baptists* he notes: "from the beginning Baptists . . . always sought for fellowship between the different churches and they were very successful in arranging for permanent organization." W. T. Whitley, *A History of British Baptists* (Philadelphia: J. B. Lippincott Company, 1923), 53.

War (1642-1649), the Parliamentary army organized various counties into "associations" for defense. Later each regiment in such military associations sent two representatives to confer with Parliament. Records confirm the extensive participation of Baptists in the New Model Army, both as commanders, troops, and chaplains. After the army disbanded, Baptists applied the familiar name and techniques of their army organization to church life, and the "association" caught on.

By 1654 the General Baptists had formed such a nationwide assembly, and they may have met even earlier. A manifesto appeared in 1654 on behalf of "many of the Messengers, Elders, and Brethren, belonging to severall of the Baptized Churches in this nation." They met in London "to consider how and which way the affairs of the Gospell of Christ, so farre as it concerns them, might be best promoted."[159]

Several things are of note in this statement. First is that the Baptists, when they first worked together by creating associations, published confessions (statements of belief in order to establish Baptist theology and practice) which the individual churches could identify with and affirm, giving doctrinal meaning to the Baptist name. This became a practice throughout Baptist history. Also, we see that the earliest Baptists were not pacifists, as many of their Anabaptist forbears were. Many Baptists fought for the parliamentary army under Cromwell during the English Civil War.[160] But likewise of note, (and most importantly for the idea of cooperation) is that the primary driving force for Baptist cooperation as the churches 'associated' together was the advancement of the gospel.[161] They met to see how they could get the gospel out by working

---

159 McBeth, *The Baptist Heritage*, 95-96.

160 See William H. Brackney, *The Baptists* (Westport, CT: Praeger, 1994), 8.

161 Characterizing the early Baptist associations, historian Robert Torbet writes: "Their purpose was framed by a desire to have fellowship between local churches and to carry out evangelistic work." Emphasis added. Robert Torbet, *A History of the Baptists* (Philadelphia: Judson Press, 1953), 72.

in concert, raising their eyes to a wider field of ministry than exclusively local church environs.

In the Catholic church, as a contrast, you don't cooperate; you just obey. If the bishop says you have a new priest, you have a new priest—there's no choice. Why? He's the bishop, a top rung in the hierarchy. That's not how it works in the Baptist church, because each person is a priest; each person in the congregation has received the Holy Spirit. Thus, cooperation between churches, who are ruled by Spirit-indwelt members, is founded on biblical soteriology (you must be born again, Jesus said) rather than man-made institutional (or territorial) logic. This is distinctive for Baptists because they don't have a pecking order or stratified top-down church organization. As we have seen, Baptists have traditionally practiced cooperation through *Associations*: regional groups of churches who agree together to reach that area for Christ and to cooperate and help each other. Conventions and denominations were developed around missions, in other words, cooperating not just regionally but throughout larger areas, as in statewide or nationwide groups, to strive together toward a common purpose, as in an international missionary effort–something big (the *great* commission to go to all nations comes to mind)—to which many churches may contribute.

So, most of the time when Baptists have been drawn together for something greater, it's for the purpose of doing missions, because they can do more together than they could as just one little church, or one big church for that matter. Thus, Baptist associations and other bigger cooperative organizations among Baptists have developed around local evangelism and overseas missions over the years. The Southern Baptist convention, as an example, is a demonstration of what can be accomplished through cooperation. Southern Baptists have been able to send over 5,000 missionaries all over the world through the International Mission Board. This is the largest missionary-sending agency in the world, and has been for a while, although a decline has been experienced in recent years. In contrast, cooperation is technically non-existent with the Roman Catholic Pope (he's the "vicar of Christ" after all). You just have obedience or compliance:Catholics must do what he says (not that they always actually do), even though the pope is basically just a glorified priest. But the New Testament says that Christians don't need an earthly priest. We have the great high priest, Jesus the Son of God who has passed through the heavens, who has sympathy for us because He has been tempted in all ways as we have, yet without sin. Because of Jesus, our high priest, all believers are called priests of God.[162] In contrast to the Roman Catholic system, Baptists believe *every believer* has the same status in Christ.

As we have noted, the idea of cooperation between individual churches is plausible only when the churches are autonomous. Yet these two distinctive principles (cooperation and autonomy) have also been held in tension through Baptist history. History has seen some within the Baptist fold veer at times so far in the direction of cooperation as to endanger the independence and autonomy of Baptist churches (by giving an association or convention too much outside authority over individual local churches). On the other hand, some have become so fiercely protective of autonomy that they have all but relinquished the privilege of working together with other Baptists (as well as with other Christian churches on special projects). For the most part, Baptists have endeavored to keep a healthy balance between the two and have made great strides in missions and evangelism via cooperating, self-governing churches.[163]

---

162 See Hebrews 4.

163 The concept of 'autonomous' churches as a biblically derived essential was defended and promoted (and probably introduced as a key ecclesiological term in Baptist life) by Baptist theologian E. Y. Mullins: "In 1898, E. Y. Mullins in the southern United States wrote authoritatively on Baptist beliefs and described much of the theological basis of the idea of autonomy. In fact, the term 'autonomy' is likely his addition to the Baptist vocabulary. He held that the government of each local church is democratic and autonomous, free and independent. But . . . he also argued for cooperation as one of the highest privileges a church could enjoy." William H. Brackney, *Historical Dictionary of the Baptists*, 2d ed. (Lanham, Maryland: Scarecrow Press, 2009), s.v. "Autonomy of the Local Church". In this summary of Mullins' influence, we see the sustaining of the two ideas of autonomy and cooperation in counterbalance, which reflects the standard Southern Baptist view.

ADONIRAM JUDSON
AND LUTHER RICE:
COOPERATION FOR MISSIONS
AMONG BAPTISTS IN AMERICA

One of the most amazing and unexpected stories of cooperation in Baptist life is that of the beginning of international missions among Baptists in America. You may be surprised to learn that this story of Baptist missions begins among the Congregationalists in New England. In the early years of the colonization of New England, the Congregationalist church was the church of Puritan Boston and Massachusetts and therefore of all New England, with the notable exception of Rhode Island.[164] For a little background: The Congregationalists were the New England Christians who experienced the Great Awakening led by Jonathan Edwards and others in the early and mid-eighteenth century. There was no unanimity concerning the revivals among the Puritans, however. Indeed, the revivals caused a schism among the Congregationalists, with those called the Old Lights being suspicious and negative toward the revivals, in opposition to the New Lights, who were in favor of the revivals. Many of these 'new light' Congregationalists became Baptists as a result. Even though the revivals that started among the Congregationalists had a positive impact on the nation, another side to the story of the New England Christians must be told.

The other side of the story is that the Congregationalists were the official state-sponsored church of Massachusetts. Even after the constitution was ratified in 1788, and the Bill of Rights in 1791, the Puritans in Massachusetts did not allow complete religious freedom, disestablishing the Congregational church, until 1833.[165] Up until that time, those who

---

164 Rhode Island was founded by a Baptist in the seventeenth century named Roger Williams, who was expelled from the Massachusetts Bay colony for what were considered revolutionary ideas, among them, religious liberty. But that is another story for another chapter.

165 See McBeth, *The Baptist Heritage*, 266. Arnold Olson gives a summary of the early colonies, which became states in the newly formed nation, as they moved toward religious liberty, stating that in Massachusetts, "the

did not conform with the Congregationalist church were persecuted by the government, including Baptists, many of whom were former Congregationalists. Congregationalists followed a Calvinistic or Reformed theological system which included baptism of infants. And yet, out of this group we find the first Baptist missionaries from America emerging. This is the unexpected story: There is a college in a little town in western Massachusetts called Williams College. There, in 1806, a group of young men began to discuss seriously the theological implications of world missions. One day in September, this group of students met near the Hoosic River in a grove of trees to continue the discussion when a thunderstorm blew up and it began to rain. They sought shelter under a nearby haystack until the storm passed, and here the discussion turned into a prayer meeting in which the students began to commit themselves to God to act upon the impulse for missionary work instead of just talking about it.[166]

One of the young men, who was a part of this group but not there the day they ducked under the haystack, expressed the same desire to act upon this new-found commitment to reach foreign lands for Christ: "I have deliberately made up my mind to preach the gospel to the heathen. I do not know, but it may be Asia."[167] This student's name was Luther Rice.

Congregational Church enjoyed full or partial establishment, as it did in New Hampshire and Connecticut. The influence and power of religion in government was further evidenced by the fact that Anglicanism was the established religion in Virginia, North Carolina, South Carolina, Maryland, and in New York City, and the three counties surrounding the city. Rhode Island led the way in Separation of Church and State and in guaranteeing the free exercise of religion. Pennsylvania and Maryland practiced religious toleration. Disestablishment of the Anglican Church in the South and Congregationalism in the North was not fully achieved until 1833." Arnold T. Olson, *Believers Only* (Minneapolis: Free Church Publications, 1964), 310.

166 See McBeth, *The Baptist Heritage*, 344.

167 William A. Carleton, *The Dreamer Cometh: The Luther Rice Story* (Home Mission Board, SBC, 1960), 21. Carleton describes Luther Rice's call to missions: "Even before his college days Luther was concerned with the condition of the heathen. In letters and in conversation he often expressed an anxious regard for their salvation. Soon after entering Williams he became closely associated with a number of young men who shared his views, and led by Samuel J. Mills, they organized a 'Society of Inquiry on the Subject of Missions.' He

The other key name to know is Adoniram Judson. He and Rice eventually became partners in the first attempt to do foreign missions by Baptists from America. As young men, both Rice and Judson ended up attending Andover Seminary in Massachusetts, along with Samuel Mills and James Richards from the 'Haystack' group out of Williams College. "These young men were attracted to each other at Andover by a common dedication to the cause of missions."[168] Propelled by Judson's leadership,[169] they all had an abiding commitment to missions and soon were pushing the Congregationalist leaders to form a sending agency to support them and transport them to foreign fields. Because of the fervor of these young men, a society was soon formed among Congregationalists called the American Board of Commissioners for Foreign Missions.

Adoniram Judson and his new wife Ann were sent by the Board to India. They departed on the ship *Caravan* in 1812. Along the way, Adoniram began anew a study of the New Testament on the issue of baptism. He had already been indirectly influenced by Baptists on his road to mis-

---

had come to feel a personal obligation to go himself as a missionary. One day during a period of prayer, alone in the woods near the college, he became very burdened for God's leadership in finding his proper place of service. He had considered foreign mission work before but had about decided to abandon the idea. As he prayed that day the words of Christ, 'Go ye into all the world and preach the gospel to every creature,' came into his mind with such clearness and power that he resolved to spend his life in mission service, whatever it might cost." Carleton, *The Dreamer Cometh: The Luther Rice Story*, 20-21.

168   Robert G. Torbet, *Venture of Faith* (Philadelphia: Judson Press, 1955), 17.

169   According to Baptist historian Robert Torbet, Judson, from Brown University, was the key leader of the missions group at Andover Seminary. Along with Rice, Mills, and Richards of the Williams College 'Haystack' group, there were three others who joined the missions group at Andover: Samuel Newell, from Harvard, Samuel Nott, Jr., from Union, and another seminarian named Edward Warren. Torbet characterizes Judson's leadership of this group: "From the first, Judson was determined to devote his life to foreign missions. The Williams men were drawn in part, at least, to work among the American Indians. It was largely the vision of Judson that directed the others of the group to a concern for peoples in land beyond the sea. He was the man of action who took decisive steps to develop an organization which might send him and his colleagues to the mission field." Torbet, *Venture of Faith*, 17.

sions.[170] He had also pondered the question of baptism during his earlier seminary studies, looking at the biblical Greek term *baptizo* as he examined the New Testament.[171] One of the motivations for his study aboard ship was that he anticipated meeting the renowned English Baptist missionary William Carey, who was already in Serampore, India. Adoniram wanted to be able to defend his Congregationalist view of baptism, which entailed baptizing whole households, including unbelievers and infants, in the mode of aspersion (sprinkling). He also did not want to cause confusion for those whom he would be attempting to reach with the gospel.[172]

---

170 Torbet tells the story of Judson's surrender to missions: "One day in September, 1809, Adoniram Judson read a sermon by Claudius Buchanan, a chaplain for the British East India Company. It was instrumental in setting the direction of his whole life. The sermon appeared in *The Massachusetts Baptist Missionary Magazine*. It had been preached at St. James Parish Church, Bristol, England, for the benefit of a 'Society for Missions to Africa and the East.' Entitled 'The Star in the East,' the sermon presented a new and compelling idea to Judson. Its appeal for missions in India gripped his imagination as nothing had ever done before. For five months he did not come to a decision. Then, one cold day in February, 1810, he was walking alone in the woods behind the seminary building when suddenly the Great Commission came into his mind. Now it held a personal meaning for his own life. That was the decisive moment. Kneeling in the snow, he resolved to become a missionary to peoples beyond the sea. As in the case of his conversion, there were several factors which influenced Judson's decision to become a foreign missionary. The immediate one seems to have been Buchanan's sermon. Certainly this was reinforced by other reading in *The Massachusetts Baptist Missionary Magazine*, which regularly carried reports of the English Baptists' [William Carey's] work at Serampore." Insertion added. Torbet, *Venture of Faith*, 16.

171 Speaking of Judson's interest in the biblical view of baptism, Torbet writes: "It was not the first time that the young missionary had been confronted with this subject. As a student in Andover Seminary, Judson's interest in the word baptizo had been aroused, while engaged in a private translation of the New Testament from Greek. In his search for the exact meaning of the Greek word, he found to his consternation that it was at variance with his understanding of it." Ibid., 20.

172 Judson's anticipation of the baptism issue as perhaps being problematic upon commencing missionary endeavors in India is summarized by one of Judson's biographers: "The Baptists and orthodox Congregationalists

So, he tackled the subject once again in order to be able to clearly present the doctrine to those to whom he would be ministering. He also wanted to be able to uphold his denominational practice, since Congregationalists were footing the bill for his mission. Looking at the New Testament in its original Greek, Judson came to the conclusion that baptism literally meant to plunge or dunk under water. The Congregationalist practice of sprinkling was never mentioned in the New Testament. This was disconcerting and somewhat alarming to Adoniram. In addition, part of the Congregationalist Board's mission for Judson was to baptize whole households rather than just individual believers. This was also something he did not find commanded in the New Testament.[173]

---

of New England had always been on friendly terms. In fact, Adoniram had met Dr. Lucius Bolles, pastor of the First Baptist Church of Salem, before departure of the *Caravan*, and had urged that American Baptists follow the example of British Baptists in forming a missionary organization. But Adoniram was not so sure about his relation with the Serampore Baptists. If they attacked the Congregational position on baptism, how could he defend it? He feared much more, however, the dilemma in which he would find himself if natives asked him to explain the difference! They might even conclude there were two competing religions, each calling itself Christian–and thus find it easier to resist conversion." Courtney Anderson, *To the Golden Shore: The Life of Adoniram Judson* (Garden City, NY: Doubleday, 1961), 132.

173 Torbet explains Judson's dilemma over baptism as a newly minted Congregationalist missionary: "But now that he was on his way to India, with instructions from the American Board to baptize 'credible believers *with their households*,' the problem took on a more urgent importance. He began to wonder how he ought to treat the unconverted children and servants of the converted when he reached his destination. He also realized that he would be obliged to defend his position before the English Baptists in Calcutta." Emphasis added. Torbet, *Venture of Faith*, 20. The Congregationalist mandate to baptize whole households primarily cites the story of the Philippian jailor in the book of Acts for scriptural authority. Baptist scholar George R. Beasley-Murray dismisses this passage as a legitimate support for household baptism: "Above all, we should return to the text of Acts and look again at the narrative of the Philippian Jailor. Here it should be admitted in candour that the statement, 'Believe on the Lord Jesus, and you will be saved, you and your household' (16.31) has been abused. It is not intended to teach that the faith of the householder suffices for his wife, children and slaves. Alford rightly

Thus, Judson came to believe that the Baptists were right about baptism. This was a genuine quandary for him, and as he discussed these things with his wife, Ann, she advised him to stay the course as a Congregationalist. There is no better way to convey the anguish and seriousness of the process of making this decision than to hear it in Ann Judson's own words in a letter home to her family from 1813, the year after the events described:

> I will now, my dear parents and sisters, give you some account of our change of sentiment, relative to the subject of baptism. Mr. Judson's doubts commenced on our passage from America. While translating the New Testament, in which he was engaged, he used frequently to say that the Baptists were right in their mode of administering the ordinance. Knowing he should meet the Baptists at Serampore, he felt it important to attend to it more closely, to be able to defend his sentiments. After our arrival at Serampore, his mind for two or three weeks was so much taken up with missionary inquiries and our difficulties with government, as to prevent his attending to the subject of baptism. But as we were waiting the arrival of our brethren, and having nothing in particular to attend to, he again took up the subject. I tried to have him give it up, and rest satisfied in his old sentiments, and frequently told him, if he became a Baptist, *I would not.* He, however, said he felt it his duty to examine closely a subject on which he had so many doubts. After we removed to Calcutta, he found in the library in our chamber many books on both sides, which he determined to read candidly and prayerfully, and

---

commented: 'καὶ ὁ οἶκός σου does not meant that *his* faith would save his household, but that *the same way was open to them as to him*: "Believe, and thou shalt be saved; and the same of thy household." That is why the word of the Lord was spoken to 'all who were in the house' (v. 32), namely that all might hear and all might believe along with him. The process is the same as that which happened to Crispus and his family: 'Crispus believed on the Lord *with his whole house*'; he did not believe for them, but they shared his faith *with* him. Such is the common pattern in Acts: the Gospel calls for faith, and both come to expression in baptism. The baptized hear and believe." G. R. Beasley-Murray, *Baptism in the New Testament* (Grand Rapids: Eerdmans, 1962), 319-120.

to hold fast, or embrace the truth, however mortifying, however great the sacrifice. I now commenced reading on the subject, with all my prejudices on the Pedobaptist [infant baptism] side. . . . But after closely examining the subject for several weeks, we were constrained to acknowledge that the truth appeared to lie on the Baptists' side. It was extremely trying to reflect on the consequences of our becoming Baptists. We knew it would wound and grieve our dear Christian friends in America–that we should lose their approbation and esteem. We thought it probable the commissioners would refuse to support us; and, what was more distressing than any thing, we knew we must be separated from our missionary associates, and go alone to some heathen land. These things were very trying to us, and caused our hearts to bleed for anguish. We felt we had no home in this world, and no friend but each other. Our friends at Serampore were extremely surprised when we wrote them a letter requesting baptism, as they had known nothing of our having had any doubts on the subject. We were baptized on the 6th of September, in the Baptist chapel in Calcutta.[174]

Obviously, the Judsons made great sacrifices to follow what they viewed as the biblical truth concerning baptism. But they were committed to finding the truth and sticking with it. Adoniram had conversed with his wife, as they were still in the thick of their consideration of the issue, and "Ann continued to hold out against becoming a Baptist. Her husband's reply was steadfast: 'But it is my duty to examine the subject; and even if I have to pay dearly for it, I hope I shall not be afraid to embrace the truth.'"[175] Adoniram embraced what he considered to be the New Testament truth about baptism so fully that he preached a sermon on baptism (soon after his own baptism) which William Carey claimed was the best sermon on baptism he'd ever heard.[176]

---

174 Insertion added. Cited in Robert A. Baker, ed., *A Baptist Source Book: With Particular Reference to Southern Baptists* (Nashville: Broadman Press, 1966), 53-54

175 Torbet, *Venture of Faith*, 21.

176 See Anderson, *To the Golden Shore*, 151. Judson would later translate

In a letter to Carey and the other Baptist missionaries in Serampore (August 27, 1812), Judson explained his change of mind and requested baptism: "My inquiries commenced during my passage from America, and after much laborious research and painful trial, which I shall not now detail, have issued in entire conviction, that *the immersion of a professing believer is the only Christian baptism.*"[177] In this request for baptism, Judson made clear that Ann had also come to the same strong belief. They concluded, based on the conviction stated above, that they had never really been baptized according to New Testament instruction: "Feeling, therefore, that we are in an unbaptized state, we wish to profess our faith in Christ by being baptized in obedience to his sacred commands."[178] It was uplifting and reassuring for the Judsons when, shortly after his arrival to India, Luther Rice, their friend and partner in the mission venture, also came to Baptist beliefs. Ann wrote: "Brother Rice was baptized several weeks after we were. It was a very great relief to our minds to have him join us, as we expected to

---

the Greek word for baptize as 'immerse' (instead of the ususal transliteration) in his translation of the Bible into Burmese because of his steadfast Baptist beliefs. One of the telling statements in Ann's letter (quoted above) to her family is that the English Baptist missionaries were 'surprised' by the Judson's request for baptism, proving that the strength of their new conviction was not in any way a result of influence by the Baptists in India, but simply a personal decision brought about by study of Scripture, as the narrative of events demonstrates. Thus, making use of Judson's own words, Torbet confirms that "this decision had not been influenced by consultation with the English Baptist missionaries. That Judson's decision had been reached privately and independently is evident from a lengthy letter which he wrote to the Third Church in Plymouth, Massachusetts, where he held his membership. In setting forth his reasons for becoming a Baptist he explained: 'I could not find a single intimation in the New Testament that the children and domestics of believers were members of the church or entitled to any church ordinance, in consequence of the profession of the head of their family. Everything discountenanced this idea. When baptism was spoken of, it was always in connection with believing. None but believers were commanded to be baptized; and it did not appear to my mind that any others were baptized.'" Torbet, *Venture of Faith*, 22.

177 Cited in Baker, ed., *A Baptist Source Book*, 54.
178 Ibid.

be entirely alone in a mission."[179] Using different words to express his thoughts, Luther Rice came to the same decision as he embraced the Baptist view, after his own careful study:[180] "I am now satisfactorily convinced that those only who give evidence of piety [Judson's words were 'professing believer'], are proper subjects, and that immersion is the proper mode of baptism."[181]

Rice was baptized on November 11, 1812. His diary entry for the day reads: "Was this day baptized in the name of the Holy Trinity. The Lord grant that I may ever find his name to be a strong tower, to which I may continually resort and find safety."[182] In a letter written describing the event the day after his baptism, Rice commented: "It was a comfortable day for my soul."[183] Rice's baptism was not only an immediate boost to the Judsons; it proved to be an auspicious moment in Baptist history. The Judsons would

---

179 Cited in Baker, ed., *A Baptist Source Book*, 54.

180 In his diary, Rice described the process of his own deliberation about the issue of baptism, considering that his friends, the Judsons, had already become Baptists: "I have just mentioned that Brother Judson has become a Baptist. As I have here with him considerable means for this purpose, I am endeavoring to investigate thoroughly the subject of the sacred ordinance of baptism. What may be the result of this inquiry, I am not able at present to say; but from the progress already made I conceive it to be possible that a revolution in my own mind, similar to that which my dear brother and sister have experienced, may take place. Should this be the case, I shall in all probability, go with them to Java. It would be peculiarly pleasing to me to be associated with them in the mission, but my affection for them can by no means determine me to become a Baptist without conviction that Baptists are in the right; nor can I on the other hand, be deterred from my conscientiously examining the subject, nor from following what really appears to be the truth; not withstanding my unpleasant considerations attending such a change of sentiment in my situation. And it is a principle with me, that truth can be no loser by the most rigorous examination, provided that examination be conducted in the fear of God with a desire to know the truth, and a disposition to do his will. May the Lord himself lead me in the way in which he would have me go." Cited in Carleton, *The Dreamer Cometh: The Luther Rice Story*, 25.

181 Insertion added. Cited in Baker, ed., *A Baptist Source Book*, 56.

182 Carleton, *The Dreamer Cometh: The Luther Rice Story*, 26.

183 Ibid.

end up in Burma, and Rice would go back to America to try to raise funds for Baptist missions, especially for Adoniram and Ann, who became nine-teenth-century religious celebrities back home. Rice never went back to the mission field. He began to organize Baptists for mission support and, in doing so, helped unite Baptists in America as never before. Adoniram himself was instrumental in calling on Baptists to unite behind the foreign mission effort.[184] Between the Judsons' riveting ongoing story of stern determination amidst bitter sacrifices on the mission field and Luther Rice's unrelenting promotion of the mission work, Baptists were galvanized to come together to form a national Baptist union.[185]

---

184 Adoniram "wrote to Dr. Baldwin [pastor of the Second Baptist Church in Boston] and to Dr. Bolles, pastor of Salem's First Baptist Church, whom he had met before sailing. Now he reminded him that, at that time, 'I suggested the formation of a society among the Baptists in America for the support of foreign missions. . . . Little did I then expect to be personally concerned in such an attempt.'" Courtney Anderson, *To the Golden Shore: The Life of Adoniram Judson*, 149. Even before his actual baptism, Judson's letter to Lucius Bolles explains his call for support among Baptists: "Within a few months, I have experienced an entire change of sentiments on the subject of baptism. My doubts concerning the correctness of my former system of belief commenced during my passage from America to this country; and after many painful trials, which none can know but those who are taught to relinquish a system in which they had been educated, I settled down in the full persuasion that the immersion of a professing believer in Christ is the only Christian baptism. Mrs. Judson is united with me in this persuasion. We have signified our views and wishes to the Baptist missionaries at Serampore, and expect to be baptized in this city next Lord's day. A separation from my missionary brethren, and a dissolution of my connection with the [Congregationalist] Board of Commissioners, seem to be necessary consequences. The missionaries at Serampore are exerted to the utmost of their ability in managing and supporting their extensive and complicated mission. Under these circumstances I look to you. Alone, in this foreign heathen land, I make my appeal to those whom, with their permission, I will call my Baptist brethren in the United States." Insertion added. Cited in Baker, ed., *A Baptist Source Book*, 55.

185 One Baptist historian, William Wright Barnes, wrote that Luther Rice, "more than any other man, may be called the organizer of the Baptist denomination in America." William Wright Barnes, *The Southern Baptist Convention: A Study in the Development of Ecclesiology* (Seminary Hill, TX, 1934), 21.

What it Means to Be a Baptist

As a result of Rice and Judson's work, along with others, over thirty Baptist delegates met at the First Baptist Church of Philadelphia on May 18, 1814, less than two years after Rice and the Judsons had left for India as Congregationalists, to form the General Missionary Convention of the Baptist Denomination in the United States for Foreign Missions. "This was the first organization of national scope for Baptists in America."[186] Since the 'General Missionary Convention of the Baptist Denomination in the United States for Foreign Missions' is rather a mouthful, the organization became known as the Triennial Convention because it met every three years. But it is instructive to note the elements contained in the longer name for this new organization. Notice that the energizing purpose, which is stated twice, is mission (going into all the world to make disciples, which rings a bell). Specifically, it is 'foreign' missions or world missions, operating through a convention in order to work together *cooperatively* as a national Baptist group to get the mission accomplished. Speaking of the importance of cooperative missions for Baptists, Baptist theologian James Leo Garrett summarizes the importance of the work of Rice and Judson:

> This belief [cooperation for missions] has served as the principal catalyst for bringing into existence a structured Baptist denomination. The so-called "Triennial Convention" was formed in Philadelphia in 1814 as a society of contributors for foreign missions, even though shortly thereafter it would also undertake home missions, prior to the formation of a separate home mission society. Luther Rice rallied support among Baptists in the United States for the support of Adoniram and Ann Judson in Burma and other foreign missionaries . . . and the result was . . . a growing sense of togetherness among Baptists.[187]

So, the beginnings of an American denomination in the United States arose out of a desire to support the spread of the gospel around the world and to achieve this by working together as Baptists.

---

186 McBeth, *The Baptist Heritage*, 344.

187 James Leo Garrett, Jr., *The Collected Writings of James Leo Garrett Jr.*, Vol. 1 *Baptists* Part 1, Ed. Wyman Lewis Richardson (Eugene, OR: Resource Publications, 2017), 36.

Michael W. McDill

THE NEW TESTAMENT FOUNDATION FOR COOPERATION BETWEEN AUTONOMOUS CHURCHES

Cooperation is demonstrated in the New Testament book of Acts as the churches worked together to send missionaries, sort out doctrinal issues (as when the church in Jerusalem sent a letter to the church in Antioch, assuring the Gentile Christians that following the Jewish law was not necessary for salvation) and help fellow Christians in need (Paul taking an offering from the churches in Greece and Anatolia to the Jewish Christians in Jerusalem). The precedence, then, for cooperating, especially to achieve the mission set for the churches by Christ Himself in the Great Commission, is clearly biblical as we read the story of the early church in the New Testament.[188] The missionary effort advanced through the lo-

---

188 In his book *Together on God's Mission*, Baptist professor Scott Hildreth nicely summarizes the biblical story, from the book of Acts, of the very earliest churches cooperating for missions: "When the church in Jerusalem heard that a large number of Gentiles were coming to faith, they sent Barnabas to Antioch. Some have interpreted this negatively, as if the Jerusalem Christians sought to control the situation. However, it is probably better to understand the church's action as sending Barnabas in a missionary capacity. Although the term missionary is not used to describe the visit, Barnabas's work seems to fit the label. First, he 'encouraged all of them to remain true' (Acts 11:23). Second, he apparently engaged in evangelism, because Luke connects his visit with the fact that 'large numbers of people were added to the Lord' (Acts 11:24). Third, Barnabas built a missionary team by seeking and then bringing Saul (Paul) to work with him in the church (Acts 11:25–26). Barnabas crossed into a different culture to evangelize, disciple, and develop local leaders. In other words, he engaged in activities that most people associate with the term missionary. By sending Barnabas as a missionary, the church in Jerusalem helped establish the church in Antioch. The next phase of the early church's mission began in Acts 11:27 when the Antioch church received word that their brothers in Jerusalem were suffering. In response to this word, they decided to send Barnabas and Paul with a financial gift. This is a significant event for two reasons. First, it shows the young church had developed an independent identity and embraced a missionary vision to minister cross-culturally. Second, during his visit to Jerusalem, Paul had an important missionary strategy meeting

that shaped his calling and future ministry. In Galatians 2, Paul recorded details of this high-level missionary consultation in Jerusalem. 'Now from those recognized as important (what they once were makes no difference to me; God does not show favoritism)—they added nothing to me. On the contrary, they saw that I had been entrusted with the gospel for the uncircumcised, just as Peter was for the circumcised, since the one at work in Peter for an apostleship to the circumcised was also at work in me for the Gentiles. When James, Cephas, and John—those recognized as pillars—acknowledged the grace that had been given to me, they gave the right hand of fellowship to me and Barnabas, agreeing that *we should go to the Gentiles and they to the circumcised*. They asked only that we would remember the poor, which I had made every effort to do.' (Gal 2:6–10, emphasis added) During this meeting, the leaders of the Jerusalem church affirmed Paul's message and agreed on a missionary strategy. Paul and Barnabas were sent to the Gentiles while Peter and the Jerusalem church leadership would continue working among the Jews. It is difficult to overstate the importance of this meeting as it relates to the mission of the early church. According to Gal 2:2, Paul initiated the conversation 'to be sure I was not running, and had not been running, in vain.' Paul was not a new convert. In fact, he had been in ministry for 14 years (see Gal 2:1), so it is inconceivable that he was worried about the content of his preaching. Instead, he seems to have been concerned about the sustainability of his missionary efforts. F. F. Bruce has rightly noted that what Paul was concerned about was not the validity of his gospel but its practicability. His commission was not derived from Jerusalem, but it could not be effectively discharged except in fellowship with Jerusalem. A cleavage between his Gentile mission and the mother-church in Jerusalem would be disastrous for the progress of the gospel. He wanted to ensure that the missionary efforts of the early churches were in concert, not competition. Paul did not view himself as an independent missionary. Rather, he seems to have understood his ministry as a collaborative, or even cooperative, endeavor. Paul and Barnabas had been sent out by the Antioch church. Now, they sought advice and endorsement from the Jerusalem church. From the earliest days of Christian missions, missionary teams operated with some degree of accountability to both major churches of their day: Jerusalem and Antioch. Even though the Bible does not record examples of consultation between the two churches, the New Testament pictures their missionary advance as the work of both churches. Their mission is God's mission, and because of this, they worked together. The story of the New Testament church's mission continues in Acts 13: 'Now in the church at Antioch there were prophets and teachers: Barnabas, Simeon who was called Niger, Lucius of Cyrene, Manaen, a close friend of Herod the tetrarch, and Saul. As they were worshiping the Lord and fasting, the

cal autonomous churches in cooperation with one another, sending missionaries, deliberating on plans and procedures, and exhibiting mutual support in order to get the job done. Again here, Baptists appear to most closely align their theology and methods with the biblical pattern. A book addressing the Baptist tradition of cooperation frames the issue scripturally, and cites an early example:

> The real question, of course, is not whether Baptists have "always done it that way" but whether it is scriptural. While it is true that in the New Testament churches were understood to be local autonomous bodies under the lordship of Christ, it is also the case that New Testament churches engaged in joint efforts for both fellowship and mission. In Acts 8 Peter and John traveled to Samaria. Philip the evangelist had been engaged in a great ministry there. When the apostles in Jerusalem heard of this work, they dispatched Peter and John to the city (Acts 8:14). We ought not to see this as a presumptuous act on the part of the Jerusalem church apostles but rather as their glad participation in and assistance to the new Samaritan Christian experience. The new work "was endorsed, received, and enthusiastically participated in by the whole church."

Holy Spirit said, "Set apart for me Barnabas and Saul for the work to which I have called them." Then after they had fasted, prayed, and laid hands on them, they sent them off.' (vv. 1–3) New Testament scholar Darrell Bock calls this 'the first steps in "missions" as the called-out and divinely directed activity of a group organized for this specific goal. This contrasts with the less-systematic work of individuals mentioned earlier. The church is becoming more organized and intentional about outreach.' In Acts 13, the Antioch church accepts the role of appointing and sending out Paul and Barnabas as a missionary team. The picture in this chapter is of different local churches sharing responsibility for the same missionary team. Though there isn't any explicit record of the churches communicating with each other about missions, Luke shows autonomous churches cooperating in the mission. The churches participated in the sending and shaping of Paul's missionary strategy: Jerusalem provided strategic consultation, and Antioch affirmed this by sending them to preach to the Gentiles." D. Scott Hildreth, *Together on God's Mission: How Southern Baptists Cooperate to Fulfill the Great Commission* (Nashville: B&H Academic, 2018), 66-68.

Upon arriving, Peter and John prayed for them, and they then were given the gift of the Holy Spirit (Acts 8:17). After the Spirit fell upon the Samaritans, Peter and John returned to Jerusalem after first preaching in other Samaritan villages (Acts 8:25), and even Philip was led by an angel to leave in order to witness to the Ethiopian eunuch (Acts 8:26-39). The Jerusalem church did not attempt to govern the Samaritans from afar but rather joined in the work in this new location, not to "supervise" it but only to share with it what it had to give.[189]

In pursuing God's agenda—getting the gospel to the world—Baptists have historically tapped the potential of independent churches working cooperatively, much as we see in the book of Acts.[190]

Although strategically the principle of cooperation is very important to Baptists, it has never been on par with other theological principles, for example the authority and sufficiency of Scripture. However, if we look a little deeper than just strategy level, we find that Christians are called to be in harmony with one another throughout the New Testament.[191] There are so many calls for unity and harmony, especially in all the epistles, that one wonders if perhaps this was one of the besetting sins of the early church. These urgent calls for unity, together with some of the indications of strife we find in the story of the New Testament churches, point to the fact that harmony and 'being of one mind' are perennial challenges for the people of

189 Chad Owen Brand and David E. Hankins, *One Sacred Effort: The Cooperative Program of Southern Baptists* (Nashville: Broadman & Holman, 2005), 65.

190 For an excellent summary of scriptural examples of New Testament churches cooperating for missions and various other reasons, see Chad Owen Brand and David E. Hankins, *One Sacred Effort: The Cooperative Program of Southern Baptists*, 65-71.

191 Baptist professor Scott Hildreth references the SBC and explains that since the subject of cooperation appears as an article in the *Baptist Faith and Message*, it is, then, an important essential distinctive for this Baptist group: "Southern Baptists did not (and do not) understand the doctrine of cooperation to be on par with more cardinal doctrines—Scripture, theology proper, Christology, soteriology, and so on. However, including cooperation among these cherished Christian doctrines indicates it is a key component of denominational identity." D. Scott Hildreth, *Together on God's Mission*, 24.

God. The strife and conceit found in the Corinthian church and its factions is a clear example. Even before any churches were established as such, we find Jesus giving a rather pointed lesson to His disciples. He exhorted them to love each other. This was couched in terms of a 'new commandment,' which He demonstrated with a memorable object lesson (washing their feet). The broader context for this teaching at the last supper is very telling. Just a few weeks before, when Jesus began His journey to Jerusalem, where the last great sacrificial events were to unfold in Jesus' mission, Scripture tells us that the disciples were arguing about who would be the greatest in the coming kingdom. This is recorded in the gospel of Luke chapter nine after Jesus had just healed a demon-possessed boy:

> And they were all astonished at the greatness of God. While everyone was amazed at all the things he was doing, he told his disciples, "Let these words sink in: The Son of Man is about to be betrayed into the hands of men." But they did not understand this statement; it was concealed from them so that they could not grasp it, and they were afraid to ask him about it. An argument started among them about who was the greatest of them. But Jesus, knowing their inner thoughts, took a little child and had him stand next to him. He told them, "Whoever welcomes this little child in my name welcomes me. And who-ever welcomes me welcomes him who sent me. For whoever is least among you — this one is great." John responded, "Mas-ter, we saw someone driving out demons in your name, and we tried to stop him because he does not follow us." "Don't stop him," Jesus told him, "because whoever is not against you is for you." When the days were coming to a close for him to be taken up, he determined to journey to Jerusalem.[192]

So here is Jesus trying to get it into the heads of the disciples that He must be betrayed to the power of men and sacrifice His life. In the passage, He is directing His steps toward Jerusalem, on purpose, to fulfill His painful mission. He has just shown His glory to Peter, James, and John through His transfiguration on the mountain, and then, having come down off

---

192 Luke 9:43-51 (CSB).

the mountain, He demonstrates His power by healing a boy tortured by demons. All of this happened, and yet His followers' concern as they went along was which one among them was the greatest. Human nature is quite breathtaking in its self-concern and self-exalting proclivity, is it not? Our capacity to miss the whole point of things is quite amazing. Jesus was as straightforward as possible in telling the disciples how His mission on earth would come to fruition, yet they were completely mystified, and too afraid (perhaps anxious not to look stupid) to ask Him directly about what He meant. This was now the second time in the gospel of Luke that He had told them about what had to take place in Jerusalem concerning His arrest and death.

If you think this episode astonishing, wait until you see the context for another debate the disciples had about which of them was the greatest:

> When the hour came, he reclined at the table, and the apostles with him. Then he said to them, "I have fervently desired to eat this Passover with you before I suffer. For I tell you, I will not eat it again until it is fulfilled in the kingdom of God." Then he took a cup, and after giving thanks, he said, "Take this and share it among yourselves. For I tell you, from now on I will not drink of the fruit of the vine until the kingdom of God comes." And he took bread, gave thanks, broke it, gave it to them, and said, "This is my body, which is given for you. Do this in remembrance of me." In the same way he also took the cup after supper and said, "This cup is the new covenant in my blood, which is poured out for you. But look, the hand of the one betraying me is at the table with me. For the Son of Man will go away as it has been determined, but woe to that man by whom he is betrayed!" So they began to argue among themselves which of them it could be who was going to do it. *Then a dispute also arose among them about who should be considered the greatest.*[193]

As noted before, this disputing among themselves strikes a stunningly dissonant note in the story describing the Lord's supper with His disciples, set forth here in the gospel of Luke. This is the moment Jesus says

---

193 Luke 22:14-24 (CSB).

He has longed for, to fellowship with and teach them before His great passion in the garden and on the cross. Yet these men are still acting utterly self-involved, so much so that they cannot remotely ascertain what Jesus is trying to tell them. They are missing the clear point He is trying to convey: He must give Himself in death so they can be redeemed by 'the blood poured out' for them. He not only tells them directly, telling them He must suffer, but gives them concrete illustrations in the bread and the cup. How God's patience is proven here!

In response, Jesus simply and patiently explains why their bickering about the greatest makes no sense in light of the generous and bounteous treasures He offers them *as a gift*. He has come as a Servant, especially through His sacrifice (pictured in the bread and wine), and as an example of the unworldly courtesy and extravagance of the kingdom of God:

> But he said to them, "The kings of the Gentiles lord it over them, and those who have authority over them have themselves called 'Benefactors.' It is not to be like that among you. On the contrary, whoever is greatest among you should become like the youngest, and whoever leads, like the one serving. For who is greater, the one at the table or the one serving? Isn't it the one at the table? But I am among you as the one who serves. You are those who stood by me in my trials. I bestow on you a kingdom, just as my Father bestowed one on me, so that you may eat and drink at my table in my kingdom. And you will sit on thrones judging the twelve tribes of Israel.[194]

Notice that Christ is *bestowing a kingdom* upon them. He is plainly presenting them with the 'greatness' they desire but don't deserve. However, the kingdom Jesus describes is one of good fellowship with the Father and the Son, eating and drinking at *His*, the King's, table—not throwing around one's weight as if more important than others like a 'lord benefactor', but enjoying the presence of God Himself, our true and only ultimate Benefactor. However, a price must be paid for this wonderful celebration dinner: the suffering of the Son. And those who reject the Son cannot enter into the Fellowship, as the reference to judgement in the text indicates.

---

194 Luke 22:25-30 (CSB).

The patience and graciousness of Jesus, sent from His Father on the great mission of mercy, which is demonstrated in these passages, reminds us that the divine expectation for us is to love one another. This was the new command given to the disciples in this very event, the Last Supper. His profound sufferings on behalf of men seeking to exalt themselves and, self-absorbed, unable to fathom His mission (and these were His most faithful followers, as He attests in the passage) was a mercy and compassion and love that baffles the customary human outlook, which prioritizes getting a leg up on the other fellow. The fact that 'while we were yet sinners' Christ 'died for the ungodly' is yet more baffling to ordinary human insight. Jesus' directive to us to 'love your enemies' is exactly what He did. No wonder the thoroughly converted man is able to see God's overwhelming mercy to him as 'amazing grace,' and thus, acknowledging God's amazing love for him, turn toward his neighbor and his brother with generosity. This generous spirit, our attempts to mimic God's *agapē* love to us, is what makes of the Christian a fisher of men, salt and light for the old sad, broken, dark, unsavory, empty world. As Jesus said, "They will know you are My disciples by your love."

So, this extended discussion of Jesus' words at the Last Supper would seem to demonstrate that the deep root of cooperation among Christians is love, which Christ Himself demonstrated. The facts surrounding His 'mission accomplished,' His death, burial, and resurrection, become for us our mission, that is, to get the gospel to the world which God loves. We are to love each other as one of the first evidences of that *agape*, a "God" kind of love, and exhibit its harmonious consequences in our lives. If we must suffer and sacrifice in our quest to love one another, then so be it. We are disciples of the One Who suffered for us, after all. The spirit of cooperation among Christians, then, is not simply for the sake of organization and effectiveness but is anchored in what the Apostle Paul claimed was 'the greatest' of spiritual gifts: voluntary, sacrificial love.

CONCLUSION

As has been observed, cooperation between churches in order to send missionaries around the world is strategically sound, grounded in New

Testament precedent. It is also an expression of harmony in the wider body of Christ, which is called for in the many commands of the New Testament to love one another. This harmony and love are themselves testimonies to the world of Jesus' love. One Baptist scholar considered cooperative missions so important that he named it as one of three key principles in Baptist life and thought which must not be abandoned, the other two being believer's baptism by immersion and religious liberty for all humans. In an essay entitled *Protect Baptist Distinctives from Extinction,* he wrote a warning identifying these three Baptist principles as "three emphases or distinctives of the people called Baptists that may be in danger of serious attrition, if not full extinction[195] Letting any of the three slide into obscurity constitutes a loss of essential Baptist identity, according to James Leo Garrett. He admonishes Baptists, particularly in this case Southern Baptists, to stand firm in a defense of believer's baptism, religious liberty, and, most importantly for the present discussion, cooperative missions:

> Practicing cooperative missions is not all that it means to be a Southern Baptist Christian, but it is highly questionable as to whether one can rightly be called a "Southern Baptist" who does not affirm and practice it. Biologists, environmentalists, and government agencies work hard to prevent those species listed as endangered from being extinct. Believer's baptism by immersion, religious freedom for all human beings, and cooperative missions! Who will prevent three major Baptist beliefs from becoming extinct among the Baptists? Will you? "Keep as your pattern the sound teaching you have heard from me, in the faith and love that are in Christ Jesus. Guard the treasure put into your charge, with the help of the Holy Spirit dwelling in us" (2 Tim 1:13–14).[196]

---

195 James Leo Garrett, Jr., *The Collected Writings of James Leo Garrett Jr.,* Vol. 1 *Baptists* Part 1, 33.

196 Ibid., 37.

Chapter 6

The Priesthood of Every Believer

The theological idea of the priesthood of the believer is that the only mediator between God and man is Jesus Christ. He has opened access to our Creator so that believers are able to come before God directly. We need no earthly mediator or priest. The Bible tells us this explicitly: "For there is one God, and one mediator between God and men, the man Christ Jesus."[197] Therefore, each believer comes into the holy presence of God Himself, just as the authorized Levitical priest would in the Old Testament. This is why the apostle Peter refers to Christians as a 'holy priesthood.'[198] Baptist scholar R. Stanton Norman helps us concisely define the idea of the priesthood of all believers: "The essential function of a priest is to stand and represent the interests and concerns of another. The concept of priesthood is integral to both the Old Testament and New Testament and finds its fulfillment in Jesus Christ, who is the Mediator and Great High Priest. According to the doctrine of the priesthood of all believers, every believer has direct access to God through Jesus Christ,

---

197 1 Timothy 2:5 (KJV). By the way, this scripture passage also shows us that He was completely human, because the Bible here calls Him "the man." In fact, the Holman Christian Standard Bible renders this verse: "For there is one God and one mediator between God and humanity, Christ Jesus, *Himself human.*" emphasis added.

198 "Coming to Him, a living stone—rejected by men but chosen and valuable to God—you yourselves, as living stones, are being built into a spiritual house for a holy priesthood to offer spiritual sacrifices acceptable to God through Jesus Christ." 1 Peter 2:4-5 (HCSB)

and the church is a fellowship of priests serving together under the lordship of Christ."[199]

THE PRIESTHOOD OF EVERY BELIEVER CONTRASTED WITH INSTITUTIONAL MEDIATION

So, we have the One Man, Jesus. He is the only Mediator. There is a clear exclusivity to His mediation here in the scripture: 'one mediator between God and men.' If Jesus is the only one, and He is very special, and He's better than even the angels and supersedes all former Old Testament high priests (according to Hebrews), then how should we perceive someone else claiming to be a mediator for God? This claim would directly contrast with scripture and thus be false, wouldn't it? There are church groups, though, that claim exactly this—that there are other mediators. For instance, the Pope of the Roman Catholic church is 'the vicar of Christ.' This means that he 'vicariously' stands in for Christ and represents Him as a physical presence in the world by virtue of his office as pope. According to the New Testament, no one represents Christ in this world except the one Jesus Himself promised, that is, the Holy Spirit: "But when the Father sends the Advocate as *my representative*—that is, the Holy Spirit—he will teach you everything and will remind you of everything I have told you."[200]

---

199   R. Stanton Norman, *The Baptist Way*, 94.

200   Emphasis added. John 14:26 (NLT). The explicit description of the Holy Spirit as representing and speaking for Christ comes in the very words of Jesus Himself, who promises the Spirit in John 16:5-15 (NKJV): "But now I go away to Him who sent Me, and none of you asks Me, 'Where are You going?' But because I have said these things to you, sorrow has filled your heart. Nevertheless I tell you the truth. It is to your advantage that I go away; for if I do not go away, the Helper will not come to you; but if I depart, I will send Him to you. And when He has come, He will convict the world of sin, and of righteousness, and of judgment: of sin, because they do not believe in Me; of righteousness, because I go to My Father and you see Me no more; of judgment, because the ruler of this world is judged. I still have many things to say to you, but you cannot bear them now. However, when He, the Spirit of truth, has come, He

The Roman church also advises that Mary, the mother of Jesus, is someone that we should pray to because she's more empathetic than Jesus (who is the fearsome and stern final Judge, as depicted in many European cathedrals), and she can tell Jesus what to do because she's His mother. One Catholic woman, interviewed on the street, captured how those who see Mary as interceder think when she said, "I feel, whenever I have a problem that I am praying, I feel that if I talk to Mary, she would have more sympathy with me. And she can understand my motives if I feel I have done something wrong, better than Jesus could or God. You know, she is kind of like the mediator for me."[201] In addition, there are other Saints you can pray to according to the Catholic authorities. For instance, there is St. Jude, who is a Saint for every apparently difficult matter, being the 'patron saint of hopeless causes.'[202] Or you could pray to St. Anthony to find your lost car keys (or any more serious loss), as the patron saint of lost things. But in doing so, would you not be asking him to *mediate* on

---

will guide you into all truth; for He will not speak on His own authority, but whatever He hears He will speak; and He will tell you things to come. He will glorify Me, for He will take of what is Mine and declare it to you. All things that the Father has are Mine. Therefore I said that He will take of Mine and declare it to you."

201 *Catholicism: Crisis of Faith*, directed by James G. McCarthy (Lumen Productions, 1991).

202 There is an actual formal prayer prescribed for Catholics when praying to St. Jude:

O most holy apostle, Saint Jude, faithful servant and friend of Jesus, the Church honoureth and invoketh thee universally, as the patron of hopeless cases, and of things almost despaired of.

Pray for me, who am so miserable. Make use, I implore thee, of that particular privilege accorded to thee, to bring visible and speedy help where help was almost despaired of.

Come to mine assistance in this great need, that I may receive the consolation and succor of Heaven in all my necessities, tribulations, and sufferings, particularly (here make your request) and that I may praise God with thee and all the elect throughout eternity.

I promise thee, O blessed Jude, to be ever mindful of this great favor, to always honor thee as my special and powerful patron, and to gratefully encourage devotion to thee. Amen.

your behalf before God?[203] The 'saints' are interesting in a sense, because they were real people in history, although many of the stories in the Catholic tradition concerning them are clearly legendary and not historical. But based on the Bible, we don't have any business praying to anyone except to God in the name of Jesus, or *to* our dear Lord Jesus, because He is the only mediator, and He *is* God. So, each individual is able to appeal directly to God, through Jesus Christ. Thus, each church member is a priest who doesn't need another human priest to stand in on his or her behalf. As one Baptist scholar wrote, "In simplest of terms, if every believer is a priest, the necessity of an official priesthood is negated."[204] As a Baptist, then, I don't believe I need any institutionally authorized priest, adjudicator, confessor, saint, sponsor, godfather, functionary, or any other human go-between or proxy to represent me before God. I have Jesus Himself, which is more than enough! He is authorized by God Himself and, as noted above, He *is* God.

Based on the fact that we have been provided with the only proper mediator to bring us into fellowship with God, the One Mediator God Himself sent, that is, His only Son, we have stumbled upon unbiblical territory should we seek any other intermediary to stand in for us as we

---

203 Doreen D'antonio, former Sister of Christian Charity, testifies to the common practice in Catholic life of seeking the mediation of dead 'saints' through prayer for assorted worries: "In the convent, we had a whole list of saints that we used for various situations. If we lost something, we would pray to St. Anthony. If we had a hopeless case in our family, maybe a relative that was a drunk or something, we would pray to St. Jude. That being a hopeless case. We would pray to St. Gerard if there was a pregnant woman in our family that needed assistance. St. Blaise if we had a sore throat. We would pray to St. Christopher . . . for traveling. . . . And in elevators. In the convent, we had an elevator for the older nuns, and in that elevator was this humongous medal of St. Christopher. It was amazing. We would have little statues of Mary and Joseph. St. Joseph for foster fathers. We would have the little statue right on the window sill, hoping and praying that statue would prevent it from raining on a particular day." *Catholicism: Crisis of Faith*, directed by James G. McCarthy (Lumen Productions, 1991).

204 Paige Patterson, "Single-Elder Congregationalism," in Steven B. Cowan, ed., *Who Runs the Church?: 4 Views on Church* (Grand Rapids: Zondervan, 2004), 141.

approach God. We believers have the privilege to come before God ourselves and 'approach the throne of grace with boldness,' as the writer of Hebrews declares.[205] Believers, then, may draw near to God with absolute confidence based on faith in our unassailable Mediator and High Priest, Jesus, the Son of God. A Baptist preacher stated the principle of the priesthood of the believer this way:

> Baptists believe in the priesthood of the believer. This means that man is responsible to God for himself and that he can and must approach God for himself. There is no hierarchy, no priest, and no human mediator between God and man. This excludes infant baptism, priestly intermediaries, and substitutes for personal faith. Man can come to God for himself! Man must come to God for himself![206]

Mankind is able to hear from and respond to God, being made in His image, possessing reason and freedom of choice. This is sometimes called soul competency or soul liberty, which is related to the idea of the priesthood of the believer in that each person must relate to God individually; no other person can serve as proxy.[207] As one Baptist teacher put it, "there is no such

---

205 Hebrews 4:16.

206 Joe T. Odle, *Why I Am A Baptist* (Nashville: Broadman Press, 1972), 98.

207 A Baptist Pastor defined soul competency as follows: "The individual is capable of dealing with God for himself. This is sometimes spoken of as soul competency. The individual needs no priest nor sponsor in approaching God. He can come directly to God without the aid of man or institution. He must deal with God for himself, for no one else can answer to God for him. There can be no proxy religion. Parents and friends may help the individual in his approach to God, but they cannot deal with God for him." J. Clyde Turner, *These Things We Believe*, 92. This privilege to approach God Himself is extended to each person by God through Christ and the good news. No other human, group, or organization has the right to extend this grace in Christ. Christ Himself extends it to anyone who will come to Him, and offers eternal life, as is well attested in the New Testament. E. Y. Mullins, who championed the idea of soul competence among Baptists in the nineteenth century, explained the concept in this way: "If there is any one thing which stands out above others in crystal clearness in the New Testament it is Christ's doctrine of the soul's capacity,

thing as proxy salvation. Salvation must be an individual experience based upon a voluntary acceptance of the gospel by personal faith."[208]

The Christian has the stupendous privilege, having responded to God in faith for salvation, to come directly into God's presence through prayer and to be assured of God's continued favor and help; all because of the mediation of Christ on the believer's behalf, secured by His finished work of redemption.[209] This is the wonderful prerogative of the believer as

---

right, and privilege to approach God directly and transact with him in religion." Edgar Young Mullins, *The Axioms of Religion*, 63. Mullins also connects this individual liberty with the very nature of the kingdom of God: "As the kingdom comes always in the first instance to the individual and can only so come; as fatherhood and sonship are relations expressive of individual and not of corporate experiences; and as there is in every regenerated life an element of privacy; as personality indeed is in every case an inner circle where outside feet may not enter, so the life of the kingdom must forever be a life of free service 'under the eye and in the strength of God.' This autonomy of the believer's life is inherent in the very idea of grace, which means that God comes into the soul to raise it into a state of moral power, and transform it into his own image. To deny the liberty and autonomy of the soul under God is to impugn grace itself." Edgar Young Mullins, *The Axioms of Religion*, 39-40.

208 W. R. White, *Baptist Distinctives*, 15. Another Baptist scholar elucidates further: "God's purpose of grace meets the free-acting human soul. He does not use force. 'No force divine doth love compel.' He does not use magic: the idea that a priest acting for God, by the recitation of certain words and the performance of certain rites, can save a soul, is contrary to the teachings of the Word of God. Salvation comes to the soul that comes to salvation. Forgiving Saviour and penitent sinner meet. Helpless man and the mighty Holy Spirit are joined in the great transaction. The man cannot save himself, but he can receive the message of hope; he cannot pluck himself as a brand from the burning, but he can lay hold by faith of the arm that is extended to save." O. C. S. Wallace, *What Baptists Believe: The New Hampshire Confession, An Exposition* (Nashville: Sunday School Board, Southern Baptist Convention, 1913), 98.

209 In addition to Catholicism, another contrast to the principle of the priesthood of all believers (something Luther himself actually championed), is the Lutheran practice of 'Confession and Absolution' (with the emphasis on the absolution, God's word of forgiveness). Lutherans hold 'Holy Absolution' in high regard and at times refer to it as a sacrament. Confession and absolution are done in private to the pastor. He is the 'confessor,' and the person confess-

a priest. The testimony of a former Roman Catholic who put his faith in Christ, having then become a Baptist pastor, is quite telling in this regard. He speaks of the freedom he felt when he left behind the intermediary claims of the Roman Church and trusted the One Mediator, God's own Son Jesus Christ:

> His priesthood superseded every other and rendered the introduction of any other not only useless, but antagonistic. His work needs not men, nor saints, nor angels to add to its efficacy or fullness; these but obscure its glory and hide its grace from a needy and sinful world. His willingness was as conspicuous as his all-sufficiency. For myself I can safely say that the intervention of priests and the invocation of saints made the impression that God reluctantly bestowed salvation. The favorite illustration of

---

ing is known as the 'penitent.' In confession, the penitent makes an act of contrition, and the pastor, acting *in persona Christi*, announces the formula of absolution. Notice this Latin phrase, indicating the pastor stands in for Christ as the auditor of confessions and giver of absolution (the pardon of God). Also, notice how unbiblical the idea of somehow paying for my sins through a religious act of contrition is, considering the *finished* work of Christ on the cross, which has been completed once and for all. Similar to the Roman Catholics, Lutherans interpret James 5:16 and John 20:22–23 as biblical evidence for this type of priestly confession. Another church which offers this type of priestly mediation is the Anglican Church. Anglican priests are available to meet parishioners to hear confession face to face and offer absolution for sins, often in their own home without official furnishings such as confessional booths as in the Roman Catholic Church. One Anglican church in Ohio explains the practice of confession, usually emphasized during special seasons of the church year: "Confession in Lent and Advent is traditional. These penitential times are natural for what is called 'auricular [hearing] confession' - private confession between a penitent and priest. Auricular Confession for Anglicans is underused. This is unfortunate since it is tremendously freeing and uplifting. Everyone thinks of it as a Roman Catholic practice but it has been a practice for Anglicans, Eastern Orthodox, and Lutherans for centuries as well. While it is not mandatory, it is encouraged." Insertion added. Lakewood Anglican Church online, (http://www.lakewoodanglican.com/blog/2017/12/4/the-sacramental-rite-of-confession).

Catholic writers, that the more friends a man has at court the better, certainly strengthens this impression. Catholic art embodies this dishonoring idea in the representation of Christ with the avenging thunderbolts poised in his hand for the world's doom, stayed by the interposition of Mary, the Queen of Heaven. Oh! strange blindness to the love and grace of him who laid down his life for the guilty and who now watches and waits for the return of sinners! . . . I shall never forget the joy which came with the truth that I could go to Christ by myself and for myself. Nobody between me and Christ. This was the Gospel. This brought peace and freedom. Many a soul-trouble has been endured since that time, but my heart treasures as its sweetest memory in life, the liberty wherewith Christ made me free.[210]

Another former Catholic, in the age of the Reformation, Anabaptist theologian Balthasar Hubmaier, expressed the same liberating principle in relation to his rejection of the interference of the Roman Church institution as interlocutor between God and humankind: "As says Paul: no other foundation can any man lay, except what is laid, which is Christ Jesus. (1 Cor. 3) . . . The church is based on this our faith and profession; *not our*

---

210 Henry McDonald, "Why Baptist and Not Roman Catholic," in J. M. Frost, ed., *Baptist Why and Why Not: Twenty-Five Papers by Twenty-Five Writers And A Declaration of Faith* (Grand Rapids: Zondervan, 1900), 73-75. Pastor McDonald comments further: "In the Roman Catholic church, salvation is promised to the unconscious infant in baptism. In many of the Reformed churches the scriptural teaching of personal repentance and faith has been obscured by theories which promise spiritual blessings, not through faith in Christ, but through natural fleshly, [familial] descent. This theory has filled the churches of Europe with the unconverted. It was this practice in the Protestant, as well as in the Catholic church, which made the religious life of America seem so strange to me. That religion is personal, that repentance and faith are essential to salvation, should be as prominent and fundamental in the organization of churches as they are distinctly taught by Christ and his apostles. An avowed faith in Jesus Christ was indispensable to church fellowship. It was the organific principle of church life as faith itself was the condition and medium of spiritual life." Insertion added. McDonald, 75-76.

faith in the church. But on the proclaimed Word of God, that God Himself is, and has become man."[211]

A Key Passage: Hebrews 4

Let's look at a key scripture regarding these ideas. Hebrews chapter four begins by talking about rest, something we all need: "Therefore, since a promise remains of entering his rest, let us fear lest any of you seem to have come short of it."[212] The author is making a distinction in the passage between rest and work, and he is speaking of eternal matters. There is a lasting, tranquil, redemptive rest given by a promise, rather than a contractual reprieve, a sort of payoff earned by works and striving. This truth is clearly one of the main emphases of the whole New Testament: faith and not works. The promise comprises the content of the offer of God (rest) which one can accept by faith. Or one may reject the promised rest in order to maintain control of one's dealings with God or gods. This is why the author of Hebrews says, "For indeed the gospel was preached to us as well as to them," meaning the people in Moses' time and in the Old Testament. The gospel was preached to them? Do you believe that? If you believe it, then you agree with the New Testament. God offered them rest in His very presence with them, which was fulfilled ultimately and fully in the incarnation. He offered rest in a promised land given them where He would be their God and dwell in their midst, a foreshadowing of the spiritual rest He offers believers through forgiveness and peace with God. The land also points to a final eschatological rest which will be fulfilled in Christ's return and in a new heaven and earth. Hebrews continues, "but the word which they heard did not profit them, not being mixed with faith in those who heard it." The author of Hebrews says the gospel was preached to them—very in-

---

211 Emphasis added. G. D. Davidson, trans. *The Writings of Balthasar Hubmaier* (1939) 231-32. Cited in Estep, *The Anabaptist Story*, 243-244.

212 Hebrews 4:1. The following discussion quotes from Hebrews 4 (NKJV).

teresting. But it didn't profit them because they didn't believe;-it wasn't mixed with faith.

Hebrews four continues: "For we who have believed do enter that rest, as He has said: 'So I swore in My wrath, They shall not enter My rest.'" Who is he talking about here? The ones who shall not enter the rest are people who don't have faith. But we who have believed do enter the rest. Entrance into God's rest, which is equated with permanent salvation wrought by God Himself in Hebrews, is by faith.[213] Continuing in the pas-

---

213 Hebrews 2:10-18 speaks of this salvation that only Christ could bring: "For it was fitting for Him, for whom are all things and by whom are all things, in bringing many sons to glory, to make the captain of their salvation perfect through sufferings. For both He who sanctifies and those who are being sanctified are all of one, for which reason He is not ashamed to call them brethren, saying: 'I will declare Your name to My brethren; In the midst of the assembly I will sing praise to You.' And again: 'I will put My trust in Him.' And again: 'Here am I and the children whom God has given Me.' Inasmuch then as the children have partaken of flesh and blood, He Himself likewise shared in the same, that through death He might destroy him who had the power of death, that is, the devil, and release those who through fear of death were all their lifetime subject to bondage. For indeed He does not give aid to angels, but He does give aid to the seed of Abraham. Therefore, in all things He had to be made like His brethren, that He might be a merciful and faithful High Priest in things pertaining to God, to make propitiation for the sins of the people. For in that He Himself has suffered, being tempted, He is able to aid those who are tempted." Hebrews 10:4-14 emphasizes the permanence of the salvation offering of Christ: "For it is impossible for the blood of bulls and goats to take away sins. Consequently, when Christ came into the world, he said, 'Sacrifices and offerings you have not desired, but a body have you prepared for me; in burnt offerings and sin offerings you have taken no pleasure. Then I said, "Behold, I have come to do your will, O God, as it is written of me in the scroll of the book." When he said above, 'You have neither desired nor taken pleasure in sacrifices and offerings and burnt offerings and sin offerings' (these are offered according to the law), then he added, 'Behold, I have come to do your will.' He does away with the first in order to establish the second. And by that will we have been sanctified through the offering of the body of Jesus Christ once for all. And every priest stands daily at his service, offering repeatedly the same sacrifices, which can never take away sins. But when Christ had offered *for all time* a single sacrifice for sins, he sat down at the right hand of God, waiting

sage, we read: "Although the works were finished from the foundation of the world." The works refer to what Jesus accomplished for believers, which God determined to achieve before creation. The writer continues:

> For He has spoken in a certain place of the seventh day in this way: "And God rested on the seventh day from all His works"; and again in this place: "They shall not enter My rest." Since therefore it remains that some must enter it, and those to whom it was first preached did not enter because of dis- obedience, again He designates a certain day, saying in David, "Today," after such a long time, as it has been said: "Today, if you will hear His voice, Do not harden your hearts."[214]

He references the creation here. This is interesting because he already noted that the works were finished at the foundation of the world. He is referring to God's rest after His six-day creation. These are matters which go back to the beginning. The beginning of God's plan, the beginning of creation, and the beginning of the people of God with Moses and on through David and his kingdom. So, this rest was what God had in mind from the beginning for those who would place their trust in Him, those who do not harden their hearts against Him.

There is an invitation in this passage emphasizing that "today" any- one who hears and believes that God offers and can impart lasting rest will receive it. This is a "God" kind of rest which is more than tempo- rary, more than just a this-worldly accommodation. The immediacy of this call, which the author of Hebrews takes from Psalm ninety-five of David, seems to be an important point. There is still a chance to enter this rest, but it comes in responding by faith: "*if* you will hear his voice." Belief, then, is one of the key motifs of this passage. We are reminded of verse three: "For we who have believed *do* enter that rest." Belief and un- belief are contrasted clearly here in the book of Hebrews, and *hearing* of the promised rest is the doorway, for entering or for turning away. This

---

from that time until his enemies should be made a footstool for his feet. For by a single offering he has perfected *for all time* those who are being sanctified." Emphasis added (NKJV).

214 Hebrews 4:4-6 (NKJV).

reminds us of Paul's affirmation that "faith comes by hearing, and hearing by the word of God." This word of the promised rest God offers, which is available to all "today" who will believe it, is equated with the salvation God offers in Christ. This faith attitude is in contrast with the Israelites, who would not believe that God would fulfill His promise to take them into the promised land, His temporal "rest" for them, and were afraid of the people living there.

Israelite Rebellion

The allusion in Hebrews to Psalm ninety-five recalls one of the first "testings" of God by His newly rescued people, the Israelites. God had already delivered them from the Egyptians through the red sea miracle. He had also provided water (He made the bitter waters sweet) and bread (manna) in response to their grumbling. Now they were complaining again for water as they continued their travels in the wilderness. Moses struck a rock, and water came gushing out to slake their thirst. Exodus seventeen gives us the story:

> The entire Israelite community left the Wilderness of Sin, moving from one place to the next according to the Lord's command. They camped at Rephidim, but there was no water for the people to drink. So the people complained to Moses, "Give us water to drink." "Why are you complaining to me?" Moses replied to them. "Why are you testing the Lord?" But the people thirsted there for water and grumbled against Moses. They said, "Why did you ever bring us up from Egypt to kill us and our children and our livestock with thirst?" Then Moses cried out to the Lord, "What should I do with these people? In a little while they will stone me!" The Lord answered Moses, "Go on ahead of the people and take some of the elders of Israel with you. Take the staff you struck the Nile with in your hand and go. I am going to stand there in front of you on the rock at Horeb; when you hit the rock, water will come out of it and the people will drink." Moses did this in the sight of the elders of Israel. He named the place Massah and Meribah because the Israelites

complained, and because they tested the Lord, saying, "Is the Lord among us or not?"[215]

The place was named Massah and Meribah, meaning "testing" and "quarreling" (rebellion). The people continued this quarreling trend all the way to the borders of the promised land. Here, on the brink of seeing God's promise of a land of their own fulfilled, they trusted their own feelings and judgments, fearing the towering Canaanites, regarding them as too strong, rather than trusting the power and faithfulness of God. This was the same God who had delivered them from Egypt with great miracles, physically manifested His presence every day and night (in the pillar of cloud or fire), and provided for their needs in the wilderness (Even when they whined for meat to indulge their culinary cravings, He supplied it).

You may remember the account from the book of Numbers. God commanded spies be sent into the land of Canaan, one from each tribe. When they returned, ten of the spies said that the land was indeed "flowing with milk and honey," but the people were too strong and their fortifications too imposing. They even saw "giants" (descendants of Anak)! AAAAAH! These spies stirred up fear and despair in the rest of the people, and they all wept for themselves. They had a pity party. They claimed it would have been better to have died in Egypt or in the wilderness than to be wiped out, along with their children, by the fearsome inhabitants of the land:

> So all the congregation lifted up their voices and cried, and the people wept that night. And all the children of Israel complained against Moses and Aaron, and the whole congregation said to them, "If only we had died in the land of Egypt! Or if only we had died in this wilderness! Why has the Lord brought us to this land to fall by the sword, that our wives and children should become victims? Would it not be better for us to return to Egypt?" So they said to one another, "Let us select a leader and return to Egypt."[216]

---

215 Exodus 17:1-7 (CSB).
216 Numbers 14:1-4 (NKJV).

Jumping to the conclusion that it was impossible to take the land, they blamed God and claimed they knew what was best. Apparently, God had made a heinous mistake in delivering them from Egypt, only to bring them here to be slaughtered by the Canaanites. The implication was that He was either incompetent, malicious, or perhaps both. Their poor children would also be victims because of God (an exaggerated slur they had also used at the waters of Meribah). What monstrous arrogance against God this was, all clothed in the garments of victimhood. Just as Solomon wrote in Proverbs, "A man's own foolishness leads him astray, yet his heart rages against the Lord."[217] No wonder the author of Hebrews characterizes these people as having an "evil heart of unbelief in departing from the living God."[218]

This Israelite rebellion would seem to characterize well the sniveling, self-pitying, yet prideful disposition common to mankind. You may have detected this sort of whining spite in your own thinking at times, being mad at God when He doesn't do things according to your expectations.[219] But two of the twelve spies, Joshua and Caleb, believed that God would fulfill His promise to His people, which demonstrates that we *can* reject the victimhood ploy that rises in us when faced with challenges and choose to be on His side. We also can believe He knows best and will bring us through to that best in the end. Today is the day to trust Him, according to Hebrews and Psalm ninety-five. The writer of Hebrews has already shown what that 'best' is (which God has in mind for us) in his demonstration of the superiority of Christ in chapters one through three. Christ is better than the angels, better than Moses, better than Joshua, and in the rest of the letter the writer shows Christ to be better than the Levitical priesthood, the tabernacle sanctuary, its sacrifices, etc. He's the best, and He's the 'rest.' The very thing we need most is the actual person of God Himself, given to us directly in Christ.

---

217 Proverbs 19:3 (HCSB).

218 Hebrews 3:12 (NKJV).

219 I confess I have often detected this sniffy, fault-finding attitude in myself, and I thank God that the remedy is contrition and confession (coming boldly before the throne of grace to obtain mercy and find grace to help in time of need) resulting in forgiveness, since God is patient and merciful toward us based on the work and mediation of Jesus Christ.

Baptist scholar E. Y. Mullins, referring to Hebrews, affirms that the better mediation of Jesus is worthy of our trust because it is lasting and constant, giving the believer a permanent position as priest because of our great High Priest:

> Priesthood, sacrifice and mediation are inwrought as idea and institution in practically all religions. Judaism provided for this fundamental religious need in its Levitical system. The epistle to the Hebrews interprets them all in terms of Christ. He is the ideal Priest, Sacrifice and Mediator. "Once for all" by the offering of himself he put an end to the necessity for the outward ritual. Henceforth all men may become priests unto God through his perfect sacrifice. Thus man's sense of sin and guilt are wiped out of his consciousness and as son and heir he "comes boldly to a throne of grace to obtain mercy and find help in time of need." Thus comes restored fellowship and union between God and man.[220]

The superiority of Jesus, then, (along with the necessity of faith) is one of the main ideas in the letter to the Hebrews. Faith in Christ is the simple theme, which accords with the tone of the whole New Testament. Trusting in Him, and not what we might think is best, is the key. He offers us what is best according to His supreme wisdom, that is, He offers Himself. Men and women on their own cannot be the judge of what is best. Adam and Eve proved this through the events associated with the Fall in the garden of Eden. It may be instructive to revisit that first event which moved mankind away from trusting their faithful God toward delusional, self-centered human judgement.

The First Rebellion

Eve interpreted eating the forbidden fruit as that which was best for her. It was pleasing to the eye, good for food, and would make her wise.[221] In

---

220 Edgar Young Mullins, *Why Is Christianity True?: Christian Evidences* (Philadelphia: American Baptist Publication Society, 1905), 406.

221 See Genesis 3:6: "So when the woman saw that the tree was good for

reaching out and taking and eating the fruit, she was claiming for herself (and Adam for himself when he ate) the authority to pass judgment on good and evil. The good was to eat the fruit, for the reasons in the text of Genesis noted above. The evil, that which was deemed worthy to be rejected, was obeying God and refraining from taking the fruit. So, to take the fruit of the tree of the knowledge of good and evil was to take to the human self what is only God's prerogative, which is to define what's best (what is good and what is evil). In eating the forbidden fruit, Adam and Eve's eyes were opened, and they saw they were naked. They weren't up to the job of judging good and evil. God is the only true Judge in these matters because of His holy character. They saw that they were weak, naked creatures (without even the protection of fur or scales that other animals possessed), and they were ashamed and sewed leaves to cover themselves. Viewing themselves through the pretension of their usurped status as judges of good and evil, they were startled to recognize their own frail nature as hairless bipeds. Physically and psychologically, Adam and Eve found that they were merely vulnerable animals who did not have the power to enforce their judgments, but even so they judged themselves with shame and fear, and hid themselves from the true Judge. Men and women still subject themselves to their own judgement in this way, resulting in the disordered schizophrenia of prideful self-disdain.

But even in their fear, they did not humble themselves before God but sought to hide, pathetically judging concealment to be their best option (another human tendency). Significantly, our passage in Hebrews four states that it is impossible to hide from God, as Adam and Eve found out: "And there is no creature hidden from His sight, but all things are naked and open to the eyes of Him to whom we must give account."[222] Yet, even in their shame, they did not give up on the program they had set for themselves to be judges of what is good and evil. When the Lord searched for them in the cool of the day (perhaps they had been in the habit of walking with Him in their lush garden, a beautiful picture of free fellowship and love between Creator and His created children), they did not run to

---

food, that it was pleasant to the eyes, and a tree desirable to make one wise, she took of its fruit and ate. She also gave to her husband with her, and he ate" (NKJV).

222 Hebrews 4:13 (NKJV).

Him for help, but when confronted with their sin, they made judgements upon each other, upon the serpent, and even upon God Himself:

> And they heard the sound of the Lord God walking in the garden in the cool of the day, and Adam and his wife hid themselves from the presence of the Lord God among the trees of the garden. Then the Lord God called to Adam and said to him, "Where are you?" So he said, "I heard Your voice in the garden, and I was afraid because I was naked; and I hid myself." And He said, "Who told you that you were naked? Have you eaten from the tree of which I commanded you that you should not eat?" Then the man said, "The woman whom You gave to be with me, she gave me of the tree, and I ate." And the Lord God said to the woman, "What is this you have done?" The woman said, "The serpent deceived me, and I ate."[223]

Notice that neither Adam nor Eve admitted their own fault but projected the blame onto someone else for this disobedience. Even in their fear and shame they kept the privilege to be judge of the situation by grotesquely accusing others rather than taking responsibility.

Adam blamed Eve, and even, implicitly, God Himself. Adam called Eve "the woman whom *you* gave me to be with me." Notice how impersonal this is, the very opposite tone from when Adam first saw Eve and exclaimed that she was "bone of his bones and flesh of his flesh."[224] Adam also appears to blame God, implying that if God had never given him this woman, the catastrophe of the fear and vulnerability he now felt wouldn't have happened. Adam must have had a moment of relief, and felt perhaps a fleeting vindication of his judgement of the situation, when God turned away from him to Eve and said, 'what is this you have done?' Of course, Eve, too, wants to pass the blame. She blames the Serpent. What Adam and Eve both say in their own defense is technically true: the woman gave Adam the fruit (as God gave Adam the woman), and Eve was definitely deceived by the Serpent. But neither took responsibility for disobeying God's explicitly worded commandment not

---

223 Genesis 3:8-13 (NKJV).
224 See Genesis 2:18-25

to eat of the tree of the knowledge of good and evil. This was a command given by their gracious Creator in the context of abundant provision and good fellowship in the happy surroundings of Eden. The fact that God so graciously gave them all they needed, including their own existence, including one another as husband and wife, including fellowship with Himself in the wondrous garden which was their home, increases the monstrosity of this rebellion. They were not rebelling against a selfish dictator but against a loving Father.

One could even say that the tree of the knowledge of good and evil itself was a gracious gift to Adam and Eve in that it gave them the option to show God that they loved Him and trusted him. Before the fall, as they continued to comply with the command to refrain from eating the fruit, they had something precious to offer back to their Creator to exhibit their love for him: their obedience. The Creator gave them the opportunity to return His lavish and gracious love for them by being trustingly submissive, and so enter into a mutual and genuinely reciprocal relationship with their Father-God. Thus, God offered a higher order of kinship to Adam and Eve than with mere created animals. This was an intimate bond, a *personal relationship*, for which the ultimate model (which unfolds more clearly in the rest of the Scripture) is the Trinity—the relation of the Godhead in Father, Son, and Holy Spirit. This mutual love completed the perfection of Eden. Adam and Eve could offer back to God the trusting obedience that they owed Him, and as the pinnacle of His creation, made in His own image, were thereby given the gift of *freely* entering into a loving relationship with God Himself. Without the prohibited tree in the garden, the God-mankind relationship would likely, and necessarily, have been of a lower order.

However, the disobedience of our first parents caused this relationship to be damaged. They had turned from God to their own designs and their own faulty judgments, placing more confidence in the word of the serpent than in their Creator, which damaged their very souls and the future of mankind. In seeking to be their own judges, Adam and Eve drifted toward folly and the nothingness of destruction, and yet the true Judge, in His mercy, sacrificed one of His precious created beings for their sakes. He covered them with clothing more permanent than sewn leaves, in the form of animal skins, to assuage their fear and shame. We cannot help but think of the coming Lamb of God when we consider this first substitutionary shedding of blood. The coming messiah would be the healer, both of the estrangement between God and mankind and of the damaged human condition with its fear and shame and arrogance and death. This is the whole point of Hebrews chapter four. We have a new way in Jesus, our High Priest, to be reconciled to God and to allow Him to be the Judge again. He is a merciful and gracious Judge.

If we accept His terms, to give up on our personal program of exalting ourselves as sovereign judges, and admit we have sinned and turn to Him for healing, we can receive the gifts of adoption and eternal life. These are overwhelmingly gracious terms, bought for us by the crushing and excruciatingly painful death of God's own Son. His sacrifice and victory restore us to our rightful place as sons and daughters of our Father in Heaven (having been forfeited by our own rebellious foolishness), and even exalting us as kings and queens over a kingdom (which we don't deserve) founded and fulfilled in reality, with God's wondrous presence at its center and radiating throughout. All this in exchange for simply giving up on our own little grimy fantasy kingdoms in which we squat in squalor as false rulers. The prodigal son comes to mind, who ended up ruling over the pig stye without even benefitting from its pitiful offerings: "He persuaded a local farmer to hire him, and the man sent him into his fields to feed the pigs. The young man became so hungry that even the pods he was feeding the pigs looked good to him. But no one gave him anything."[225] Jesus tells us that the young man *'came to his senses'* and decided to go home and humble himself before his father. What would the father do or say? Of course, we know the answer. He dashes toward him with warm acceptance and open arms, enthusiastically celebrating his return. What lavish love and grace is given for arrogant, entitled rebels who repent:

> So he returned home to his father. And while he was still a long way off, his father saw him coming. Filled with love and compassion, he ran to his son, embraced him, and kissed him. His son said to him, "Father, I have sinned against both heaven and you, and I am no longer worthy of being called your son." But his father said to the servants, "Quick! Bring the finest robe

---

225 Luke 15:15-16 (NLT).

in the house and put it on him. Get a ring for his finger and sandals for his feet. And kill the calf we have been fattening. We must celebrate with a feast, for this son of mine was dead and has now returned to life. He was lost, but now he is found." So the party began.[226]

The Great High Priest

While human beings were in the process of destroying themselves, God was revealing His unfolding plan of redemption centered in His Son, the lion of kingly sound judgement (Jesus said, "I AM the truth") and the lamb of suffering and sacrifice. The triumphant King, the Lion of Judah, has overcome death on our behalf so that we need not fear. As Hebrews chapter two says, "Inasmuch then as the children have partaken of flesh and blood, He Himself likewise shared in the same, that through death He might destroy him who had the power of death, that is, the devil, and release those who through *fear of death* were all their lifetime subject to bondage."[227] The Lamb of God, who is worthy and worshiped in heaven, has taken our shame upon Himself, and our sins are washed away, and we are cleansed in His blood. As Hebrews ten says, "But when Christ had offered for all time a *single sacrifice* for sins, he sat down at the right hand of God, waiting from that time until his enemies should be made a footstool for his feet. For by a single offering he has *perfected for all time* those who are being *sanctified*."[228] Being perfected for all time is a pretty nice benefit! What a profusely generous gift this is, simply received by faith! And this gift God offers is for His haughty little human enemies, who had usurped God's authority in disobedience. In other words, Christ died for the ungodly. Those whining, victim-playing, lying, pronouncers of judgment like Cain, the first murderer who executed judgment on his own brother simply because he was jealous. These are the people God loved and sent His Son to die for.

This picture of human nature is clear in Scripture: "For from within, out of the heart of man, come evil thoughts, sexual immorality, theft, murder, adultery, coveting, wickedness, deceit, sensuality, envy, slander,

---

226 Luke 15:20-24 (NLT).
227 Emphasis added. Hebrews 2:14-15 (NKJV).
228 Hebrews 10:12-14 (ESV).

pride, foolishness. All these evil things come from within, and they defile a person."[229] What a world we live in, with billions of these little tin gods wandering about the planet behaving as if they were much more important and powerful than they really are. Each one can clearly see that he or she will die and yet invests absolutely in this temporary life, seeking his or her own benefit (often at the expense of others whom they claim are loved-ones) as if knowing indisputably what is best. Even the shaggy, vile, and godless twentieth-century poet Charles Bukowski, a denizen of the city of Los Angeles, could see this sad state of the human condition: "We're all going to die, all of us, what a circus! That alone should make us love each other but it doesn't. We are terrorized and flattened by trivialities, we are eaten up by nothing."[230] Yet God overcame this nothingness through His love for us. Christ died for us 'while we were yet sinners' in this sorry state of selfishness and conceit which leads inevitably to death. He entered into the very consequence of our wicked rebellion, that is, death itself, and blew it apart with His goodness and power in the resurrection: "Death has been swallowed up in victory."[231] That is why the writer of Hebrews exhorts his readers to enter into the rest God offers, which is trusting God's power, promise, and finished work in Christ, and thus entering into the very presence of God Himself to find grace and mercy.

---

229 Mark 7:21-23 (ESV). The great Baptist preacher Charles Spurgeon expressed it this way, in light of temptation: "All the sea outside a ship can do it no damage till the water enters and fills the hold. Hence, it is clear, our greatest danger is within. All the devils in hell and tempters on earth could do us no injury, if there were no corruption in our own natures. The sparks will fly harmlessly if there is no tinder. Alas, our heart is our greatest enemy; this is the little home-born thief, Lord, save me from that evil man, myself!" Cited in Augustus Hopkins Strong, *Systematic Theology: A Compendium and Commonplace-Book*, Vol. 2 (Philadelphia: Griffith & Rowland Press, 1907), 589.

230 Charles Bukowski, *The Captain Is Out to Lunch* (New York: Harper Collins), 10.

231 "When this corruptible is clothed with incorruptibility, and this mortal is clothed with immortality, then the saying that is written will take place: *Death has been swallowed up in victory. Death, where is your victory? Death, where is your sting?* Now the sting of death is sin, and the power of sin is the law. But thanks be to God, who gives us the victory through our Lord Jesus Christ!" 1 Corinthians 15:54-57 (HCSB).

These are the theological underpinnings, built on the firm foundation of the gospel of Christ and Him crucified, which brace up the great principle of *the priesthood of every believer*. Each believer is a priest who comes before God bravely, like a favored child, not due to any underlying merit but simply because of God's love and mercy. Now we hear the crescendo of Hebrews chapter four:

> Seeing then that we have a great High Priest who has passed through the heavens, Jesus the Son of God, let us hold fast our confession. For we do not have a High Priest who cannot sympathize with our weaknesses, but was in all points tempted as we are, yet without sin. Let us therefore come boldly to the throne of grace, that we may obtain mercy and find grace to help in time of need.[232]

The inherent value of the believer who obtains mercy is shown most resplendently in the lengths God was willing to go to save us, not in any boasting we might do to demonstrate our worth, or by any works we might display to earn it. So, we come boldly before the throne of *grace*, right into God's presence, because we have a high priest who has passed through the heavens, who is representing us there. Everyone who has believed and entered into this rest can appeal to God without going through any other person on earth. Why? Because I already *have* a Mediator, someone who is representing me before the great God of wrath and judgement, and of love and mercy, and that is Jesus, His Son. In other words, we have a *great* High Priest, and therefore we don't need a mere human priest. We have *the* One Man, our God-anointed representative, *the* Great High Priest and blameless, perfect Lamb of God.[233] Any mortal man claiming to stand in

---

232 Hebrews 4:14-16 (NKJV).

233 One of the obvious reasons no mortal man can represent another to the Holy God is that we are all corrupt. The Levitical priests in the Old Testament had to be cleansed with water and with sacrificial blood in order to represent their fellow Israelites. They had to be consecrated with elaborate ceremonies and wear special clothing and accoutrements. And they were appointed by God Himself, foreshadowing the perfect priest which was to come, the Messiah Himself who was without sin. Baptist theologian Augustus Strong

for or represent Jesus to us is, by definition, an imposter. This great truth is clearly explicated here in Hebrews in what is one of the key passages regarding the Priesthood of the Believer.

The Promised Rest

As we look at Hebrews chapter four, we may ask: what is the nature of the rest that God promises? Since it is so intimately associated with Christ and His status as our High Priest, it would appear evident that this promised rest is a biblical analogy for our reconciliation with God, the fact that we can enter into the very presence of our Holy God, because of Christ. We are finally at home and can rest from our laborious and empty self-seeking journey when we find Christ. He himself promised His disciples that He would go and prepare a place for them in the Father's house.[234] There is a final resting place for all those who place their trust in Jesus. The Father's house, to be home with our Creator, our Heavenly Father, is the rest which Jesus offers and the Father promised. That rest, which is in Christ for eternity, was pictured in the rest that God offered the Israelites in promising them their own land and the peace of settling there. But this was only a picture. Hebrews makes it clear that the ultimate rest, that Sabbath rest patterned after God Himself who

---

wrote concerning humanity's universal imperfection: "Every man knows himself to have come short of moral perfection, and, in proportion to his experience of the world, recognizes the fact that every other man has come short of it also. Chinese proverb: 'There are but two good men; one is dead, and the other is not yet born.' . . . Dr. Jacob Chamberlain, the missionary, said: 'I never but once in India heard a man deny that he was a sinner. But once a Brahmin interrupted me and said: "I deny your premises. I am not a sinner. I do not need to do better." For a moment I was abashed. Then I said: "But what do your neighbors say?" Thereupon one cried out: "He cheated me in trading horses"; another: "He defrauded a widow of her inheritance." The Brahmin went out of the house, and I never saw him again.'" Augustus Hopkins Strong, *Systematic Theology: A Compendium and Commonplace-Book*, Vol. 2, 575.

234 "Let not your hearts be troubled. Believe in God; believe also in me. In my Father's house are many rooms. If it were not so, would I have told you that I go to prepare a place for you? And if I go and prepare a place for you, I will come again and will take you to myself, that where I am you may be also." John 14:1-3 (ESV).

rested from His creative work in the beginning, is offered as a gift to those who have faith in Christ. He writes: "For if Joshua had given them rest, then He (David) would not afterward have spoken of another day. There remains therefore a rest for the people of God. For he who has entered His rest has himself also ceased from his works as God did from His."[235]

Thus, salvation and eternal life with God is not our work to accomplish, but something promised from the Old Testament days, and prefigured in God's relationship with the Israelites, and realized in Christ. Each person who trusts Christ enters into that long-promised rest. The believer stops trying to find rest by his own efforts and simply receives from Christ the finished fact, from His great labors in His first coming, that we now belong in the Father's house. Establishing our own righteousness based on our own faulty judgements is only a fool's errand. Accepting God's righteousness as a gift, and all the riches that come with being a child of God, is to forsake any and all of my own works and efforts to justify myself and *earn* salvation.[236] So, Hebrews four verse ten says that we

---

235 Hebrews 4:8-10 (NKJV).

236 The mistake of attempting to establish one's own righteousness is clearly communicated in Paul's epistle to the Romans as he discusses his hope for his own Jewish brothers and sisters: "Brethren, my heart's desire and prayer to God for Israel is that they may be saved. For I bear them witness that they have a zeal for God, but not according to knowledge. *For they being ignorant of God's righteousness, and seeking to establish their own righteousness, have not submitted to the righteousness of God.* For Christ is the end of the law for righteousness to everyone who believes. For Moses writes about the righteousness which is of the law, 'The man who does those things shall live by them.' But the righteousness of faith speaks in this way, 'Do not say in your heart, "Who will ascend into heaven?"' (that is, to bring Christ down from above) or, '"Who will descend into the abyss?"' (that is, to bring Christ up from the dead). But what does it say? 'The word is near you, in your mouth and in your heart' (that is, the word of faith which we preach): that if you confess with your mouth the Lord Jesus and believe in your heart that God has raised Him from the dead, you will be saved. For with the heart one believes unto righteousness, and with the mouth confession is made unto salvation. For the Scripture says, 'Whoever believes on Him will not be put to shame.' For there is no distinction between Jew and Greek, for the same Lord over all is rich to all who call upon Him. For 'whoever calls on the name of the Lord shall be saved.'" Emphasis added, Romans 10:1-13 (NKJV).

who have entered His rest by faith also forsake our own works: "For he who has entered His rest has himself also ceased from his works as God did from His." Baptist scholar Albert Mohler explains:

> How do we enter this Sabbath rest? The whole letter of Hebrews tells us: by believing in Jesus Christ, the Lord of the Sabbath. Joshua led Israel into the land, but Jesus leads his people into God's true eschatological rest. Verse 10 elaborates on this. We rest from our works and enter God's rest when we trust in Christ. We no longer have to live our lives trying to "prove" our righteousness before God. Instead, we "rest" from that labor because Christ has already proved that righteousness on our behalf.
>
> Like John 3:16, Hebrews 4:10 powerfully captures the message of the gospel in a single verse. The gospel is not morality. The gospel is not external religion. Nor is it a seven-step program for obtaining a better life. The gospel is the message of Christ's accomplishments on our behalf so that we might "rest" from our works by trusting in his work. When we trust in Christ's work, we rest from trusting our own.[237]

We can find rest for our souls in Christ! We may as well "get real" and admit that our own works, relying on our own judgements, are not going to make us righteous, and receive this wonderful rest which comes through childlike trust in God.

The Old Testament makes it clear that our righteous works "are as filthy rags."[238] Jesus declared that we must be perfect as our Heavenly Father is perfect. This is impossible by our own efforts. But a perfect righteousness from God through Christ can be received through faith. Just as Abraham believed God's promise, "and it was credited to Him as righteousness," so we can believe in Christ, the fulfillment of the promise, and re-

---

237 R. Albert Mohler, Jr., *Exalting Jesus in Hebrews* (Nashville: B&H Publishing, 2017), 58-59.

238 "But we are all as an unclean thing, and all our righteousnesses are as filthy rags; and we all do fade as a leaf; and our iniquities, like the wind, have taken us away." Isaiah 64:6 (KJV).

ceive undeserved righteousness and life.[239] It is not our own heart condition or self-righteous efforts that can make us holy. Only God can do it. In fact, Christ *is* our righteousness![240] John Bunyan, the famous seventeenth-century author of *Pilgrim's Progress*, and the pastor of the Bedford Baptist Church in England, expressed this wonderful truth as a personal testimony:

> But one day as I was passing into the field, with some dashes on my conscience, fearing yet that all was not right, suddenly this sentence fell upon my soul, "Your righteousness is in heaven." I thought I saw with the eyes of my soul Jesus Christ at God's right hand. There was my righteousness. Wherever I was, or whatever I was doing, God could not say of me that I lacked His righteousness, for that was ever before Him. Moreover, I saw that it was not my good frame of heart that made my righteousness better, nor yet my bad frame that made my righteousness worse, for my righteousness was Jesus Christ Himself, "the same yesterday, today, and for ever."[241]

We might as well admit that our own "righteousness" will never do and be free of our*selves*, rejoicing with our brother John Bunyan that Christ is our righteousness. Jesus said, "seek first the kingdom of God, and *His righteousness.*" He was essentially saying "I, the righteousness of God, am before you; seek Me."

Only the beauteous perfection of the holy Son of God will avail us, and He gives it as a freely offered gift. We cannot fool God, although we are

---

239 Genesis 15:6.

240 "Brothers, consider your calling: Not many are wise from a human perspective, not many powerful, not many of noble birth. Instead, God has chosen what is foolish in the world to shame the wise, and God has chosen what is weak in the world to shame the strong. God has chosen what is insignificant and despised in the world—what is viewed as nothing—to bring to nothing what is viewed as something, so that no one can boast in His presence. But it is from Him that you are in Christ Jesus, who became God-given wisdom for us—our righteousness, sanctification, and redemption, in order that, as it is written: The one who boasts must boast in the Lord." 1 Corinthians 1:26-31 (HCSB).

241 John Bunyan, *Grace Abounding to the Chief of Sinners,* paragraph 229.

often successful in fooling others, and even ourselves. He knows what's really in our hearts. That is why the writer of Hebrews characterizes the word of God as a sword which can read our hearts and minds. He declares that nothing is hidden from God, to whom we are accountable. "For the word of God is living and powerful, and sharper than any two-edged sword, piercing even to the division of soul and spirit, and of joints and marrow, and is a discerner of the thoughts and intents of the heart. And there is no creature hidden from His sight, but all things are naked and open to the eyes of Him to whom we must give account."[242] What a relief to come out of hiding, as Adam and Eve should have done, and throw ourselves on the Mercy of God, throwing over and discarding our own estimates of ourselves (as the apostle Paul says: comparing themselves among themselves, they were foolish) and submitting to the truth of His atoning judicial decision in the cross and thus on the mercy of our loving, gracious Savior, the true Judge and true Sacrifice, Jesus Christ.[243] No wonder the writer of Hebrews encourages us to be diligent to enter, by faith alone, this wonderful *rest* which was promised and fulfilled by God Himself.

SALVATION ASSURANCE

As we have seen, the principle of the priesthood of every believer is opposed to sacerdotalism (from the Latin, *sacerdotalis* "of or pertaining to a priest," from *sacerdos* [genitive *sacerdotis*] "priest," literally "offerer of sacrifices," from *saceros* "priest," so referring to a priest). The Catholics, and even many Protestants, held on to this idea that you need some sort of earthly human church representative to administer official rites to you in order to stay right with God. But what do you need to stay right with God? Jesus on the cross and resurrected—that's all you need. In many churches, to this day, the priest is the intermediary or mediator, and therefore, by

---

242 Hebrews 4:12-13 (NKJV).

243 Paul describes people who try to build themselves up by their own judgements: "For we dare not class ourselves or compare ourselves with those who commend themselves. But they, measuring themselves by themselves, and comparing themselves among themselves, are not wise." 1 Corinthians 10:12 (NKJV).

being the functionary of the church, conveys grace through his ministrations and sacraments, as in the Roman Catholic Church, Eastern Orthodox, and High Anglican. Baptists are not sacramentalist or sacerdotalist. Baptists would argue that the priesthood of the believer is a distinctly Baptist precept in the sense that Baptists have historically taken this truth more seriously by rejecting a sacramental (in other words, salvation through rituals and rites) approach to belief. That's why, when we connect this to the ordinances, we don't call them sacraments, and we don't believe that they do anything except remind us about what God has already done in Christ.

And what are the ordinances? Baptism and the Lord's Supper. Only two. As a contrast, we can inquire as to how many sacraments are in the Catholic church: Seven. But we don't find those in the New Testament. For Baptists, the ordinances, which are given to us by Christ Himself, are symbols: they don't actually provide grace in any sense; they are not magical; they're not sacraments, but they're memorials of the salvation already accomplished by Christ. And what did He say as He was on the cross? "It is finished." In Greek, it is *"tetelestai."* This points to the once-and-for-all nature of the substitutionary atonement finished at the cross. If this one sacrifice is enough, as the writer of Hebrews makes plain, then any other supposed conduits of grace through church ceremonies are illegitimate and could even be characterized as hindrances to true grace, God's grace in Christ alone. Thus, for Baptists, the ordinances simply point us to the completeness of the sacrifice of Christ because, as Isaiah the prophet said, "all our sins are laid upon Him."[244] He was punished in our place: "But He was pierced for our offenses, He was crushed for our wrongdoings; The punishment for our well-being was laid upon Him, And by His wounds we are healed."[245]

Now, along with this, I want to mention a controversial subject in some Christian circles, and that is eternal security. We know that Jesus said this: "For God so loved the world that he gave his only begotten son that whosoever believeth in him should not perish but have everlasting

---

244 "All we like sheep have gone astray; We have turned, every one, to his own way; And the LORD has laid on Him the iniquity of us all." Isaiah 53:6 (NKJV).

245 Isaiah 53:5 (NASB).

life."[246] Now what is the quality of the life given to those who believe? Everlasting. Enough said. It's not a life that you can forfeit or throw away; it's everlasting. And that life, through the Holy Spirit's presence (God Himself in you) is a gift. So, a wonderful assurance of salvation is observable in the undeserved gift of life everlasting and is connected with the Priesthood of all Believers. Any believer, who has perfect access to God Himself because of his or her wondrous mediator, Christ, has genuine and permanent security. Why? Because the believer has entered into the promised rest. He is not looking at himself and his works, or lack thereof, anymore. The rest that God has already given to me from my works, and the freedom that I know I can do nothing to save myself—so that it's sheer grace to me—was received when I heard that good news, believed, and, thus, was saved. Very simple. Like a little child. Remember, Jesus used the little child as one of His favorite pictures typifying those who enter His kingdom. This simple faith in response to Jesus' promise of life is illustrated in Jesus' friend Martha right before the raising of her brother Lazarus from the dead:

> When Jesus arrived, He found that Lazarus had already been in the tomb four days. Bethany was near Jerusalem (about two miles away). . . . Then Martha said to Jesus, "Lord, if You had been here, my brother wouldn't have died. Yet even now I know that whatever You ask from God, God will give You." "Your brother will rise again," Jesus told her. Martha said, "I know that he will rise again in the resurrection at the last day." Jesus said to her, "I am the resurrection and the life. The one who believes in Me, even if he dies, will live. Everyone who lives and believes in Me will never die—ever. Do you believe this?" "Yes, Lord," she told Him, "I believe You are the Messiah, the Son of God, who comes into the world."[247]

---

246 John 3:16 (KJV).

247 John 11:17-27 (HCSB). It is interesting to note that this exchange between Jesus and Martha happens *before* the Lazarus miracle, which confirmed Jesus' claim to *be* the Resurrection and the Life and the giver of everlasting life to those who believe (as Martha confesses: He is the Son of God).

Jesus seems pretty clear about the everlasting quality of the life He offers here. The only thing He desires from Martha, which He pointedly urges her to express, is belief.

Salvation through faith in Christ, then, is a gift, and salvation equals everlasting life. Thus, that gift cannot be taken away, since the promised word of the Giver, who *is* the Resurrection and the Life, cannot be challenged or reversed. It's a pretty good gift, isn't it? So, when I have doubts about my salvation, what am I doubting? If you have doubts about your salvation, it usually has to do with your own errors. "Am I good enough? Did I do the thing I should have?" All of that has been put to rest in the death of Christ. No, you weren't good enough; Jesus had to die for you. That's the whole point: we'll never be good enough, but He still gave you, as a gift, eternal life—the best gift anybody could ever bestow on anyone else. This is because all of my sin that I have committed or ever will commit was laid upon Him and done away with in His death. This is called good news! The gospel itself *is* eternal security. As the apostle John wrote, "I have written these things to you who believe in the name of the Son of God, so that you may know that you have eternal life."[248]

So, the righteousness of God, which brings eternal life, is given me as a gift because of faith. If I am righteous, then I'm right with God. This is forever, and cannot be taken away, because it is Christ Himself. He is my righteousness,[249] and He is my representative before God forever as my High Priest. Eternal security is not necessarily strictly a Baptist

---

248 1 John 5:13 (HCSB).

249 "God has chosen what is insignificant and despised in the world—what is viewed as nothing—to bring to nothing what is viewed as something, so that no one can boast in His presence. But it is from Him that you are in Christ Jesus, who became God-given wisdom for us—*our righteousness*, sanctification, and redemption, in order that, as it is written: The one who boasts must boast in the Lord." Emphasis added. 1 Corinthians 1:28-31 (HCSB). "'Behold, the days are coming,' says the LORD, 'That I will raise to David a Branch of righteousness; A King shall reign and prosper, And execute judgment and righteousness in the earth. In His days Judah will be saved, And Israel will dwell safely; Now this is His name by which He will be called: *THE LORD OUR RIGHTEOUS-NESS.*'" Emphasis added. Jeremiah 23:5-6 (NKJV).

distinctive, since other protestant groups hold to this doctrine, but Baptists have always had strong elements and traditions of teaching that the promise from God of eternal life for those who believe is inviolable. In other words, it's not going to be taken back. God will not go back on His word; nothing can be done against it. The gift of eternal life through faith in His Son is *His* proclamation, and so believers are secure and assured of life forever with God: "The Lord promised that everlasting life is *the present possession* of believers. 'He who believes in Me *has* everlasting life,' the Lord said (John 6:47, emphasis added). *Has.* That's present tense."[250] As the Apostle Paul said concerning his own death, "To be absent from the body is to be present with the Lord."[251]

Another proclamation Jesus made about salvation in John chapter three was that there need be no fear of condemnation. The famous passage, John 3:16, is part of the interview with Nicodemus when Jesus tells him, "you must be *born again*, born from above;" in other words, you need a new life:

> Nicodemus answered and said to Him, "How can these things be?" Jesus answered and said to him, "Are you the

---

250 Shawn Lazar, *Assurance Made Simple* (Denton, TX: Grace Evangelical Society, 2019), 11.

251 2 Corinthians 5:8. Paul also insisted that Titus, the young pastor in Crete, accentuate firmly to the believers there this hope of eternal life, based on the finished work of Christ: "But when the kindness of God our Savior and His love for mankind appeared, He saved us—not by works of righteousness that we had done, but according to His mercy, through the washing of **regeneration and renewal** by the Holy Spirit. He poured out this Spirit on us abundantly through Jesus Christ our Savior, so that having been justified by His grace, we may become heirs with the **hope of eternal life**. This saying is trustworthy. I want you to insist on these things." Emphasis added. Titus 3:4-8a (HCSB). Likewise, Jude, in his letter warning against false teachers, emphasized eternal life in his exhortation to the believers near the end of the epistle: "But you, dear friends, as you build yourselves up in your most holy faith and pray in the Holy Spirit, keep yourselves in the love of God, *expecting the mercy of our Lord Jesus Christ for eternal life.*" Emphasis added. Jude 20-21 (HCSB). These are but two examples of the importance of eternal life given through God's grace in Christ, which is emphasized throughout the New Testament.

teacher of Israel, and do not know these things? Most assuredly, I say to you, We speak what We know and testify what We have seen, and you do not receive Our witness. If I have told you earthly things and you do not believe, how will you believe if I tell you heavenly things? No one has ascended to heaven but He who came down from heaven, that is, the Son of Man who is in heaven."[252]

He's talking about Himself—I came from heaven, so I know what I'm talking about here, about life and about being born again. In fact, I'm the key to it all. "And as Moses lifted up the serpent in the wilderness, even so must the Son of Man be lifted up, that whoever believes in Him should not perish but have eternal life."[253] He says this in verse fifteen and He repeats the promise in verse sixteen, referring to *everlasting* life: "For God so loved the world that He gave His only begotten Son, that whoever believes in Him should not perish but have everlasting life." *Whoever.* Whoever has the traditionally approved theology should not perish, but have everlasting life? Whoever is baptized into a Christian denomination at birth? Whoever is helpful to all the people around them should not perish and have everlasting life? Whoever has a deeply moving religious experience should not perish? No, just whoever believes in Him, whoever trusts Jesus.

But let's notice also verse seventeen: "For God did not send His Son into the world to condemn the world, but that the world through Him might be saved." Into the world, *into* this place with all of us sinful people, *not to condemn the world*—all of us people—but that He might save it, save *us*. If we believe, we're no longer condemned! So how do we get out of the 'condemned' column (which means you must perish)? Just by childlike faith. That's the only way. And then you go into this other column called 'everlasting life,' and you're not condemned any more. So why on earth would that everlasting life ever be taken away if, because of the blood of Christ, you're not condemned? The blood of Christ is so precious that the salvation it brings could never be taken away. So, if you are not condemned, then you need not perish. Thus, eternal security. In verse eigh-

---

252 John 3:9-13 (NKJV).
253 John 3:14-15 (NKJV).

teen Jesus goes on and clinches the argument, and of course He's talking about Himself: "He who believes in Him is not condemned; but he who does not believe is condemned already, because he has not believed in the name of the only begotten Son of God." So, faith leads to salvation, which, in its essence, is eternal life, being born again, having the Holy Spirit dwell within you permanently, and that can't be taken away, thus you can't 'lose' your salvation. Spiritual birth, like physical birth, only happens once and cannot be undone. And the new birth is a birth into the *gift* of everlasting life for all of us who deserve condemnation.

If we have trust in Christ, there is no fear of condemnation. What a relief! What gratitude wells up within us when we grasp this unmistakable truth. Eternal life is given as a gift to those who simply believe, with humble trust, in Jesus' power and work. This is the quality of life that God offers through Jesus Christ—eternal, the sort of life that only God can give, the 'God' kind of life, that cannot be overcome. Can anyone overcome God's life? Can anyone kill God? No. He allowed Himself, as a man, to be killed to be our sacrifice, but death could not hold Him. This is the kind of life Jesus offered the Samaritan woman at the well— He called it living water, a spring of life that doesn't run out, eternally flowing. And, as we have noted, the letter of Hebrews says believers are 'perfected for all time.'[254] Believers, then, have instant access with God Himself at any time, each being part of a royal priesthood. Thus, as an old Baptist preacher once wrote, "All notions of a needed 'priesthood,' to bring us into connection with Christ, must yield to the truth that Christ is ever with us."[255] The author of Hebrews confirms our security in Jesus Christ when he proclaims:

> But this man, because he continueth ever, hath an unchangeable priesthood. *Wherefore he is able also to save them to the uttermost that come unto God by him, seeing he ever liveth to make intercession for them.* For such an high priest became us, who is holy, harmless, undefiled, separate from sinners, and made higher than the heavens; Who needeth not daily, as

254 Hebrews 2:14-15.
255 Ezekiel Gilman Robinson. Cited in Augustus Hopkins Strong, *Systematic Theology: A Compendium and Commonplace-Book*, Vol. 3, 969.

those high priests, to offer up sacrifice, first for his own sins, and then for the people's: for this he did *once*, when he offered up himself. For the law maketh men high priests which have infirmity; but the word of the oath, which was since the law, maketh the Son, who is consecrated *for evermore*.[256]

CONCLUSION: THE PRIESTHOOD OF EVERY BELIEVER AS INTEGRAL TO BAPTIST PRINCIPLES

The Priesthood of the Believer is an important theological principle connected with all of the Baptist distinctives discussed in previous chapters. First, it is crucial to the idea of Biblical authority because each believer can study and read Scripture for himself without the interference or need of an official priestly guide, ecclesiastical council, or spiritual guru of any sort. The New Testament tells us that each believer is born again and thus indwelt by the Holy Spirit. Believers, then, are not in need of a human guide or authority to read and attempt to interpret Scripture, since the Holy Spirit will "guide us into all truth."[257] Reliance

---

256 Emphasis added. Hebrews 7:24-28.

257 In the gospel of John, Jesus promised His disciples the Holy Spirit as their guide for truth and associated the Spirit's guidance with His own words and with the Father's. No disciple could miss the fact that the Old Testament was where they learned the words of the Father, which were their Scriptures. Jesus appealed to the Scripture as the ultimate authority over and over. The New Testament is also promised here as the continuing word from Jesus and the Father through the Holy Spirit disclosed to the apostles: "But now I go away to Him who sent Me, and none of you asks Me, 'Where are You going?' But because I have said these things to you, sorrow has filled your heart. Nevertheless I tell you the truth. It is to your advantage that I go away; for if I do not go away, the Helper will not come to you; but if I depart, I will send Him to you. And when He has come, He will convict the world of sin, and of righteousness, and of judgment: of sin, because they do not believe in Me; of righteousness, because I go to My Father and you see Me no more; of judgment, because the ruler of this world is judged. I still have many things to say to you, but you cannot bear them now. However,

on the Holy Spirt as we approach Scripture is an important principle of *hermeneutics (the science and art of interpretation)*, which acknowledges God Himself as the source of truth. However, this reliance is not a guarantee that the individual believer will interpret well. Historical-grammatical hermeneutical principles must be employed in order to treat the Bible according to its nature and, thus, read it in the proper literary and historical context in which it was written. It is not a book of spiritual secrets or magic power but a book explaining objective truth through historical events and teaching. It is, of course, inspired by God Himself, "breathed out" by the Holy Spirit, as the apostle Paul says in his letter to Timothy. But it must be approached and studied according to what it is, that is, written-down language in a real-world context. Thus grammatical, literary, and historical rules of interpretation apply.

So, we have the Scripture, which has behind it the authority of "thus sayeth the Lord," as we see explicitly with the prophets. But we have also the living God Himself who has promised to guide us into truth by the Holy Spirit. The two must remain together, since the truth is God's word and God's Word (Jesus) is the truth. One simply cannot spiritually baptize his own ruminations or experiences by proclaiming and declaring them to be God's word or Holy Spirit-inspired. Any word from a man must be *checked by the Scriptures, which cannot be broken,* according to Jesus (who proclaimed Himself to be the Truth). You see how the Scriptures affirm Jesus, and Jesus the Scriptures. Luke wrote in his gospel that Christ said the Scriptures were all about Him.[258] In addi-

---

when He, the Spirit of truth, has come, He will guide you into all truth; for He will not speak on His own authority, but whatever He hears He will speak; and He will tell you things to come. He will glorify Me, for He will take of what is Mine and declare it to you. All things that the Father has are Mine. Therefore I said that He will take of Mine and declare it to you." John 16:5-15 (NKJV) The same Spirit of Truth promised here is that Spirit of life which dwells within the believer today and desires to still glorify Christ by guiding us toward truth, which is accessible to us in the Old and New Testaments.

258 "Now that same day two of them were going to a village called Emmaus, about seven miles from Jerusalem. They were talking with each other about everything that had happened. As they talked and discussed these things with each other, Jesus himself came up and walked along with them; but they

were kept from recognizing him. He asked them, 'What are you discussing together as you walk along?' They stood still, their faces downcast. One of them, named Cleopas, asked him, 'Are you the only one visiting Jerusalem who does not know the things that have happened there in these days?' 'What things?' he asked. 'About Jesus of Nazareth,' they replied. 'He was a prophet, powerful in word and deed before God and all the people. The chief priests and our rulers handed him over to be sentenced to death, and they crucified him; but we had hoped that he was the one who was going to redeem Israel. And what is more, it is the third day since all this took place. In addition, some of our women amazed us. They went to the tomb early this morning but didn't find his body. They came and told us that they had seen a vision of angels, who said he was alive. Then some of our companions went to the tomb and found it just as the women had said, but they did not see Jesus.' He said to them, 'How foolish you are, and how slow to believe all that the prophets have spoken! Did not the Messiah have to suffer these things and then enter his glory?' And beginning with Moses and all the Prophets, he explained to them what was said in all the Scriptures concerning himself. As they approached the village to which they were going, Jesus continued on as if he were going farther. But they urged him strongly, 'Stay with us, for it is nearly evening; the day is almost over.' So he went in to stay with them. When he was at the table with them, he took bread, gave thanks, broke it and began to give it to them. Then their eyes were opened and they recognized him, and he disappeared from their sight. They asked each other, 'Were not our hearts burning within us while he talked with us on the road and opened the Scriptures to us?' They got up and returned at once to Jerusalem. There they found the Eleven and those with them, assembled together and saying, 'It is true! The Lord has risen and has appeared to Simon.' Then the two told what had happened on the way, and how Jesus was recognized by them when he broke the bread. While they were still talking about this, Jesus himself stood among them and said to them, 'Peace be with you.' They were startled and frightened, thinking they saw a ghost. He said to them, 'Why are you troubled, and why do doubts rise in your minds? Look at my hands and my feet. It is I myself! Touch me and see; a ghost does not have flesh and bones, as you see I have.' When he had said this, he showed them his hands and feet. And while they still did not believe it because of joy and amazement, he asked them, 'Do you have anything here to eat?' They gave him a piece of broiled fish, and he took it and ate it in their presence. He said to them, 'This is what I told you while I was still with you: Everything must be fulfilled that is written about me in the Law of Moses, the Prophets and the Psalms.' [Notice that the whole

tion, Luke lauded the Bereans as 'noble' in the book of Acts when they were daily examining the Scriptures *for themselves* in response to the gospel message which Paul proclaimed.[259] Apparently, Paul did not take offense, hand over heart, and say, 'What, you don't believe me? Did I not just tell you of my experiences on the road to Damascus when Christ Himself appeared to me? Is that not bona fide enough authority for you? You had to check the Scriptures?' No, Paul's fellow missionary, Luke, praised them for checking his gospel message with their scriptures, the Old Testament. All this to show that the Scripture and the indwelling Holy Spirit are all the believer needs to commence, and then continue, to know the truth. Believers need no Roman Catholic magisterium or special 'anointing' or sublime reverend or masterly teacher or priest or synod or any other man or manmade authority to seek and understand the truth. No theological or spiritual gurus need apply. Believers are a 'royal priesthood'[260] who have instant access to God Himself through Christ in prayer and possess the same God-given authoritative Scriptures to which Jesus and the apostles appealed.

In chapter two, we discussed the principle of Believer's baptism. This Baptist distinctive is also connected with and undergirded by the theological truth of the priesthood of every believer. The mere fact, with believer's baptism, that a believer is *already* a believer when baptized shows that no human clergy, institution, or church denomination is needed to authorize entrance into salvation. The believer is already

---

Old Testament is represented here by this tripartite expression: Law, Prophets, Psalms. Also notice that Jesus' own words are equated with and founded upon the truth of Scripture, by Jesus Himself.] Then he opened their minds so they could understand the Scriptures. He told them, 'This is what is written: The Messiah will suffer and rise from the dead on the third day, and repentance for the forgiveness of sins will be preached in his name to all nations, beginning at Jerusalem. You are witnesses of these things. I am going to send you what my Father has promised; but stay in the city until you have been clothed with power from on high.'" Luke 24: 13-49 (NIV).

259 "Now the Berean Jews were of more noble character than those in Thessalonica, for they received the message with great eagerness and examined the Scriptures every day to see if what Paul said was true." Acts 17:11 (NIV)

260 1 Peter 2:9.

saved through his faith response to the gospel and the activity of the life-giving Holy Spirit, promised by Christ for all who believe in Him. He is then baptized, and upon that demonstration of faith is publicly enrolled in the local church, a body of believers. Believers are saved in order to be in the church (the group of saved people) and so are baptized, NOT baptized in order to be in the church and so saved. This means we enter into the blessings of salvation through belief in Christ's finished work as our one and only Mediator, with nothing else added. No institutional sanction or ecclesiastical mediation is needed for salvation. Thus Christian baptism, instituted by Christ, is for believers only, who are given priestly status so that each is able to enter directly into the presence of the Holy God through their Savior Jesus, the Great High Priest and sacrificial Lamb of God.

The priesthood of the believer is also related to two other Baptist principles: the believers' church and congregational rule. Because the church does not control or dole out salvation, and because we do not need a human priest or churchly governing body to represent us before God, Baptists believe that the church is a body of believers vested with authority to govern themselves. They are able as an assembled body to approach God directly and serve Him together. Baptist theologian R. Stanton Norman discusses the connection between the concepts of the priesthood of every believer and congregationalism: "Of particular significance to the doctrine of the priesthood of all believers is the concept of the gathered church, or congregationalism. Each church is comprised of believers who have been redeemed by Christ and now serve together as priests. . . . As the people of God the church is now a 'royal priesthood' (1 Pet. 2:9) and ministers corporately in the name of Christ."[261]

Francis Wayland, a nineteenth-century Baptist leader, regarded the priesthood of all believers, congregational rule, the role of the pastor, and even religious liberty, as interconnected principles in Baptist belief:

---

261 R. Stanton Norman, *The Baptist Way: Distinctives of A Baptist Church* (Nashville: Broadman & Holman, 2005), 96. Norman stresses the perspective that the priesthood of every believer must be placed in a corporate context, with authority ultimately belonging to Christ: "This doctrine refers to believers gathered together under the lordship of Christ, not to individual believers serving God alone." *The Baptist Way*, 96.

Michael W. McDill

As a natural and inspired consequence of the doctrine of the spirituality of the church, we have ever held to that of the universal priesthood of believers. We have always proclaimed that every child of God has the right, in his own person, of drawing near to God through the intercession of the one only Mediator and High Priest. Hence we reject all notions of the necessity of human mediators, and with it, all belief in the holiness of a priesthood, and in general of an ecclesiastical caste. While we believe that men are to be set apart for the duties of the ministry in whom we see the evidence of ministerial gifts, yet, that it is the church itself—by which I mean not the clergy, but the whole body of Christians—which sets them apart; and that when thus appointed to this work, they are, by this act, rendered no better or holier than their brethren. They are not thus made lords over God's heritage, but servants of the church, appointed to minister in spiritual things. They have no authority, either individually or collectively, to legislate for their brethren, but are, in all respects, just as any other believers, subject to the law of Christ. This, in a country like our own, where the press is free and the church can not wield the arm of the state, may seem a matter of secondary moment. But let any one cast his eyes over the past history of Christianity, and observe the universal tendency of teachers of religion to constitute themselves into a priesthood, to assert dominion over the conscience, and to use the power which they have usurped for their own advantage, and to the extinction of piety, and he will, I think, come to a very different conclusion. No more fatal error has, in all ages, dogged the footsteps of the church of Christ, than the belief in the official holiness of the teacher of religion, and the necessity of a human mediator, in some sort, to appear on our behalf before God. From this belief have been developed those various forms of ecclesiastical hierarchy, which now, with their appalling weight, press down the masses of Europe, and hold them bound in the fetters of spiritual ignorance and sin.[262]

---

262 Francis Wayland, *Notes on the Principles and Practices of Baptist Churches* (New York: Sheldon, Blakeman & Co., 1857), 131-132.

Each believer, being a priest who comes before God through our great High Priest, and being indwelt by the Holy Spirit, needs no extraneous authority from any elite body or special minister within the church in order to understand scripture or approach God or, as a body of believers (each a priest before God), to organize or discipline the church. The church, then, is ruled by the congregation, as we have outlined in chapter four.

Associated with the principle of congregation rule, and thus the autonomy of each local church, cooperation for missions (the subject of chapter five) is also connected with the priesthood of every believer. This can be seen in that there is no human hierarchy over churches, only Christ, who is the head of the church and who commanded us to make disciples in all the world. The *Baptist Faith and Message* defines the church in the following way, connecting the mission of the church with each member's accountability to Christ:

> A New Testament church of the Lord Jesus Christ is an autonomous local congregation of baptized believers, associated by covenant in the faith and fellowship of the gospel; observing the two ordinances of Christ, governed by His laws, exercising the gifts, rights, and privileges invested in them by His Word, and seeking to extend the gospel to the ends of the earth. *Each congregation operates under the Lordship of Christ* through democratic processes. In such a congregation, *each member is responsible and accountable to Christ as Lord.*[263]

No priestly class or ecclesiastical power structure is needed to pursue God's mission as churches in cooperation. As D. Scott Hildreth writes, "As Baptists, we believe in the autonomy and sufficiency of the local church. As Southern Baptists, we also believe these convictions do not mandate [strict] independence. Rather, we fully embrace the idea that God's will for us mandates working together. Cooperation is our denominational identity."[264] So, we see that accountability is to Christ, not to any human

---

263 Emphasis added. *Baptist Faith and Message,* 2000. This is the statement of faith of the Southern Baptist Convention.

264 Insertion added. D. Scott Hildreth, *Together on God's Mission,* 74.

middleman or intermediary, so that the mission of churches to make disciples, which can be pursued in cooperation with one another, is founded on the principle of the priesthood of every believer.

Hildreth adds "Cooperation is more than a programmatic value. As we have seen, cooperation between churches fits perfectly with God's intention for his people. Local Southern Baptist churches, though completely autonomous, are commissioned to participate in God's global mission. We worship one God with one mission. Each local church is not permitted to create its own mission. Thus, cooperation is not merely pragmatic or programmatic. It is fundamental to full participation in God's mission."

Chapter 7

Religious Liberty

Religious Liberty or Freedom of Conscience refers to the notion that no man or power or institution on earth can demand someone believe or think a certain way, and thus none should have power to force any person to profess or behave in a prescribed manner in religious or spiritual matters. In other words, no authority can have power over your thoughts, your beliefs, and your conscience, and actions which are contrary to your conscience, your sense of right and wrong, should not be forced upon you by threat of punishment. This freedom in religion would exclude, of course, as an example, the adherent of Islam who may want to follow his religious belief by committing acts of terror. Religious liberty as a concept does not include the right to harm others by following your "conscience" in support of a particular religion. In fact, religious liberty, as a principle, prohibits the idea of the use of force or coercion in any religious matter whatsoever. Jesus and His disciples never made use of force or aggression, whether government-sanctioned force or the violence of terrorism, in order to advance the kingdom of Christ. When Jesus told Pilate, the representative of Roman might, "My Kingdom is not of this world," He explicitly separated the Christian movement from any worldly identity, except for local groups of followers called churches. Plainly, no worldly institution or authority can be identified with Christ because He claimed *all* authority in heaven and earth as His own, and by that authority did not make a new earthly kingdom (that will come later) but simply sent His disciples to make more disciples of *all nations*.

One of the principles undergirding the believers' church, essential to Baptist beliefs as we have seen, is that each *member* (and remember that this is a term associated with a biblical analogy, the body, connoting a spiritual community) is a priest before God. This idea is repeatedly affirmed in the New Testament. No single person or inner circle of persons is to impose their will upon the church, as we have noted already. All church members appeal to the Scriptures. All decide what the church will do together because every member is equal, and all are believed to be indwelt by the Holy Spirit. Baptist theologian Augustus Strong declared: "Since each regenerate man recognizes in every other a brother in Christ, the several members are upon a footing of absolute equality."[265] This leads to the affirmation that authority in the church is ceded to the congregation itself: the members decide the matters that concern the church, according to the Scriptures. No outside authority, including any government or state power, holds sway over the church as a body. With this logic, we see that Religious Liberty, an important and precious Baptist distinctive, is undergirded by Baptist ecclesiology, which is based on Scripture. Thus, a state church of any sort is incompatible with Baptist beliefs concerning religious liberty, resulting in an affirmation of a crucial associated principle: separation of state and church. The Baptists have been some of the most unwavering apologists for religious freedom on the scene of history. As historian William R. Estep notes, Baptists are "historically the most ardent shapers and defenders of religious liberty in the English-speaking world."[266]

In addition, a believers' church is possible only where believer's baptism is practiced, since baptism of believers is the entryway for a church consisting of believers only. Thus, we observe that two of the cornerstones of Baptist belief, believer's baptism and believers' church, are related to the principle of religious liberty in Baptist theology. Oxford historian Christopher Hill explained: "The theological starting-point of . . . the Baptists, was subversive of a state Church. For adult baptism meant that each individual, when he reached the years of discretion, decided for himself what Church he would belong to. It denied that every child born

---

265 Augustus Hopkins Strong, *Systematic Theology: A Compendium and Commonplace-Book*, Vol. 3, 898.

266 William R. Estep, *Religious Liberty: Heritage and Responsibility* (North Newton, Kansas: Bethel College, 1988), 3.

in England automatically became a member of the Church of England."[267] Believer's baptism is, and always has been, irreconcilable with the state church (which always features infant baptism). The Anabaptists found, to their harm, that fierce devotion to a state church, a medieval idea which excluded religious liberty, could not be rooted out of Europe even by the celebrated Reformation of the sixteenth century. The Reformers realized that they, and their reforms, would be destroyed were they to regard a state-established church as unbiblical, and so simply carried forward the tyranny that had been the norm for more than a thousand years, beginning with Constantine in the fourth century. Those enforcing the state-church schema, including religious leaders, did not refrain from dealing violently with those that dissented, whom they considered enemies of society. The first English Baptists in the early seventeenth century, such as Thomas Helwys, were likewise persecuted, imprisoned, and even gave their lives on occasion (as did the Anabaptists in far greater numbers during the Reformation period) because they stood solidly for religious liberty and against the state church.[268]

---

267 Christopher Hill, *The Century of Revolution* (New York: Norton, 1961), 167.

268 Reformed scholar (thus not necessarily partial to Baptist promotional statements) Sanford Cobb summarized well the essential role the Anabaptists and Baptists played in the rise of Religious Liberty in the modern west: "But among the few and scattered European voices for religious liberty, heard in the two hundred and fifty years from the day of Luther, the place of honor is undoubtedly to be accorded to the Anabaptists. Their doctrine is one of the most remarkable things which appeared in that wonderful age. It comes to speech with a clearness and fulness which suggest a revelation, just as to Luther dawned justification by faith, soul enlightening and uplifting. And, no less notable, this doctrine came at the very opening of the Reformation, in the year 1524, just after the famous Diet of Worms and while Luther was secluded in the Wartburg. The doctrine, making a thorough distinction between the kingdom of nature and the kingdom of grace, insisted that freedom of conscience and of worship was fundamental, and that religion should be entirely exempt from the regulation or interference of the civil power, so that a man's religion should not work his civil disability. Besides this, they declared also that the Church should be composed exclusively of the regenerate, membership therein to be conditioned, not upon residence or birth, but upon the work of grace in the heart. In

What it Means to Be a Baptist

As was noted in chapter one, early Baptist leader Thomas Helwys likely died in Newgate Prison in London before 1616. His great crime was contending for religious freedom and separation of church and state in a recent work entitled *A Short Declaration of the Mistery of Iniquity*. Helwys had led a small company of Baptists back to England and established the first Baptist church on English soil in 1612. This group had been part of the very first Baptist church, which had been constituted in 1609 in Amsterdam, Holland by Helwys and John Smyth: "Helwys . . . and about a dozen others felt it their duty to return to London, in spite of the danger, and bear their witness there. In Spitalfields [a district in London] they established the first Baptist church on English ground . . . . Helwys soon

---

this last point they anticipated, by more than two centuries, that distinction . . . which shattered the union of Church and State in America. There can be but one mind as to the grandeur of the doctrine thus propounded by the Anabaptists, nor as to the immense blessings which it finally conferred upon the world. This is the great contribution to Christian thought made by this one among the Protestant sects. To the honor of its descendants it should also be noted that they ever clung tenaciously to these principles so early declared. Thus, the English Baptists at Amsterdam, in 1611, made it an article of faith that — 'The magistrate is not to meddle with religion or matters of conscience, nor compel men to this or that form of religion; because Christ is the King and Lawgiver of the Church and conscience.' And when, in the following century, the struggle for religious liberty took place in America, among the various Churches the Baptists were most strenuous and sturdy in its defence. They divide the honors, indeed, with the Quakers. But while the Quakers were immovable in their passive resistance to intolerance, the Baptists added to such virtue the active energy which overcomes. But upon the world of the early Anabaptists their doctrine smote with a voice of alarm. In Romanist and Protestant alike it aroused disgust and anger, seeming to strike at the foundations of both Church and State. And not without reason. It was too radical, and neither princes nor people were ready to recognize its vital and enlightening principle. For them it meant disorder and revolution without good ends or stable aims, merely for disorder's sake. . . . The poor enthusiasts [Anabaptists] were hunted and slain like wild beasts. With curious and bitter irony, the Protestant Canton of Zurich decreed that all 'rebaptizers and rebaptized,' should be drowned. Thus the new and glorious life was eclipsed to reappear after long waiting in America." Insertion added. Sanford Hoadley Cobb, *The Rise of Religious Liberty in America: A History* (New York: Macmillan, 1902), 63-65.

found himself in Newgate prison, for he had brought with him from Holland a book he had written—*The Mistery of Iniquity*—which he began to circulate, and which insisted, for the first time in England, on the right of universal religious liberty."[269] The book was an appeal to the King of England, James I, in which Helwys bluntly laid out his principles of religious liberty: "Our Lord the King is but an earthly King, and he hath no aucthority as a King but in earthly causes, and if the King's people be obedient and true subjects, obeying all humane laws made by the King, our lord the King can require no more : for men's religion to God is betwixt God and themselves : the King shall not answer for it, neither may the King be judg betwene God and Man. Let them be heretickes, Turcks, Jewes, or whatsoever, it apperteyenes not to the earthly power to punish them in the least measure."[270]

Helwys apparently tried to present the book to the king in person. When this was not possible, he sent a copy to King James which he autographed with a personal note, a bold step in a time when personal liberty and freedom of conscience were discouraged and punished, and when kings were seen to have a divine right to rule. The following hand-written inscription to the king, in which he dares to instruct and warn the potentate, seems almost reckless, yet proves Thomas Helwys had the courage of his convictions, a quality which is perhaps rare in our times, or any other for that matter:

> Heare O King, and dispise not ye command of ye poore, and let their complaints come before thee. The King is a mortall man, and not God therefore hath no power over ye immortall soules of his subjects, to make lawes and ordinances for them, and to set spirituall Lords over them. If the King have authority to make spirituall Lords and lawes, then he is an immortal God and not mortall man. O King be not seduced by deceivers to sin so against God Whom thou oughtest to obey, nor against thy poore subjects who ought and will obey thee in all things with

---

269 Insertion added. Ernest A. Payne, *The Free Church Tradition in the Life of England*, rev. ed. (London: SCM Press, 1951), 42.

270 Thomas Helwys, The Mistery of Iniquity (1612), 69. Cited in Payne, *The Free Church Tradition in the Life of England*, 43.

body life and goods, or let their lives be taken from ye earth. God save ye King.[271]

Wherever they have been planted, Baptists have struggled against government-established churches. The first Baptist churches, launched in the early seventeenth century by English Separatists (Protestants who were *separating* from the Anglican state church), pleaded earnestly for religious liberty *for all* in the environment of stern Anglican governance. As Separatists, and then Baptists, they were outlawed because of their noncompliance with the Church of England.[272] But instead of knuckling under, they spoke

---

271 From the flyleaf on an old copy of Helwys, The Mistery of Iniquity. Cited in McBeth, *The Baptist Heritage,* 103-104. McBeth provides useful background and commentary on Helwys' daring work on religious freedom: "Helwys was . . . a major spokesman for religious liberty. He wrote *A Short Declaration of the Mistery of Iniquity* soon after returning to England. Helwys chose the inopportune time of 1612 to plead for religious liberty in England. That year Bartholomew Legate and Edward Wightman were burned in London for heresy, and officials threatened that others might also 'frie at a Stake.' The title of the book shows that Helwys was caught up in the apocalyptic enthusiasm of the times. Among Separatists the almost universal interpretation of Revelation 13 was that the first beast represented the Roman Church, the second beast the Anglican Church. In *The Mistery*, Helwys attacked the Church of England for aping Rome, the Puritans for compromise, and the Separatists for making only a partial separation. However, the book's major thrust was its consistent, courageous, and, at times, quite eloquent plea for full religious liberty for all, perhaps the first such plea in the English language. Helwys held that 'none ought to be punished either with death or bonds for transgressing against the spiritual ordinances of the New Testament, and that such Offences ought to be punished onely with spirituall sword and censures.' He denied the validity of civil punishment for spiritual offences. He demanded for Baptists, and for all others, the 'blessed liberty, to understand the Scriptures with their own spirits.' Helwys was ahead of his time in asking religious liberty for all people." McBeth, *The Baptist Heritage,* 102-103.

272 The following is a helpful summary describing the situation of the early Baptists with respect to the state church in England: "Early Baptists faced severe persecution both from the state church and from the government. English law required all citizens aged sixteen and over to attend the Church of England. They had to worship according to the liturgy set out in the Church's Prayer Book,

out against this church-state religious oppression. The earliest Baptist leader, John Smyth (Thomas Helwys' pastor in Amsterdam) declared, "That the magistrate is not by virtue of his office to meddle with religion, or matters of conscience, to force or compel men to this or that form of religion, or doctrine: but to leave Christian religion free, to every man's conscience, and to handle only civil transgressions (Rom. xiii), injuries and wrongs of man against man, in murder, adultery, theft, etc., for Christ only is the king, and lawgiver of the church and conscience (James iv. 12)."[273] This is a superbly succinct statement of religious liberty written in 1612, part of an early Baptist statement of faith. Not only does it lay out the simple idea that government officials (magistrates) have no authority over religious belief or individual conscience, it also advocates the separation of church and state by declaring that the government's power is limited to 'civil transgressions, injuries and wrongs of man against man.' Smyth insists on this limitation of government to civil (not spiritual or religious) matters based on Romans thirteen, in which the apostle Paul lays out the God-given role of earthly government. Baptist historian Leon McBeth comments on Smyth's statement: "Despite its brevity, this is one of the most complete statements of

---

and believe the doctrines set out in the Thirty-nine Articles, which was the official creed. The Conventicle Act, a law passed in 1664, seemed aimed especially at Baptists. The law forbade any religious meetings of dissenters with more than four persons present outside of family members. This made Baptist meetings for worship illegal, and when caught the Baptists could be fined and/or sent to prison. As a result, the jails and prisons in England were filled with Baptists. John Bunyan, a Baptist pastor famous for writing *Pilgrim's Progress,* spent twelve years in jail in Bedford for his refusal to stop preaching. At times the Baptists tried to meet secretly, or at least did not publicize their meetings. They sometimes set teenage boys to watch outside their meetings to warn the group if government officials came near. For a time the English government paid a reward to any citizen who reported on an illegal 'conventicle.' Baptists had to be on guard against spies and bounty hunters who tried to discover their meetings and turn them in to the authorities. In response to this persecution, the Baptists set out a number of tracts and treatises on religious liberty. Drawing from Scripture, history, and logic the Baptists argued that the soul should be free to respond to God without coercion." E. Eugene Greer, Jr., ed. *Baptists: History, Distinctives, Relationships* (Dallas, Texas: Baptistway Press, 2007), 13

273 Lumpkin, ed., *Baptist Confessions of Faith*, 140.

religious liberty of that generation. Smyth and early Baptists advocated complete liberty for all. Although the confession does not use the terms 'separation of church and state,' that concept is clearly present."[274]

Let's dig a bit more into this key passage of Scripture cited by Smith, found in Romans chapter thirteen, concerning the believer's relationship with the state, with its important implications for religious liberty. The apostle Paul places any authority a government may have under God's control. God gives power to those who govern for His own good purposes. This makes sense because God is good. Government's role is prescribed by God in order that people might live in peace and security, and not in a lawless chaos incapable of curtailing human evil. Paul writes to the followers of Christ in Rome, the center of the governing power in the Mediterranean world of his time, and the same power that authorized the execution of Jesus of Nazareth in Judea:

> Let every person be subject to the governing authorities. For there is no authority except from God [granted by His permission and sanction], and those which exist have been put in place by God. Therefore whoever resists [governmental] authority resists the ordinance of God. And those who have resisted it will bring judgment (civil penalty) on themselves. For [civil] authorities are not a source of fear for [people of] good behavior, but for [those who do] evil. Do you want to be unafraid of authority? Do what is good and you will receive approval and commendation. For he is God's servant to you for good. But if you do wrong, [you should] be afraid; for he does not carry the [executioner's] sword for nothing. He is God's servant, an avenger who brings punishment on the wrongdoer. Therefore one must be subject [to civil authorities], not only to escape the punishment [that comes with wrongdoing], but also as a matter of principle [knowing what is right before God]. For this same reason you pay taxes, for civil authorities are God's servants, devoting themselves to governance. Pay to all what is due: tax to whom tax is due,

---

274 H. Leon McBeth, ed., *A Sourcebook for Baptist Heritage* (Nashville: Broadman Press, 1990), 70.

customs to whom customs, respect to whom respect, honor to whom honor.[275]

Note here that determining the standard for what is right and wrong is not given to the civil authority but is found in God, the highest authority, and present in humans through His work in the conscience. The punishment meted out by the earthly government is for earthly wrongdoing (against other earthlings, in other words humankind, as John Smyth pointed out in his statement), and thus the state authorities are instituted by God for our temporal protection against evildoers. Ultimate issues of faith, salvation, and final judgement (with which the conscience and God Himself have to do) are clearly not in the purview of the civil government, which receives any legitimacy it possesses from God in the first place.

Religious liberty and freedom of conscience can also be deciphered in this passage, since we answer to God, not to any other man, for our consciences and for whether or not we trust and honor Him. Whatever authority may be claimed by any man or group of men, it does not reach the level of God's authority. His is absolute, while government merely derives its authority from God as His servant, the earthly punisher of evil deeds. Thus, no man can cleanse my conscience or acquit me of my evil thoughts, nor should any earthly authority punish me for my wrong (or right) beliefs concerning spiritual things. This is why John Smyth also refers to James chapter four which says, "God alone, who gave the law, is the Judge. He alone has the power to save or to destroy. So what right do you have to judge your neighbor?"[276] Thus, God is the ultimate judge who has the power and authority of salvation or damnation in the end. As the author of Hebrews declares, "Nothing in all creation is hidden from God. Everything is naked and exposed before his eyes, and *he is the one to whom we are accountable*."[277] In this ultimate sense, no man can judge another, and so James asks a rhetorical question of one who presumes to judge another's status before God: 'who are you' to make such a judgement? The context for this, in James' letter, is a warning against speaking evil of one another, in oth-

---

275 Romans 13:1-7 (Amplified Bible).
276 James 4:12 (NLT).
277 Hebrews 4:13 (NLT).

er words, defaming the character of a brother in Christ. Pronouncing as evil the actions and motivations, the conscience, of another person is ultimately the prerogative of God. Thus, passing judgement on another's inner character is a judicial decision that only God is allowed to make. We do not have the level of knowledge God has to discern people's motivations and thoughts; and we are corrupt ourselves and thus faulty in our thinking. Who are we, as James asks, to declare our brothers' hearts evil?

Notice, too, in this early Baptist formulation of religious liberty, that the theological concept that recognizes Christ as the unequaled head of the church undergirds the whole statement. If Christ is the final authority for the church, then no other earthly power should assume that role. Any authority in the world which claims to be head of the church (as Henry VIII did, for instance, in sixteenth-century England) is illegitimate. The last phrase in Smyth's statement, "for Christ only is king and lawgiver of the church and conscience," which bears the full weight of the argument for religious freedom, references the book of James. As we have noted, James indicates that placing myself above the judgements of God by making character judgements about my brother is tantamount to usurping God's place as the highest Judge: "Brothers and sisters, do not slander one another. Anyone who speaks against a brother or sister or judges them speaks against the law and judges it. When you judge the law, you are not keeping it, but sitting in judgment on it."[278] James argues that slandering my brother and condemning him as evil is to judge the law itself. This is because I am making myself out to be the final authority and thereby displacing the law of God. When I judge another person, I am in essence saying that I am a higher authority than God and His standard of judgment in the law, and that whoever I am criticizing is accountable to my standards of judgment in some way. James makes it clear this judgmental attitude is repulsively inappropriate for a believer.

In the final analysis, each person is accountable *to God* for his sins. As Thomas Helwys urged King James to consider in 1612: "O let the lord king judge, is it not most equal that men should choose their religion themselves, seeing that they only must stand themselves before the judg-

---

278 James 4:11 (NIV).

ment seat of God to answer for themselves?"[279] The believer's appropriate perspective, therefore, is one of humility, and recognition that God is the final authority. The believer not only respects God as the ultimate Judge but also acknowledges that Christ is the only head and highest authority for the church. This acknowledgment, in addition to promoting brotherly love and harmony in the church, operates as a safeguard for congregational independence. No man, whether in the church or outside, as in the state, can have the final say over the Christian's faith and conscience, only Christ, the King of kings (Who, thank God, provides those who believe with undeserved grace and forgiveness gained by His sufferings). As Thomas Helwys enquired of King James:

> Does the king not know that the God of Gods and Lord of Lords has under him made our lord the king an earthly king and given him all earthly power, and that he has reserved to himself a heavenly kingdom, "a kingdom that is not of this world"..."neither are the subjects of his kingdom of this world?"...Yet this king [Christ] was in the world and his subjects are in the world, and that with this kingdom our lord the king has nothing to do (by his kingly power) but as a subject himself; and that Christ is King alone, only high priest and chief bishop; and there is no king, no primate, metropolitan, archbishop, lord spiritual, but Christ only, nor may be, either in name or power to exercise authority one over another.[280]

This biblical precept leaves the church, as a body of believers directly subject to Jesus' authority, free from earthly control, not only from the government, but also from any other traditional usurpers that may encroach on this liberty (e.g. popes, bishops, cardinals, priests, prelates, presby-

---

279 Thomas Helwys, *A Short Declaration of the Mystery of Iniquity* (1612). Cited in Joseph Early, Jr., ed., *Readings in Baptist History: Four Centuries of Selected Documents* (Nashville: B&H Publishing, 2008), 16.

280 Insertion added. Ibid., 15-16. Note how Helwys states the same principles which Smyth had, based on Romans 13, that God is the administrator over earthly powers and governments. He also quotes Jesus' words before Pilate concerning His kingdom, which have been referred to in the discussion above.

ters, canons, councils, synods, ecumenical committees, monastic orders, ministerial organizations, ecclesiastical offices, conference presidents, deacon boards, domineering preachers, vertical apostles, reverend doctors, spiritual gurus, popular authors, religious scholars, denominational elites, faith communities, renewal movements, social advocates, cultural influencers, twitter prophets, etc.), and so the principle of church autonomy is affirmed, along with religious freedom.

A relationship can also be observed, in Smyth's statement, between religious freedom and another important Baptist principle: biblical authority. Since we have the very words and teachings of Christ, our Lawgiver and King, in the New Testament, it might be said that biblical authority and religious liberty are connected in a more crucial way than it would appear at first glance. Baptists have traditionally regarded the Bible, being the Word of God, as the highest tangible authority for the Christian, considering all others as human creations and thus not entirely dependable. Christians who believe that Scripture is the only reliable foundational authority will be vigilant to exclude all other authorities when it comes to truth about God and, therefore, about eternity and temporality. This exclusion would apply especially to any cultural, political, governmental, or other traditional man-made authority. Practically, this would mean checking the statements and actions of earthly authorities as to their alignment with Scripture. To find any authority other than Scripture prevailing in church life or supplanting true doctrine is to forfeit Christian liberty.

To ensure liberty for believers, the Baptist has traditionally urged state officials to ensure liberty of conscience *for all*. This is not simply enlightened self-interest but has been considered by Baptists as a biblical principle in view of the fact that Jesus and the Apostles never forced people to believe, but always invited them to repent and submit to the gracious authority of Christ. Leo Pfeffer, a scholar who specialized in the study of religious freedom and issues of church and state, when looking at the American scene, stated that "the Baptists were the denomination by far most vigorous in the struggle for religious freedom and separation of church and state."[281] Edward Frank Humphrey affirms the unique role the Baptists played in the fight for religious freedom in America:

---

281 Leo Pfeffer, *Church, State, and Freedom.* Rev. ed. (Boston: The Beacon Press, 1967), 101.

The Baptists were chiefly instrumental in establishing the American principle of the non-interference of the state with religion, Religious Liberty. Other sects, notably the Presbyterians, were energetic and effective in demanding their own liberties; the Quakers and the Baptists agreed in demanding liberty of conscience and worship, and religious equality before the law, for all alike. But the active labor in this cause was mainly done by the Baptists. It is to their consistency and constancy in the warfare against the privileges of the powerful "standing Orders" of New England and of the moribund establishments of the South, that we are chiefly indebted for the final triumph of the principle of separation of church and state, — one of the largest contributions of the New World to the cause of civilization and Christianity.[282]

---

282 Edward Frank Humphrey, *Nationalism and Religion in America: 1774 – 1789.* (New York: Russell & Russell, 1965), 320-321. A short catalog of similar statements, giving Baptists the lion's share of the credit for the achievement of religious liberty in America, is collated by Baptist professor William Pinson: "People in the United States enjoy as great a degree of religious freedom as that found anywhere in the world. Knowledgeable people of various nationalities and denominations have praised the Baptist role in providing such freedom.

George Bancroft, an American historian in the 1800s, wrote, 'Freedom of conscience, unlimited freedom of mind, was from the first, the trophy of the Baptists.'

The British historian Herbert S. Skeats stated, 'It is the singular and distinguished honour of the Baptists to have repudiated, from their earliest history, all coercive power over the consciences and the actions of men with reference to religion.'

The German historian-philosopher Georg Gottfried Gervinus in his *Introduction to the History of the Nineteenth Century*, in reference to the colony of Rhode Island founded by Baptists, observed, 'Here in a little state the fundamental principles of political and ecclesiastical liberty practically prevailed before they were even taught in any of the schools of philosophy in Europe.'

Frank S. Mead, a Methodist historian, declared of Baptists, 'They are God's patriots, putting allegiance to Him always above allegiance to Caesar. Freedom of conscience and complete divorce of Church

Another author stressed the importance of the Baptists in securing religious liberty in America, especially those in Virginia, by quoting Baptist Elder John Leland: "Some realization of the determined and effective work of the Baptists in the cause of religious freedom may be gained by Leland's statement in 1790 that the matter 'has been so canvassed for fourteen years, and has so far prevailed, that in Virginia, a politician can no more be popular without the possession of it, than a preacher who denies the doctrine of the new birth. . . ,'"[283]

THE BAPTIST STRUGGLE FOR RELIGIOUS LIBERTY IN VIRGINIA

The Baptist call for universal religious freedom in Virginia was expressed in the General Committee of Virginia Baptists' appeal to the newly elected President, George Washington, in 1789. In a letter to the President

---

and State! How they have suffered for that! They have faced mockery and mud, fines, whippings, and iron bars; they have been burned at the stake and pulled on the rack, but they have held to it.'

William Warren Sweet, American historian, wrote, 'But justice compels the admission that Jefferson's part in this accomplishment [of religious liberty] was not so great as that of James Madison, nor were the contributions of either or both as important as was that of the humble people called Baptists.'

Leo Pfeffer, jurist and church-state scholar, noted, 'The Baptists were the most active of all the colonial religious bodies in their unceasing struggle for religious freedom and separation.'

In 1884 Henry C. Vedder in *Baptists and Liberty of Conscience* wrote that the 'glory of the Baptists' was their fervent support of religious liberty for everyone.'

Baptists have trumpeted religious liberty long and loud and endured terrible persecution in order to help provide it for everyone, not just themselves." William M. Pinson, Jr., *Baptists and Religious Liberty: The Freedom Road.* (Dallas: BaptistWay Press, 2007), 9-10.

283 Anson Phelps Stokes, *Church and State in the United States.* Vol. 1 (New York: Harper & Brothers, 1950), 375.

full of praise for his military leadership in guiding the young nation to victory in their Revolution, these Virginia Baptists reminded him of their concern that full religious liberty be ensured for all citizens. Virginia, as a colony, had been under the thumb of the government-established Anglican church, and Baptists were not allowed to preach or meet without approval from the authorities. William Estep provides a helpful summary of the situation in Virginia:

> In no colony was the Anglican Church as firmly established as in Virginia. Fines were levied for the lack of church attendance or the refusal to have an infant baptized or for making derogatory remarks about an Anglican minister. Almost from the very beginning of the Separate Baptist presence in Virginia, Baptist preachers met with violence from both mobs, often led by Anglican clergymen, and the magistrates, who arrested and imprisoned them.[284]

When Baptist leaders were squeezed by red tape and fines, which were insurmountable to most of them, they simply preached and worshiped anyway. They were arrested, persecuted, whipped or stoned, and then thrown in prison, where they often drew large crowds while preaching through the bars of their cells.[285]

---

284 William R. Estep, *Religious Liberty: Heritage and Responsibility.* (North Newton, KS: Bethel College, 1988), 76.

285 An article from the *Journal of the American Revolution* describes the persecution of the Baptists (and other dissenters) in Virginia in the colonial period: "While taxes and other fees supported Anglican priests' salaries, their glebe lands [land set aside to support and house a priest, owned by a parish church] and their churches, dissenters often gathered secretly in individual homes and were fined for not attending mandatory Anglican services. Anglican marriages were performed by numerous Anglican priests, marriages between dissenters, however, required either finding a minister of their faith (usually only one dissident minister was permitted per county), or paying a substantially higher fee than an Anglican would to an Anglican priest for the same service. Worse, county clerks were under no obligation to record such ceremonies in county marriage registries, although marriage license applicants were nevertheless required to pay the filing fee for a license. And those were just a few of

What it Means to Be a Baptist

One Virginia Baptist preacher, John Waller, wrote of his sufferings in a letter from prison in 1771. He describes a Baptist service that was subsequently broken up by local authorities:

> Last Saturday whilst brother William Webber was addressing the congregation from James II;18, there came running towards him, in a furious rage, Captain James Montague, a magistrate of the county, followed by the parson of the parish, and several others, who seemed greatly exasperated. The magistrate, and another, took hold of brother Webber, and dragging him from the stage, delivered him, with Wafford, Robert Ware, Richard Falkner, James Greenwood and myself, into custody, and commanded that we should be brought before him for trial. Brother Wafford was severely scourged . . . . I may inform you that we were carried before the above magistrate, who, with the parson and some others, carried us, one by one, into a room, and examined our pockets and wallets for fire-arms, &c., charging us with carrying on a mutiny against the authority of the land. Finding none, we were asked if we had license to preach in that county; and learning we had not, it was required of us to give bond and security not to preach any more in the county, which we modestly refused to do, whereupon, after dismissing brother Wafford, with charge to make his escape out of the county by twelve o'clock the next day on pain of imprisonment . . . the rest of us were delivered to the sheriff, and sent to close jail. . . . Blessed be God, the sheriff and jailor have treated

---

the civil abuses. Among the catalog of physical abuses suffered by dissidents were physical assaults, imprisonment for preaching without a license; imprisonment for preaching to the enslaved, assaults upon their churches by fire or disruption, and assaults upon their congregations, to which their petitions to the General Assembly as well as other documents give legions of evidence. At least six Baptist ministers, for example, were in Culpeper County's jail, according to a letter written by James Madison, writing from his home in adjoining Orange County." Insertion added. Alex Colvin, "Religious Liberty in Virginia: How 'Dissenters' Parlayed Oppression into Freedom," *Journal of the American Revolution* (October 2016): 2.

us with as much kindness as could have been expected from strangers. May the Lord reward them for it! Yesterday we had a large number of people to hear us preach; and among others, many of the great ones of the land, who behaved well, while one of us discoursed on the new birth. We find the Lord gracious and kind to us beyond expression in our afflictions. We cannot tell how long we shall be kept in bonds; we therefore beseech, dear brother, that you and the church supplicate night and day for us, our benefactors and our persecutors.[286]

Waller did stints in prison three more times after this, the last one in 1774 for some sixty days until he finally paid fines in order to be released. He and several others had been arrested "for preaching and expounding the Scriptures contrary to law."[287] These incarcerated preachers "from the beginning to the end of their imprisonment, preached twice during the week, gave godly advice to those who visited them, read the Scriptures a great deal, and prayed almost without ceasing."[288] The time in prison was a trial to Waller and his fellow Baptist pastors, despite their faithfulness to preach and minister: "John Waller in his journal wrote that they passed through various fiery trials, their minds being harassed by the enemy of souls."[289]

The narrative of the sufferings of John Waller, as he represents the painful struggle for religious liberty in colonial Virginia, includes an astonishing twist which connects to modern times. The very courthouse where Waller and other Baptists were put behind bars was bought by the Centennial Baptist Church of Tappahannock, Virginia, where the church first began meeting in 1875. The website of the current Beale Memorial Baptist Church of Tappahannock in Virginia has the following historical information on its website concerning the courthouse used by the Baptist Church as its meeting place:

---

286   Cited in Baker, ed., *A Baptist Source Book*, 33-34.

287   Court record of Essex County Virginia, proceedings of the twenty-first day of March, in the year of our Lord 1774. Cited in E. Wayne Thompson and David L. Cummins, *This Day in Baptist History: 366 Daily Devotions Drawn from the Baptist Heritage* (Greenville, South Carolina: Bob Jones University Press, 1993), 103.

288   *This Day in Baptist History*, 103.

289   Ibid.

What it Means to Be a Baptist

Beale Memorial Baptist Church has a long and rich history in Tappahannock, Virginia. The church was founded in 1875 by the Reverend Frank Browning Beale. It was then known as Centennial Baptist Church, named in honor of our nation's first centennial. Later, the church's name was changed to Beale Memorial to reflect appreciation to its founding pastor. Beale originally met in the old Essex County Courthouse, a colonial structure on the National Register of Historic Places. The current structure contains the original walls of the old courthouse (originally constructed in 1728). In 1875 the Tappahannock Baptists organized Centennial Baptist Church. The building had been the scene in 1774 of the trial and sentencing to jail of four Baptist ministers for "preaching and expounding the Scriptures contrary to law." Beale's story is connected to the struggle for religious liberty in the British colonies. It's remarkable that a Baptist congregation would one day meet where Colonial Baptist ministers were tried for simply being Baptist, and sharing the Gospel.[290]

Baptist historians Wayne Thompson and David Cummins eloquently encapsulate this story of a courthouse jail where Baptist preachers were held in Virginia that later became a Baptist Church: "The old brick courthouse building where these men were arraigned as lawbreakers . . . is now a Baptist Church. The walls of the building that resounded with the condemnation of Baptist preachers for preaching the gospel of Jesus Christ have reverberated for many years now with the proclamation of that gospel and the songs of praise to its Author."[291]

To fill out this improbable but true tale, we should go back a bit in time. John Waller was first imprisoned in 1768. His path toward that event is intriguing. He was born in 1714 from a respectable family and studied law, but became a gambler and was known as "Swearing Jack Waller." According to Baptist historian Richard B. Cook, "It was frequently remarked, that there could be no deviltry among the people, unless he was at the head of it. Once he had three warrants served on him, at one

---

290 https://www.bealembc.org/history.
291 This Day in Baptist History, 104.

time."[292] In addition to these "failings may be added his fury against the Baptists."[293] After years of "unbridled inclinations to vice," he happened to serve on the grand jury which heard the case of Lewis Craig, who came before them for preaching illegally, probably the first Baptist preacher apprehended for this 'crime' in Virginia.[294] When given the opportunity to address the jury, preacher Craig gave a personal testimony of sorts. He said, "I thank you, gentlemen of the grandjury, for the honour you have done me. While I was wicked and injurious, you took no notice of me; but since I have altered my course of life, and endeavored to reform my neighbors, you concern yourselves much about me."[295]

Upon observing his calm spirit and hearing his words, John Waller marveled at Craig's attitude of humility, combined with his boldness and humor, in addressing the jury in this way. He wondered what it was about the man that struck him so much. He possessed a quality which Waller had never encountered before. "He thought within himself, that he could be happy if he could be of the same religion as Mr. Craig."[296] Through this encounter, Waller began to attend Baptist meetings, felt conviction for his sin, became a believer, and was baptized in 1767. He began to preach immediately and was faithful to do so, even in the face of persecution and imprisonment, as we have seen, until he died in 1802. In the year after his baptism, 1768, he was thrown into jail along with Lewis Craig, the man God had used to change the course of his life and lead him to Christ.

---

292 Richard B. Cook, *The Story of the Baptists in All Ages and Countries* (Baltimore: H. M. Wharton, 1884), 223.

293 Ibid.

294 Ibid. Leon McBeth places Baptist pastor Lewis Craig in historical context, describing the persecution in colonial Anglican Virginia: "Beginning in the 1760s, Baptists in Virginia were whipped, fined, beaten by mobs, jailed, and/or exiled in an attempt to control them. Between 1768 and 1777, at least thirty Baptist preachers in Virginia were imprisoned, whipped, or stoned. Most of these were Separates. Apparently Lewis Craig was the first Baptist preacher hauled before the court for preaching in Virginia." McBeth, *The Baptist Heritage,* 270.

295 Cited in Lewis P. Little, *Imprisoned Preachers and Religious Liberty in Virginia* (Lynchburg, Va.: J. P. Bell Company, Inc., 1938), 6.

296 Cook, *The Story of the Baptists,* 224.

What it Means to Be a Baptist

Baptist historian H. Leon McBeth tells us that this 1768 event was the first time Baptists were imprisoned for preaching the gospel in Virginia, an opening salvo in an aggressive attempt to silence dissenters during this period: "Waller was included with Craig and several other Baptists who were cast into the Fredericksburg jail in Spotsylvania County for preaching. This was the first recorded imprisonment of Baptists in Virginia, but many other examples followed."[297] The courtroom scene which led to their jail time was intense: "At court they were arraigned as disturbers of the peace; on their trial, they were vehemently accused by a lawyer, who said to the court, 'May it please your worships these men are great disturbers of the peace, they cannot meet a man upon the road, but that they must ram a text of Scripture down his throat.'"[298] When arrested, they were told they would be set free if they agreed not to preach again for a whole year. They refused and were locked up, though Craig took the opportunity to preach through the grating of his cell to large crowds which gathered, defying his persecutors.[299] The preaching of these Baptists through the bars was so effective, the authorities finally let them go free just to be rid of them.[300]

The story of Baptist preacher John Waller provides immediate historical background for the letter (mentioned above) which Virginia Baptists sent to President Washington, written only a decade or so after these events.[301] Not only was Waller repeatedly thrown in jail, he was also beat-

---

297 McBeth, *The Baptist Heritage*, 270.

298 Robert B. Semple, *A History of the Rise and Progress of the Baptists in Virginia* (Richmond: Published by the author, 1810), 415-416.

299 Thomas H. Appleton Jr., "Lewis Craig (ca. 1737–by 1825)," *Dictionary of Virginia Biography*, (Library of Virginia, 2006).

300 "Morgan Edwards records that they made 'very serious impressions on the minds of eleven heads of families and their domesticks [domestics] with many others. The populace doing everything they could invent to keep the people off and to plague the prisoners, till at last they let them out in order to get rid of them.'" Cited in *This Day in Baptist History*, 234.

301 Waller's story is helpfully placed in a wider historical context by Cambridge historian David Reynolds: "Although not directly political, evangelicals were socially subversive and the potential threat they posed to the social order was evident when the Baptists hit Virginia around 1770. Traditional Anglican services there were largely a recital of the Book of Common Prayer; local parsons operated at the beck and call of the big landowners. A celebrated

en on several occasions and flogged with a horse whip.[302] These struggles and sufferings lead us to understand the seriousness with which Baptists in America viewed the enshrining of religious liberty, along with its companion principle, separation of church and state, in the governing documents of the new nation. The Baptists were determined that clear statements be written into the constitution of the United States so that no one would be treated as they had, simply because their beliefs differed in certain respects (believer's baptism etc.) from those sanctioned by the colonial government. The pertinent section of the 1789 letter to Washington in which the Virginia Baptist General Committee expresses their concerns regarding religious liberty (and the new United States constitution) runs as follows:

Baptist preacher in Virginia was John Waller (known before his conversion as 'swearing Jack'), who, one Sunday in April 1771, started a service only to see the parson and some other local worthies riding up. As Waller was praying, according to one observer, they pulled him off the stage, 'Beat his Head against the ground,' and then 'Carried him through a Gate that stood some Considerable Distance,' where the sheriff gave him twenty lashes with his horsewhip. But when Waller was released, he 'Went Back Singing praise to God, Mounted the Stage & preached with a Great Deal of Liberty.' Roughing up the preachers had little effect, however. By 1772 maybe 10 percent of Virginia's population was Baptist." David Reynolds, *America, Empire of Liberty: A New History of the United States* (New York: Basic Books, 2009), 38.

302 An account given by Waller of this physical abuse is described in the book, *Imprisoned Preachers and Religious Liberty in Virginia*: "While conducting a worship service in a home the following persecutions were perpetrated on Waller: 'While he was singing the Parson of the Parish would keep running the end of his horse whip in his mouth, laying his whip across the hymn book, etc. When done singing he [Waller] proceeded to prayer. In it he was violently jerked off the stage; they caught him by the back part of his neck, beat his head against the ground, sometimes up, sometimes down, they carried him through a gate that stood some considerable distance, where a gentleman gave him something not much less than twenty lashes with his horse whip. After they carried him through a long lane they stopped in order for him to dispute with the parson. The parson came up, gave him abominable ill language, and away he went with his clerk and one more. Then Brother Waller was released, went back singing praise to God, mounted the stage and preached with a great deal of liberty.'" Little, *Imprisoned Preachers and Religious Liberty in Virginia*, 230-231.

What it Means to Be a Baptist

When the Constitution first made its appearance in Virginia, we, as a society, had unusual strugglings of mind, *fearing that the liberty of conscience, dearer to us than property or life, was not sufficiently secured. Perhaps our jealousies were heightened, by the usage we received in Virginia, under the regal government, when mobs, fines, bonds, and prisons were our frequent repast.* Convinced, on the one hand, that without an effective National Government, the States would fall into disunion and all the consequent evils ; and, on the other hand, *fearing that we should be accessary to some religious oppression, should any one society in the Union preponderate over the rest* ; yet, amidst all these inquietudes of mind, our consolation arose from this consideration,—the plan must be good, for it has the signature of a tried, trusty friend, and if religious liberty is rather insecure in the Constitution, 'the Administration will certainly prevent all oppression, for a WASHINGTON will preside.' According to our wishes, the unanimous voice of the Union has called you, sir, from your beloved retreat, to launch forth again into the faithless seas of human affairs, to guide the helm of the States. May that Divine munificence, which covered your head in battle, make you a yet greater blessing to your admiring country in time of peace. Should the horrid evils that have been so pestiferous in Asia and Europe, faction, ambition, war, perfidy, fraud, and *persecution for conscience sake*, ever approach the borders of our happy nation, may the name and administration of our beloved President, like the radiant source of day, scatter all those dark clouds from the American hemisphere.[303]

The letter was written by John Leland (1754–1841), a key Baptist leader in both New England and Virginia, especially concerning the struggle for religious freedom, with signatures affixed of the members of the Virginia Baptist General Committee.

---

303 Emphasis added. L. F. Greene, ed., *The Writings of the Late Elder John Leland: Including Some Events in His Life* (New York: G. W. Wood, 1845), 53.

Leland and the Baptists were concerned that the constitution, which had just recently been ratified, was weak on the matter of the guarantee of religious freedom. A bill of rights was needed to ensure this and other freedoms the new federal government would be obligated to protect. As the bill of rights was in its development, the Virginia Baptists' letter appealed to Washington, as the new president, to protect freedom of conscience in his new administration. Washington's response was as encouraging as it was eloquent:

To the General Committee, representing the United Baptist Churches in Virginia.

Gentlemen,—I request that you will accept my best acknowledgments for your congratulation on my appointment to the first office in the nation. The kind manner in which you mention my past conduct, equally claims the expression of my gratitude.

After we had, by the smiles of Divine Providence on our exertions, obtained the object for which we contended, I retired, at the conclusion of the war, with an idea, that my country could have no farther occasion for my services, and with the intention of never entering again into public life. But when the exigencies of my country seemed to require me once more to engage in public affairs, an honest conviction of duty superseded my former resolution, and became my apology for deviating from the happy plan which I had adopted.

If I could have entertained the slightest apprehension that the Constitution framed by the Convention where I had the honor to preside, might possibly endanger the religious rights of any ecclesiastical society, certainly I would never have placed my signature to it ; and if I could now conceive that the general government might even be so administered, as to render the liberty of conscience insecure, *I beg you will be persuaded, that no one would be more zealous than myself, to establish effectual barriers against the horrors of spiritual tyranny, and every species of religious persecution.*

What it Means to Be a Baptist

For you, doubtless, remember, *I have often expressed my sentiments, that any man, conducting himself as a good citizen, and being accountable to God alone for his religious opinions, ought to be protected in worshiping the Deity according to the dictates of his own conscience.*

While I recollect with satisfaction, that the religious society of which you are members, have been, throughout America, uniformly, and almost unanimously the firm friends to civil liberty, and the persevering promoters of our glorious revolution ; I cannot hesitate to believe, that they will be the faithful supporters of a free, yet efficient general government. Under this pleasing expectation, I rejoice to assure them, that they may rely upon my best wishes and endeavors to advance their prosperity.

In the meantime, be assured, gentlemen, that I entertain a proper sense of your fervent supplications to God for my temporal and eternal happiness.

I am, gentlemen, your most obedient servant,

GEORGE WASHINGTON.[304]

President Washington was clearly an advocate of religious liberty, and his response to their letter would have reassured Baptists in Virginia that, at least while Washington was chief executive, freedom

---

304 *The Writings of the Late Elder John Leland*, 54-55. It is important to note here that Washington witnesses to the Baptist contribution to the revolution in America. Baptists were big supporters of the new nation and of independence. They were willing, as were many others, to put their lives on the line for this new freedom. As far as Baptist allegiance to the nation is concerned, we should note that the Pledge of Allegiance to the United States was written by a Baptist: "The Pledge of Allegiance was written in 1892 by a Baptist minister from Boston named Francis Bellamy, who was ordained in the Baptist Church of Little Falls, New York. He was a member of the staff of The Youth's Companion, which first published the Pledge on September 8, 1892, in Boston, Massachusetts. Public-school children first recited it during the National School Celebration on the 400th anniversary of Columbus' discovery of America, October 12, 1892, at the dedication of the 1892 Chicago World's Fair. The words 'under God' were taken from Abraham Lincoln's Gettysburg Address, '...that this nation, under God, shall have a new birth...'" William J. Federer, *The Ten Commandments and their Influence on American Law* (Amerisearch, 2002), 47-48.

of conscience would have its day. One scholar asserts that Washington was unshakable in his belief in religious freedom: "In all the letters that Washington wrote to the many religious groups that contacted him, one of the main points he stressed was America's religious liberty for all. European history was filled with religious intolerance, perpetrated all too often in the name of Christianity. But Washington saw the United States as an asylum where such bigotry would not gain a foothold."[305]

But the Baptists of Virginia longed to have a clearer and more permanent indication that religious freedom would be foundational to the governing of the new American States. Estep describes the Baptist feeling of the time:

> The Baptists were clearly upset with the new Constitution without a bill of rights. The General Committee met . . . in Goochland County on March 7, 1788 and drew up their

---

305 Peter A. Lillback, *George Washington's Sacred Fire* (Bryn Mawr, PA: Providence Forum Press, 2006), 481-482. The author provides additional evidence of Washington's dedication to freedom of conscience: "As the first president under the well-reasoned American Constitution, Washington was given an enlightened pulpit from which to speak concerning his views of religious liberty, even to the clergy. Accordingly, President Washington wrote on January 27, 1793 to ecclesiastical leaders . . . in Baltimore . . . . Therein, Washington boasted of America's triumph over superstition, 'We have abundant reason to rejoice that in this Land the light of truth and reason has triumphed over the power of bigotry and superstition, and that every person may here worship God according to the dictates of his own heart. In this enlightened Age and in this Land of equal liberty it is our boast, that a man's religious tenets will not forfeit the protection of the Laws, nor deprive him of the right of attaining and holding the highest Offices that are known in the United States.' This conviction came after two or three centuries of wars of religion within outwardly Christian denominations–Catholics vs. Protestants–Protestants vs. other Protestants. . . . Writing to Benedict Arnold on September 14, 1775, and speaking of Roman Catholics in Canada, he affirmed: 'Prudence, policy, and a true Christian spirit will lead us to look with compassion upon their errors without insulting them.' He wrote to his soldiers on July 9, 1776, immediately after receiving a copy of the Declaration of Independence: 'The General hopes and trusts, that every officer and man, will endeavour so to live, and act, as becomes a Christian Soldier, defending the dearest Rights and Liberties of his country.'" *George Washington's Sacred Fire*, 481-482.

list of reasons why they could not support the Constitution without further guarantees of religious liberty. First of all, they declared:

> There is no Bill of Rights. Whenever a number of men enter into a state of society, a number of individual rights must be given up to society, but there should be a memorial of those not surrendered, otherwise every natural and domestic right becomes alienable, which raises Tyranny at once, and this is as necessary in one Form of Government as in another.

After pointing out other rights not explicitly protected by the Constitution, Leland, in the tenth objection, enlarged upon the first:

> What is clearest of all — Religious Liberty, is not sufficiently secured. No religious test is required as a qualification to fill any office under the United States, but if a majority of Congress with the President favour one system more than another, as much as they please, and if oppression does not ensue, it will be owing to the mildness of Administration, and not to any Constitutional defence, and if the manners of people are so far corrupted, that they cannot live by Republican principles, it is very dangerous leaving Religious Liberty at their mercy.[306]

Through this and other appeals, they got what they were pleading for in the first amendment of the Bill of Rights (ten amendments that were added to the constitution by Congress on December 15, 1791), which reads, "Congress shall make no law respecting an establishment of religion, or prohibiting the free exercise thereof; or abridging the freedom of speech, or of the press; or the right of the people peaceably to assemble, and to petition the

---

306   Estep, *Religious Liberty: Heritage and Responsibility*, 78-79.

Government for a redress of grievances."[307] This was the clear statement the Baptists were seeking. John Leland described the time after religious liberty was secured in the following manner: "Heaven has restrained the wrath of man, and brought auspicious days at last. We now sit under our vines and fig-trees, and there is none to make us afraid."[308]

John Leland played a pivotal role in the development and ratification of religious liberty in America. He was born in Massachusetts and became a Baptist preacher there before migrating south to Virginia in 1777, where he was an itinerant preacher and pastor of several small Baptist churches. He was one of the key leaders for Virginia Baptists in the late eighteenth century, that crucial period which gave rise to the birth of the United States, involving the revolutionary war, the ratification of the constitution, and the addition of the Bill of Rights. Leland was instrumental in championing the Bill of Rights, including freedom of religion, as addendums to the constitution. During his time in Virginia, he was a vocal champion of freedom of conscience among Baptists. He conferred and negotiated with James Madison and Thomas Jefferson to secure religious freedom for all in the new nation. William Estep characterizes the alliance between these men of Virginia:

> It was Leland's friendship with Thomas Jefferson and James Madison that helped to form a coalition of Baptists and Deists in the common cause of religious liberty. Jefferson represented the rationalistic approach with its concern for freedom from all forms of tyranny over the minds of men, characteristic of the French Enlightenment. Leland's concern, on the other hand, was that of Roger Williams and the English Baptists who were convinced that the gospel itself was predicated upon an uncoerced response. Theirs was primarily a religious stance derived from their understanding of the New Testament. Thus, strong advocates of religious lib-

---

307 U.S. Constitution, amend. 1.

308 *The Writings of the Late Elder John Leland,* 107. Leland is referring to Micah 4:4, which reads, "But everyone shall sit under his vine and under his fig tree, And no one shall make them afraid; For the mouth of the Lord has spoken." (NKJV)

erty from two widely divergent ideological premises joined forces which eventually forged the basic freedom provisions of the new nation.[309]

James Madison had vehemently bewailed the state of affairs in Virginia in a letter to a friend in 1774: "That diabolical Hell conceived principle of persecution rages among some and to their eternal Infamy the Clergy can furnish their Quota of Imps for such business. This vexes me the most of any thing whatever. There are at this [time?] in the adjacent County not less than 5 or 6 well meaning men in close Gaol for publishing their religious Sentiments which in the main are very orthodox."[310] In 1788, Leland consulted with Madison regarding the Baptists' concerns that religious freedom be plainly stated as a God-given right in the foundational legal documents of the new nation. Leland had suggested that he would seek candidacy to the ratifying convention for the new constitution in order to vote it down due to its lack of clear provision for liberty of conscience. As a result of this consultation, Leland and the Baptists agreed to support Madison as candidate for Virginia to ratify the constitution, in return for a promise to add a Bill of Rights that would include a guarantee of religious liberty. According to Jack Manley, "The election of James Madison to the Virginia Convention to ratify the federal Constitution is attributed directly to the efforts of Leland, and his influence was clearly behind Madison's introduction of the

---

309   William R. Estep, *The Lord's Free People in a Free Land: Essays in Baptist History in honor of Robert A. Baker* (Fort Worth: Evans Press, 1976), 149.

310   *The Papers of James Madison, vol. 1, 16 March 1751 – 16 December 1779*, ed. William T. Hutchinson and William M. E. Rachal (Chicago: The University of Chicago Press, 1962), 104–108. Leland's frank assessment of the Virginia colony's Anglican church establishment was in accord with Madison's: "The church of England, in Virginia, has no discipline but the civil law. The crimes of their delinquent members are tried in a court-house, before the judges of the police, their censures are laid on at the whippingpost, and their excommunications are administered at the gallows." *The Writings of the Late Elder John Leland*, 107. Part of Leland's point here is that these "disciplinary" tactics for church matters are found nowhere in the New Testament. Obviously, Christ and His apostles never commanded coercion, punishment, or any other force of state law in church discipline.

First Amendment to the Constitution, which guaranteed the separation of church and state."[311]

Leland's concern came from a realization that in all of history, the union of church and state had always resulted in man's traditions cruelly coercing consciences, leading to inauthentic faith[312] and to the criminalization of those who were perhaps simply in need of church discipline:

> But almost all Christian nations and states, since the reign of Constantine, have sought to establish national churches : in order to effect which, they have brought in all the natural seed of the professors into the pales of the church, making no difference between the precious and the vile ; and from this foundation they have appealed to the laws of state, instead of the laws of Christ, to direct their mode of discipline. What a scandal it is to the Christian name to see church discipline executed in a court-house, before the judges of the police—to see censures given at the whipping-post, and excommunica-

---

311 Jack Manley, "Leland, John," in *Encyclopedia of Southern Baptists*, vol. 2, ed. Norman Wade Cox and Judson Boyce Allen (Nashville: Broadman Press, 1958).

312 John Ragosta elaborates on the importance of authentic faith, particularly for Baptists, in light of a state church model: "Theologically, the necessity of a completely free acceptance of God was central to the eighteenth-century evangelicals, especially the Baptists. The implication was that any endorsement of religion by government, even a declaration in favor of Christianity, would tend to encourage religion based on the power and authority of government, rather than God, interfering with that free will offering. Leland explained that 'if a creed or faith, established by law was ever so short and ever so true; if I believed the whole of it with all my heart, should I subscribe to it before a magistrate, in order to get indulgence, preferment or even protection, I should be guilty of a species of idolatry, by acknowledging a power, that the head of the church, Jesus Christ, has never appointed.' The whole notion of a national religion was to suggest that in some way adherents to that religion were more patriotic or better citizens, thereby influencing religious choices, an anathema to evangelicals." John A. Ragosta, *Wellspring of Liberty: How Virginia's Religious Dissenters Helped Win the American Revolution and Secured Religious Liberty* (Oxford: Oxford University Press, 2010), 141.

tions at the gallows ;* and for smaller breaches, to be admonished by a sheriff's seizing and selling cows, etc., or wiping off the admonition by a pecuniary mulct! Yet such has been, and still is the case, even in New England, that has made her boast of religion and liberty.†

---

* The Baptists and Newlights have been imprisoned, fined, and whipped, and witches and Quakers have been hung in Massachusetts.

† Seizing and selling, for ministerial tax, is still practised in many towns to this day.[313]

---

313 *The Writings of the Late Elder John Leland*, 217. A 'mulct' is a monetary fine or compulsory payment. Later in his writings, Leland elaborates concerning the evils of the state when punishing those who fail to follow its religious dictates: "But when I see a man with the insignia of his office, arrest a fellow-man for non-attendance on worship, or labor or amusement on Sunday, it strains every fibre of my soul. Who that ever read the New Testament, which describes the meekness, patience, forbearance and sufferings of the first Christians, would ever have expected to see those who call themselves Christians, avail themselves of such weapons to suppress vice and support Christian morality? The spirit seems to be the same that influenced Peter to draw his sword and cut off the ear of one who did not reverence Christ; or, like that which stimulated James and John to command fire to come down from heaven and consume those who would not receive the blessed Saviour. The first was ordered to put up his sword ; and the last were rebuked, with 'ye know not what manner of spirit ye are of.' It reminds me of an instance which took place with one of [British general] Burgoyne's men, who professed to be a zealous Christian. The man, hearing an American speak irreverently of religion, exclaimed, 'How I hate him—I will kill him, because he does not love my blessed Jesus.' About two centuries past, the spirit of witchcraft and witchburning ran through a considerable part of the world, like a raging plague. The rulers used to reason thus : 'God will burn wizards and witches in the next world, and we who are God's representatives, must burn them in this world.' But it is thought that the following reasoning would have been better : 'God is merciful to the poor, deluded creatures, and lets them live, and we will imitate him.' So in regard to those improperly called sabbath breakers. If they commit overt acts—if they assault the life, liberty or property of any man, let them be punished by law. But if their only error is not worshipping where, when, and as you do, your only weapon is fair reasoning with them. If God lets

Baptist scholar James Leo Garrett provides a summary of Leland's thought: "Constantine's 'error' had been his putting 'the same fatal dagger' used to put to death Christians into the hands of Christians; hence 'the shocking monster of *Christian nation*.' Human beings ought not to surrender conscience to government because everyone 'must give an account of himself to God,' conscience is 'to be kept sacred by God,' . . . and 'religion is a matter between God and individuals.'"[314] This was a philosophy of Christian history that was out of phase with the traditional Protestant understanding, which retained the state church system. Neither Luther nor Calvin nor any other Protestant reformer countenanced genuine religious liberty: "None of the Protestant churches—neither the Lutheran Evangelical, the Zwinglian, the Calvinist Reformed, nor the Anglican—were tolerant or acknowledged any freedom to dissent."[315] The territorial church, with full dedication to

---

them live, though in disregard of Sunday solemnities, let not man kill them." Insertion added. *The Writings of the Late Elder John Leland*, **444**.

314 James Leo Garrett, Jr., *Baptist Theology: A Four-Century Study* (Macon: Mercer University Press, 2009), 162.

315 Perez Zagorin, *How the Idea of Religious Toleration Came to the West* (Princeton: Princeton University Press, 2003), 82. The following represents a rather brutal but essentially accurate portrayal of Luther and Calvin as regards their willingness to coerce by threat of punishment, and indeed inflict persecution on others, who merely disagreed religiously: "Luther was not generally tolerant. He hated Judaism and the Jewish people and was the author of a number of anti-Semitic tracts. He was, needless to say, highly intolerant of Catholicism. Although at first he advocated preaching and persuasion rather than the use of force to eliminate Catholic worship, he soon came to maintain, as he told the elector of Saxony in 1525, that it was the duty of rulers and public authority to suppress the Catholic Mass as an outward abomination and blasphemous crime. His advice to the German princes who embraced Protestantism was that they compel their subjects to submit to religious instruction and allow them to hear only authorized preachers. Such compulsion, he held, did not infringe the freedom of faith, because no one was forced to believe but all were required to listen to the word of God. He gave no weight to the argument of Catholics who appealed to their right of conscience to celebrate Mass, since their conscience was not guided by Scripture and was thus merely 'a conscience in appearance.' Although he held that the word of God in Scripture was the sole Rule of Faith,

persecuting 'heretics,' was the societal norm for Protestants, following the Constantinian model that dominated the Middle Ages, especially in Western Europe via Roman Catholic Popery. No wonder Leonard Verduin remarks upon an early American Baptist's "appraisal of Calvin . . . Roger Williams... said of Calvin and Beza that 'these excellent men endeavor (as James speaks) to bring forth from the same fountains sweet water and bitter, which is monstrous and contradictory.'"³¹⁶

---

he implicitly arrogated to himself the right to be the Scripture's infallible interpreter. Toward Protestants he showed himself very intolerant of the Swiss theologian Zwingli, the spiritual leader of the Reformation in Zurich, and of those called 'Sacramentarians,' to whose doctrine denying Christ's physical presence in the Eucharist, or sacrament of the altar, he was violently opposed. . . . He was also fiercely intolerant of the new sects of Spiritualists, Anabaptists, Antinomians, and others to which the Reformation gave birth and which insisted on separation from the Protestant state churches. While the cruel persecution of the Anabaptists at the hands of Protestant authorities occasionally troubled him, he considered them guilty of blasphemy and sedition and therefore deserving of death. In a letter of 1541 he made the comment that he 'could not conceive of any reason by which toleration could be justified before God,' and this statement may be regarded as a definitive expression of his attitude on the subject. Calvin, as a Protestant leader, was as intolerant as Luther, if not more so, since he always maintained that heretics should be punished and killed if necessary. He had none of Luther's human warmth, spontaneity, or peasant humor. A man of severe and inflexible character, he succeeded in dominating everyone around him by virtue of his intellectual power and theological learning, his literary skill and polemical ability, and his single-minded will as a Protestant disciplinarian, educator, and organizer." Zagorin, *How the Idea of Religious Toleration Came to the West*, 76-77.

316 Leonard Verduin, *The Anatomy of a Hybrid: A Study in Church-State Relationships* (Grand Rapids: Eerdmans, 1976), 223. Edwin Gaustad encapsulates Williams' view of Calvin's state church in Geneva: "Well, some say, look at Geneva in Switzerland. There, under the leadership of John Calvin, even Protestants had created a solid union of church and state. He had looked at Geneva, Williams replied, and he did not like what he saw. For it implied that the ordinances of the church might 'be given by Christ to any civil state, town, or city,' and that, said Williams, 'I confidently deny.' We must not allow ourselves to get hung up on John Calvin, he argued, any more than on Moses. The new Israel is a spiritual community only; the old Israel has passed away, to be replaced

ROGER WILLIAMS AND
THE NEW ENGLAND BAPTISTS:
BOLD APOLOGISTS OF RELIGIOUS FREEDOM

Roger Williams (1603–1683), that notable champion of Religious Liberty early in the history of colonial America, expressed a similar historical philosophy which regarded (as John Leland would more than a century later) the Constantinian establishment of the state church as injurious to Christian freedom and vitality:

> The unknowing zeal of Constantine and other emperors did more hurt to Christ Jesus [and] his crown and kingdom than the raging fury of the most bloody Neros. In the persecution of the latter, Christians were sweet and fragrant, like spices pounded and beaten in mortars. But those good emperors, persecuting some erroneous persons (like Arius) and advancing the professors of some truths of Christ (for there was no small number of truths lost in those times) and maintaining their religion by the material sword, I say by this means Christianity was eclipsed and the professors of it fell asleep. Babel was ushered in, and by degrees the gardens of the churches of saints were turned into the wilderness of whole nations, until the whole world became Christian, or "Christendom."[317]

---

not by a nation but by a church. How long will it take for kings and bishops, for governors and magistrates to get this message? They have now had some 1,600 years; that should have been long enough for Christ's words to sink in: 'My Kingdom is not of this world.'" Edwin S. Gaustad, *Roger Williams: Prophet of Liberty* (New York: Oxford University Press, 2001), 96-97.

317 James Calvin Davis, ed., *On Religious Liberty: Selections from the Works of Roger Williams* (Cambridge, Mass.: Belknap Press, 2008), 121. Edwin Gaustad elaborates on Williams' historical view of the curse of the state church: "Beginning with the Roman emperor, Constantine in the fourth century, the fatal habit developed of defending spiritual truths with physical force. The emperor Nero, who in the first century burned Rome and burned Christians,

What it Means to Be a Baptist

To his own harm, Williams had bucked the Puritan authorities in Massachusetts, confronting their heavy-handed state-church establishment with a call for complete freedom of conscience. For this, and for insisting that the Natives in the region be compensated for the land the English acquired, Williams was banished in October 1635 from the Massachusetts Bay Colony, surviving a harsh winter only because the local Indians, whom he had befriended, took him in.[318] He experienced first-hand, in

---

proved to be a better friend to true Christianity than was Constantine, for Nero did not corrupt the church by mixing religion and politics together to such an extent that one could not pry them apart. But Constantine introduced a fatal confusion into Christ's religion, said Williams, when he created this political-religious, messy mixture called Christendom. It is because of Christendom that we have come to speak of Christian nations, Christian states, Christian institutions. For Williams, there were no such things. There was only Christianity, a truth that dwells only in the hearts and souls of women and men. It is not found in kingdoms, for kingdoms do not convert, do not receive the grace of God, do not enter into heaven. So the time had come to undo what Constantine, 1,300 years before, had done. The state had its proper role and the churches theirs. The state might assist the church only in the sense that it maintained peace and order in the society. The church might assist the state only in the sense that it might 'cast a blush of civility and morality' upon its citizens. . . . This should be perfectly clear, perfectly simple to all, Williams believed. For to act in any other way was 'to turn the world upside down.' Then the garden of the church became indistinguishable from the weeds of the world. Religion could no longer be separated from politics, and Christ, the good shepherd, could no longer keep the wolves away from his sheep." Gaustad, *Roger Williams: Prophet of Liberty*, 95-97.

318 A book entitled *The Indomitable Baptists* recounts Williams' story of exile: "The court had allowed him six weeks to prepare to leave the colony. . . . Many friends came to visit him, usually at night, to offer sympathy and wish the family well. . . . One day a close friend brought Williams a secret message from Governor Winthrop. The Boston authorities were planning to seize Williams and put him aboard a ship bound for England . . . Williams decided he would not be a martyr if he could escape and continue his fight for liberty of conscience. That night he bundled himself in his greatcoat, stuffed some food into his pockets, kissed his wife and baby good-by, and stole out into the darkness. A storm was blowing up and by midnight it had turned into a blizzard. Williams headed eastward toward Narragansett Bay, shuffling along the drifting snow covered fields

New England, the results of a state-church union which he believed to be a 'Christian' monstrosity which had stalked and slouched through all the years since Constantine: "When Christianity began to be choked, it was not when Christians lodged in cold prisons, but down beds of ease, and persecuted others."[319]

So we see a consistency between Baptist leaders separated by almost 150 years concerning a perspective on religious freedom: "Like Roger Williams, Leland pursued his argument to its logical conclusion: If the government had no authority over religious matters, then the State had no power to provide for ministers, to enact Sabbath laws, to pay military chaplains, or to exclude from office adherents of any religion. In his estimation, the notion of a Christian commonwealth was absurd."[320] In 1644, Williams had published his famous treatise on religious freedom, *The Bloudy Tennent of Persecution*, in which he wrote: "And however in civil things we may be servants unto men, yet in divine

---

and through forests. It grew bitter cold and the wind howled and shrieked about him. During the next day, utterly exhausted and nearly frozen, he reached a camp of the Narragansett Indians. Greeting him as a brother, these friends took him in, fed him, thawed him out, and insisted that he remain in hiding with them. Through all the rest of that winter the exiled minister stayed with his Indian benefactors, sharing their food and their shelter, telling them more about the Great Spirit. . . . During the winter the exiled parson had made a momentous decision. He would establish his own colony, and it would be open to all who wanted to live in the enjoyment of religious freedom." O. K. Armstrong and Marjorie M. Armstrong, *The Indomitable Baptists: A Narrative of Their Role in Shaping American History* (Garden City, NY: Doubleday, 1967), 49-50.

319 *On Religious Liberty: Selections from the Works of Roger Williams*, 122.

320 Thomas J. Curry, *The First Freedoms: Church and State in America to the Passage of the First Amendment* (Oxford: Oxford University Press, 1986), 176. Curry ranks John Leland with Roger Williams, the formidable (and earliest) defender of religious liberty, as unmatched advocates of freedom of conscience and separation of church and state in America: "Others in America at the time would have agreed with Leland's opposition to establishment of religion; but no religious figure would have transcended his contemporary cultural milieu and followed the logic of his thought to such sympathetic imaginative conclusions. Indeed, until Leland no religious thinker matched the thought on Church and State of Roger Williams of the previous century." Curry, *The First Freedoms*, 182.

and spiritual things the poorest peasant must disdain the service of the highest prince. *Be ye not the servants of men*, 1 Cor. vii."[321] In *The Bloudy Tennent*, Williams told the story of the English Baptist pastor John Murton (1583–1626). Murton had succeeded Thomas Helwys as pastor of the first Baptist church in England after Helwys died in prison. According to Williams, Murton wrote his own statement urging freedom of conscience while he, in turn, was imprisoned in London. He wrote it in milk on the paper that was used as a bottle stopper, and this was smuggled out and browned over a fire by a friend who then transcribed Murton's thoughts with conventional paper and ink.

Murton, who evidently was influential for Williams, had also declared the fallibility of princes when it came to authority (and especially the meting out of punishment!) over spiritual matters: "The wisdom of God foresaw, that seeing the mysteries of the gospel are such spiritual things as no natural men though they be princes of this world, can know them; he left not kings and princes to be lords and judges thereof, seeing they are subject to err. But he left that power to his beloved Son, who could not err; and the Son left his only deputy, the Holy Ghost, and no mortal man whatsoever."[322] Making a direct appeal to King James, Murton clarified his views further, speaking as a pastor and leader of early Baptists in England:

> Not that we any way desire for ourselves or others, any the least liberty from the strict observation of any civil, temporal, or human law, made or to be made, for the preservation of your majesty's person, crown, state, or dignity; for all that give not to Caesar that which is his, let them bear their burden. But we only desire, that God might have that which is his,

---

321 Roger Williams, *The Bloudy Tennent of Persecution* (1644). Cited in Joseph Early, Jr., ed., *Readings in Baptist History*, 22

322 John Murton, *A Most Humble Supplication of Many of The King's Majesty's Loyal Subjects, Ready to Testify All Civil Obedience, by the Oath of Allegiance, or Otherwise, and That of Conscience; Who are Persecuted (Only for Differing in Religion), Contrary to Divine and Human Testimonies, 1620* in Edward Bean Underhill, *Tracts on Liberty of Conscience and Persecution, 1614 — 1661* (London: J. Haddon, 1846), 227.

which is the heart and soul in that worship that he requireth, over which *there is but one Lord*, and *one Lawgiver, who is able to save it, or to destroy it*, which no mortal can do. It is not in your power to compel the heart ; you may compel men to be hypocrites, as a great many are, who are falsehearted both towards God and the state ; which is sin both in you and them. The vileness of persecuting the body of any man, only for cause of conscience, is against the word of God and law of Christ..[323]

Murton spent thirteen years in prison, most likely using the time to write the above, which is found in his treatise of 1620 entitled *A Most Humble Supplication*. He most likely died in prison in 1626. The fact that Roger Williams cited *A Most Humble Supplication* and relayed the details of Murton's imprisonment speaks to Williams' esteem for Murton as an example of undaunted courage in defending religious liberty among Baptists in England, which Williams continued to do in the American colonies of New England.[324]

---

323 John Murton, *A Most Humble Supplication in Underhill, Tracts on Liberty of Conscience and Persecution,* 192. Speaking of esteem for Murton, one historian writes this: "JOHN MURTON, who replaced Thomas Helwys, exhibited more than ordinary talents as an author. He published . . . an elaborate address to the King for liberty of religion, headed : "A most humble supplication of many of the kings Majestys loyal subjects—who are persecuted only for differing in religion." . . . It is not surprising that a church, presided over by so zealous a man as John Murton, numbered, about 1626, already one hundred and fifty members, in spite of fierce persecutions by the State-church. . ." The author writes this tribute respecting Murton and Helwys and other early Baptist defenders of religious freedom: " — for this truth alone, professed by them, though at the risk of imprisonment and even of their lives, they are entitled to a place of honor among the advocates of true progress, true toleration, and true freedom." Jacob Gijsbert de Hoop Scheffer, *History of the Free Churchmen Called the Brownists, Pilgrim Fathers and Baptists in the Dutch Republic, 1581-1701* (Ithaca, NY: Andrus & Church, 1922), 178, 184.

324 This connection between Williams and Murton is noted in Baker and Landers, *A Summary of Christian History.* Williams arrived in New England "in February 1631, about six months after Boston was settled and named. Williams is significant not only as the organizer of perhaps the first Baptist church

What it Means to Be a Baptist

While not as celebrated, Roger Williams' colleague in early colonial America, John Clarke (1609–1676), was perhaps just as significant for the cause of religious liberty urged by the Baptists. Like Williams, Clarke perpetuated in New England the Baptist struggle for liberty, as Smyth, Helwys, and Murton had in Old England. His notable and effective work, *Ill Newes from New England*, was influential on both sides of the Atlantic for exposing the heinous nature of state-church force and its persecution of religious dissension. Early in the seventeenth century, only a few Baptist leaders in England and New England were contending, and suffering, for full freedom of conscience. Part of the full title of Clarke's work is *Ill newes from New-England, or, A narative of New-Englands persecution wherin is declared that while old England is becoming new, New-England is become old*, indicating that the first cracks in the ice of state control of religion were being seen in England while in the American colonies of New England there was in place a tyranny over conscience which was hardened and hardening. To illustrate his contention that the authorities in the new land were oppressors, both civil and religious, Clarke told the story of his own imprisonment and the whipping at the post of fellow Baptist Obadiah Holmes.

In July 1651, on a mission of mercy, two Baptist ministers, Clarke and Holmes, along with a deacon, were visiting a blind and aging fellow

---

in America but also because of his advanced views. Religious liberty, separation of church and state, and democracy were condemned almost universally on both sides of the Atlantic in 1631, except by a few General Baptists in England and Williams in America. Only a decade later and after a political and constitutional revolution in England did dissenters other than Baptists champion such ideas. Where did Williams get such notions? Perhaps a clue is found in his writings. He preserved a story about the second pastor of the first Baptist church in London, John Murton, an early contemporary of Williams. This tale speaks of how Murton wrote Baptist tracts from prison by using milk and paper bottle stoppers for writing paper. A confederate outside browned the dried milk to rescue Murton's writings. He died in London about 1626 when Williams was about twenty-seven years of age. Perhaps there is a larger context for this anecdote that Williams alone remembers from Murton, for some of Williams's ideas were those of Thomas Helwys, first pastor of the church, and of John Murton." Robert A. Baker and John M. Landers, *A Summary of Christian History* (Nashville: Broadman & Holman, 2005), 344-345.

Baptist in the Massachusetts Bay Colony, having traveled up from Rhode Island (the only territory featuring religious liberty in New England). As a consequence, they were arrested, put on trial, and sent to prison. Before the trial, Clarke and Holmes were taken against their will to a Puritan Congregational church service, where they refused to remove their hats as a protest. Clarke made a short speech after the service explaining why they refused to doff their hats, claiming that they were compelled to attend and declaring that the church was not constituted according to the New Testament. This, obviously, did not ingratiate them to the Puritan authorities. At the trial, the governor spoke against the Baptists, as Clarke records in his *Ill Newes*:

> At length the Governour stept up, and told us we had denyed Infants Baptism, and being somewhat transported broke forth, and told me I had deserved death, and said he would not have such trash brought into their jurisdiction; moreover he said, you go up and down, and secretly insinuate into those that are weak, but you cannot maintain it before our Ministers, you may try, and discourse or dispute with them, &c. To this I had much to reply, but that he commanded the Jaylor to take us away.[325]

---

325 John Clarke, *Ill Newes from New-England: or a Narrative of New-Englands Persecution...Also four conclusions touching the faith and order of the Gospel out of his Will and Testament, confirmed and justified* (London: Printed by Henry Hills, 1652), 33. A context for this outburst from the Massachusetts governor is provided by Clarke's biographer Louis Franklin Asher: "It would seem to appear by the arrest warrant that the Puritan Elders seized this opportunity to vent their wrath on Clarke and Holmes for their past missionary work in the vicinity of the Puritan Congregational churches. Off and on for several years, Clarke had baptized converts from the Puritan Congregationalists. Since the warrant contained more than simply the charge of frequenting an illegal worship service, but also included several other past grievances—all of a religious nature—this would further suggest Puritan religious intolerance." Louis Franklin Asher, *John Clarke (1609-1676): Pioneer in American Medicine, Democratic Ideals, and Champion of Religious Liberty* (Paris, Arkansas: Baptist Standard Bearer, 2004), 59.

Clarke, desiring greatly to respond to this challenge and debate one of
the Puritan ministers, appealed in writing to the authorities to do so. He
never got the chance, however, for an anonymous benefactor paid his fine,
and he was freed from prison and went back home to his family in Rhode
Island. Obadiah Holmes refused an offer to have his fine paid, and was
thus marched to the Boston Common to be punished after spending two
months in prison. He was publicly flogged with a three-braided whip.

Clarke records Holmes' description of his beating. As he was
stripped of his shirt to receive the lashing, he spoke to the crowd, then
endured the punishment willingly, giving God credit for helping him:

> I told them moreover, the Lord having manifested his love
> towards me, in giving me repentance towards God, and Faith
> in Jesus Christ, and so to be baptized in water by a Messen-
> ger of Jesus into the name of the Father, Son, and Holy Spir-
> it, wherein I have fellowship with him in his death, buriall,
> and resurrection, I am now come to be baptized in afflictions
> by your hands, that so I may have further fellowship with my
> Lord, and am not ashamed of his sufferings, for by his stripes
> am I healed ; And as the man began to lay the stroaks upon
> my back, I said to the people, though my Flesh should fail, and
> my Spirit should fail, yet God would not fail ; so it pleased the
> Lord to come in, and so to fill my heart and tongue as a vessell
> full, and with an audible voice I brake forth, praying unto the
> Lord not to lay this Sin to their charge, and telling the peo-
> ple, That now I found he did not fail me, and therefore now I
> should trust him for ever who failed me not ; for in truth, as
> the stroaks fell upon me, I had such a spirituall manifestation
> of Gods presence, as the like thereto I never had, nor felt, nor
> can with fleshly tongue expresse, and the outward pain was
> so removed from me, that indeed I am not able to declare it to
> you, it was so easie to me, that I could well bear it, yea and in a
> manner felt it not, although it was grievous, as the Spectators
> said, the Man striking with all his strength (yea spitting on
> his hand three times, as many affirmed) with a three-coarded
> whip, giving me therewith thirty stroaks ; when he had loosed

me from the Post, having joyfulnesse in my heart, and cheer-
fulnesse in my countenance, as the Spectators observed, I told
the Magistrates, you have struck me as with Roses ; and said
moreover, Although the Lord hath made it easie to me, yet I
pray God it may not be laid to your charge.[326]

This spectacle so moved some of the onlookers that they crowded around
Holmes, after his thrashing, to shake his hand.[327]

This state of affairs in Puritan Massachusetts did not improve for
some time. A century or so later was heard still another vigorous Baptist
voice crying out for religious freedom in the spiritual wilderness of New
England, that of Isaac Backus (1724–1806). He was, in New England, the
chief champion of liberty of conscience for all in the period leading up
to and after the establishment of the United States as a nation. He, like
Roger Williams and John Leland, was of the opinion that the initiation of
the absurdity of "Christendom," a this-worldly Christian kingdom, had
been the Constantinian embrace of Christianity by the Roman Empire in
the fourth century:

---

326 Clarke, *Ill Newes from New-England*, 47-48.

327 Clarke describes the joyous response of a number of those who witnessed Holmes' punishment in this way: "Whilst he (through the spirit of the
Lord that rested upon him) bore these bloody strokes with so cheerfull a spirit
as if he felt them not, divers of the standers by, beholding it, were so affected
with joy, that when he was loosed could not forbear to come to him, and to
shake him by the hand, thereby to manifest their rejoycing with him, that the
Lord had supported him ; but information hereof being given to the Magistrates, warrants were sent forth (as is reported to the number of 13) whereup-
on some through fear were fain to hide themselves, and being strangers, to
hasten away, or change their habit, two of them were taken as aforesaid, that
is to say John Spur, and old John Hazell, and committed to prison." Clarke, Ill
Newes from New-England, 52. Asher tells us: "Following the public beating of
Holmes, two bystanders, John Hazel and John Spur, approached Holmes and
shook his hand. As a result of this encouraging gesture, both men were arrested
and later fined for giving aid and comfort to a lawbreaker. Hazel was an elderly
man and—perhaps due to the grueling ordeal of incarceration—died before he
arrived home following his release." Asher, *John Clarke (1609-1676)*, 63-64.

What it Means to Be a Baptist

Nothing is more evident, both in reason, and in the Holy Scriptures, than that religion is ever a matter between God and individuals ; and therefore no man or men can impose any religious test, without invading the essential prerogatives of our Lord Jesus Christ. Ministers first assumed this power under the Christian name ; and then Constantine approved of the practice, when he adopted the profession of Christianity as an engine of State policy. And let the history of all nations be searched, from that day to this, and it will appear that the imposing of religious tests hath been the greatest engine of tyranny in the world.[328]

He wrote further, bluntly characterizing the harmful results of this "greatest engine of tyranny" in the long centuries since the union of church and state was first introduced: "Constantine brought the sword into the church to punish heretics, and to support religious ministers ; and blood and slavery, deceit and cruelty, have followed those superstitions ever since, though many good men have been ensnared in those ways."[329] Although he grew up a strict Calvinist, Backus testified he was 'born again' at the age of seventeen during the Great Awakening revivals.[330] He eventually became a Baptist pastor in Middleborough, Massachusetts. He was the author, in 1773, of a clear and effective treatise advocating for the idea of separation of church and state entitled *An Appeal to the Public for Religious Liberty Against the Oppression of the Present Day.*

---

328 Isaac Backus, *A History of New England: With Particular Reference to the Denomination of Christians Called Baptists,* Vol. 2, 2nd ed. (Newton, Mass.: Backus Historical Society, 1905), 336.

329 Backus, *A History of New England*, Vol. 2, 406.

330 James Leo Garrett, speaking of the revivals, reports that "the newly converted had become aware how many unconverted persons held church membership," and that Backus had been baptized as an infant in his local Congregational church. "When two of his church members began to set forth antipedobaptist views, Backus initially resisted and only slowly became convinced of their validity. After struggle by 1751 he came to reject infant baptism and subjected himself to believer's immersion." *Baptist Theology: A Four-Century Study,* 154-155.

This call for religious liberty grew out of the experiences of the Baptists in New England, and from Backus' own family's experience of religious oppression. In fact, the authorities in Connecticut threw Backus' aging mother, Elizabeth, in jail for failing to pay the state church tax. The tax collectors came to her door one evening as she sat by the fire reading the Bible. She was quite ill at the time, but the officers still demanded she pay the tax for the state support of the Congregational churches, confronting her in her own home. She refused to pay and was taken off to prison. In his book *A History of New England with Particular Reference to the Denomination of Christians Called Baptists*, Backus wrote, "Among the many instances that discovered how tenacious our oppressors were of their taxing power to support worship, take the following . . . Connecticut still kept pace with . . . Massachusetts in oppression, of which the place of the author's nativity now exhibited a striking example. A widow [his mother] who had withdrawn from their worship seven years, and steadily attended and supported worship in another church, gives so clear an account of it, that her letter is here presented to the reader, without adding or diminishing a word."[331] Backus then presented the whole letter from his mother regarding the events surrounding her imprisonment, in which she wrote: "My Dear Son : I have heard something of the trials amongst you of late, and I was grieved, till I had strength to give up the case to God, and leave my burthen there. And now I would tell you something of our trials. Your brother Samuel lay in prison twenty days. October 15, the collectors came to our house, and took me away to prison about nine o'clock, in a dark rainy night. Brothers Hill and Sabin were brought there the next night. We lay in prison thirteen days . . ."[332]

The letter from Backus' mother to Isaac is dated November 4, 1752. These sorts of events had already been the norm for Baptists and other dissenters in New England for a good while, as is seen in the early example of Clarke and Holmes in the seventeenth century. In his *History*, Backus had also "recorded at length the persecution that Baptists endured in the first decades of the 1700s, primarily for their refusal to pay the tax levied by the government for the support of the Congregational

---

331 Backus, *A History of New England*, Vol. 2, 96-98.
332 Ibid., 98-99.

churches. The government of Massachusetts confiscated property and imprisoned men and women on numerous occasions, often for paltry sums of unpaid taxes."[333] According to historian Thomas Curry, the Baptists were technically exempt from these taxes and so were in the right to refuse to pay. He writes, "In theory Massachusetts had long exempted Baptists from paying toward the support of the established churches, but in fact the authorities—particularly after the increase in the number of Baptists there following the Great Awakening—found all kinds of legal loopholes through which to harass them and extract taxes from them for the support of the Congregational system."[334] Connecticut church authorities were up to the same tricks, resulting in Widow Backus' jail time, so that 'Connecticut still kept pace with . . . Massachusetts in oppression,' as Isaac Backus had asserted.

To sense the spirit of these early Baptists in their struggle for freedom, it may be instructive to read the words of Elizabeth Backus and sense the faith expressed by a courageous grandmother in the eighteenth century, even amidst persecution, as she continued her letter to her son Isaac:

> We lay in prison thirteen days, and then set at liberty, by what means I know not. Whilst I was there a great many people came to see me ; and some said one thing and some another. O the innumerable snares and temptations that beset me, more than I ever thought on before ! But, O the condescension of heaven ! though I was bound when I was cast into this furnace, yet was I loosed, and found Jesus in the midst of the furnace with me. O then I could give up my name, estate, family, life and breath, freely to God. Now the prison looked like a palace to me. I could bless God for all the laughs and scoffs made at me. O the love that flowed out to all mankind ! Then I could forgive as I would desire to be forgiven, and love my neighbor as myself. Deacon Griswold was put into

---

333 Pinson, *Baptists and Religious Liberty*, 53.

334 Curry, *The First Freedoms*, 131. In 1728, an Act was passed by the General Court of Massachusetts, exempting Baptists from the tax, but that was the personal tax only; the property tax was still liable. See Torbet summary of exemption laws 234-235.

prison the 8th of October, and yesterday old brother Grover, and [they] are in pursuit of others ; all which calls for humiliation. This church hath appointed the 13th of November to be spent in prayer and fasting on that account. I do remember my love to you and your wife, and the dear children of God with you, begging your prayers for us in such a day of trial. We are all in tolerable health, expecting to see you.

These from your loving mother,

ELIZABETH BACKUS.[335]

Some twenty years later, Backus wrote his *Appeal to the Public for Religious Liberty,* in which he maintained, "It appears to us that the true difference and exact limits between ecclesiastical and civil governments is this, That the church is armed with *light and truth*, to pull down the strongholds of iniquity, and to gain souls to Christ and into His Church.... While the state is armed with the *sword* to guard the peace, and the civil rights of all persons and societies, and to punish those who violate the same."[336]

---

335 Backus, *A History of New England*, Vol. 2, 99. Baptist historian Leon McBeth characterizes this episode of heavy-handedness on the part of the Connecticut Congregationalists as quite a whopper as mistakes go: "Probably the state church made one of their biggest mistakes when they imprisoned Elizabeth Backus, a widow and mother to Isaac Backus, the major spokesman for religious liberty in New England. Mrs. Backus, like her son, had left the state church to become a Baptist and was behind on her church taxes. When the officers came for her late one night, she was sick, wrapped in quilts to promote perspiration, sitting by the fire reading her Bible. They hauled her away to jail despite her condition. . . . Probably few letters from a mother to her son had greater impact. The Widow Backus was well-respected, and her case attracted widespread attention, all unfavorable to the standing order. Apparently the state minister was only too glad to see Mrs. Backus released and her damaging witness momentarily silenced. One may only surmise the extent to which this family incident hardened the resolve of Isaac Backus to break the state church monopoly over religion." McBeth, The Baptist Heritage, 257-258.

336 Isaac Backus, *An Appeal to the Public for Religious Liberty, Against the Oppressions of the Present Day* (Boston: John Boyle, 1773), 13.

CONCLUSION:
FREEDOM MEANS SEPARATION

The "exact limits" described above by Backus are what we know today as separation between church and state. Backus delineates the sphere of the church as touching men's souls, to gain them for Christ, and the sphere of the secular government as pertaining to civil society, to punish those who are uncivil and criminal, who tread upon the rights of other individuals. This is important to Baptists because the state is never to dictate to people's souls, to control their relationship, or lack thereof, to God. The spiritual is not the sphere over which the state has any oversight or authority. In the early twentieth century, E. Y. Mullins expressed this principle: "For its own ends the state is sovereign. But those ends do not include the religious life of the individual at all. Hence, the civil and religious life of persons belong to different spheres entirely. The right of every soul to direct access to God is an inalienable right, with which the state must not interfere."[337] The same sentiment is reflected in George W. Truett's eloquent address regarding these matters, which he delivered to a global Baptist meeting on the eve of World War II, in 1939:

> In the very nature of the case there can be no proper union of church and state, because their nature and functions are utterly different. Jesus stated the principle in the two sayings, *"My Kingdom is not of this world,"* and *"Render unto Caesar the things that are Caesar's, and unto God the things that are God's."* When therefore, the state seeks to play mentor to the church, or the church to the state, a Pandora's box of evils will be loosed upon the people.

> *"Let Caesar's due be paid*
> *To Caesar and his throne;*
> *But consciences and souls were made*
> *To be the Lord's alone."*[338]

---

337 Mullins, *Baptist Beliefs*, 73.
338 George W. Truett, "The Baptist Message and Mission for the Life of

the World" (Atlanta, Georgia: *Official Report of the Sixth Baptist World Congress,* 1939) 27-28. Cited in Estep, *Why Baptists?*, 43. This principle cuts both ways in that we understand that the state is not spiritual, and neither is the church worldly, as indicated by the idea that neither should 'mentor' the other. Truett's words, again, ring through the decades as representative of a vital Baptist belief regarding ecclesiology: "Concerning the church, Baptists hold that it is a Divine institution, not evolved from the changing conditions of society, but expressing the mind of Christ; that it is an enduring institution, adapted to all times and climes; that it is the custodian of the truth, to hold and teach it to the end of time, and to all peoples. They hold that a church of Jesus Christ is a spiritual institution, and that it is pure democracy, without disbarment of franchise to any member, on the ground of nationality, race, class or sex." Emphasis added. Truett, "The Baptist Message and Mission for the Life of the World", 28. Cited in Estep, *Why Baptists?*, 43-44. This idea that there is no social differentiation in the church reflects the words of Paul in Galatians, "For you are all sons of God through faith in Christ Jesus. For as many of you as were baptized into Christ have put on Christ. There is neither Jew nor Greek, there is neither slave nor free, there is neither male nor female; for you are all one in Christ Jesus." Galatians 3:28 (NKJV). Truett (1867-1944) was pastor of the First Baptist Church, Dallas Texas from 1897 to 1944. He is quoting here, at the end of the citation, from a hymn by the English nonconformist pastor Isaac Watts (1674-1748), published in 1806. It runs as follows:

> *Eternal Sovereign of the sky,*
> *And Lord of all below;*
> *We mortals to thy majesty*
> *Our first obedience owe.*
>
> *Our souls adore thy throne supreme,*
> *And bless thy providence,*
> *For magistrates of meaner name,*
> *Our glory and defence.*
>
> *Kingdoms on firm foundations stand,*
> *While virtue finds reward;*
> *And sinners perish from the land*
> *By justice and the sword.*
>
> *Let Caesar's due be ever paid*
> *To Caesar and his throne;*
> *But consciences and souls were made*
> *To be the Lord's alone.*

Conclusion

Baptists and the Key of Biblical Liberty

As we have seen, Baptists in America have labored, despite punishment and persecution, for freedom of conscience for all. Mere toleration while maintaining an established church, although better than religious tyranny and persecution, would never do for Baptists. Likewise, early English Baptists constantly cried out for complete religious freedom and were imprisoned and even martyred for these efforts. According to Baptist historian William Estep, this was not merely due to a concern for personal or denominational religious freedom, but was founded upon a belief in a principle of spiritual freedom, that of each person's ability to freely respond to the gospel:

> The seventeenth century English and American Baptists were convinced that the proclamation of the gospel was predicated upon an uncoerced response. It was their unqualified conviction that the God revealed in Jesus Christ is a God of the invitation who invites the heavy laden to come to Him, but forces no one to accept the invitation. Coercion in matters of faith, Roger Williams warned the Puritans, in England and New England, makes hypocrites but no Christians. Only a voluntary response of faith in Christ under the convicting and converting power of the Holy Spirit results in genuine conversions. Thomas Helwys argued that religion is a personal matter between God and the individual, therefore, *"the King shall not answere for it, neither may the King be jugd betweene God and man. Let them be heretikes, Turks, Jewes or whatsoever, it ap-*

229

pertenynes not to the earthly power to punish them in the least measure." Such a concept of the gospel demands freedom from the coercive powers of both church and state.[339]

Thus we see that, for the Baptist, the free offer of the gospel, the personal invitation to come to Christ, is foundational to the call for a free church in a free state as far as religious liberty is concerned.

The emphasis on freedom in the New Testament is quite telling in this regard. Jesus said the truth would set us free. Paul, in his letter to the Galatians, maintains that believers are called to be free. Freedom from law and from sin and from death. Freedom in order to love. This is the state of life which is envisioned in the New Testament. The counterintuitive wisdom here is that we submit to our proper Lord, that is, God Himself through His Son, in order to be truly free; free from the tyranny of man and any temporary, worldly, self-glorifying system, however religious it may appear to be. Whether the Sanhedrin, the Roman Inquisition, the Puritan commonwealth, Anglican state church, Muslim caliphate, or any other religious state, even the modern totalitarian secular movement with its own progressive religiosity and twisted ethic—none of these are able to set a man free and accord him his proper God-given dignity. They are all tyrannical systems where cabals of elites control others in order to secure their own power, however pure their self-perceived motivations may be. The gate-keepers of favor and prosperity in any of these systems apportion to themselves the greatest part of the benefits, which they control in the name of God or Allah or The People or The Workers or "Democracy." Those who defy the system are persecuted, imprisoned, tortured, and liquidated.

It is instructive to note that the New Testament features the testimony of a former persecutor of the kind described above. This is found in the book of Galatians, a very personal and revealing letter written by the Apostle Paul. Paul testifies, "I advanced in Judaism beyond many of my contemporaries in my own nation."[340] Here, surely, is the ambitious man who gravitates toward power in his chosen belief system. He is also the 'true believer,' as Paul wrote that he saw himself as "more exceeding-

---

339 Estep, *Why Baptists?*, 39.
340 Galatians 1:14 (NKJV).

ly zealous for the traditions of my fathers" than even many of the most devoted of his fellow Israelites.[341] This portrait of his former self is the background for his persecuting career, which he describes as "my former conduct in Judaism, how I persecuted the church of God beyond measure and tried to destroy it."[342] It is for this reason that Paul refers to himself as the chief of sinners. Yet, as demonstrated in his own case, this acknowledgment of sin serves to accentuate the mercy and grace that are at the heart of the gospel Paul preached:

> And I thank Christ Jesus our Lord who has enabled me, because He counted me faithful, putting me into the ministry, although I was formerly a blasphemer, a persecutor, and an insolent man; but I obtained mercy because I did it ignorantly in unbelief. And the grace of our Lord was exceedingly abundant, with faith and love which are in Christ Jesus. This is a faithful saying and worthy of all acceptance, that Christ Jesus came into the world to save sinners, of whom I am chief. However, for this reason I obtained mercy, that in me first Jesus Christ might show all longsuffering, as a pattern to those who are going to believe on Him for everlasting life. Now to the King eternal, immortal, invisible, to God who alone is wise, be honor and glory forever and ever. Amen.[343]

Paul is trying to clarify in these passages in Galatians that the gospel is not just another system of man-made religious rules and devotion with a duly authorized elite ruling class, but is a word of forgiveness from heaven itself. It is because of pure mercy and love from Christ that this former persecutor of Christ and His people is forgiven, and then called to declare this "longsuffering" grace of God, the God who patiently offers us eternal life even in the face of our insolence. Thus both the persecutor and the persecuted are called to be freed by God's grace in Christ.

No human tradition, however prestigious, is capable of generating or maintaining this kind of freedom. The freedom of God's grace and re-

---

341 Galatians 1:14 (NKJV).
342 Galatians 1:13 (NKJV).
343 1Timothy 1:12-17 (NKJV).

newal into eternal life is not something any man or group of men can achieve. This is Paul's great contention as he opens his epistle to the Galatians: "As we have already said, so now I say again: If anybody is preaching to you a gospel other than what you accepted, let them be under God's curse! Am I now trying to win the approval of human beings, or of God? Or am I trying to please people? If I were still trying to please people, I would not be a servant of Christ. I want you to know, brothers and sisters, that the gospel I preached is not of human origin."[344] This gospel, then, is God's doing and is thus free from the despotic oppression of any human religious or ideological system. "For I neither received it from man, nor was I taught it," Paul says, "but it came through the revelation of Jesus Christ."[345] The source of the good news preached by Paul is no mere man, but God Himself and His beloved Son, whom He anointed our Savior. It is a salvation from heaven and not from this world.

This idea that Christ is the ultimate representation and revelation of God has always been one of the keys to Baptist faith, and to the New Testament emphasis on freedom from the traditions of men. William Estep writes concerning Baptist belief:

> Baptist confessions declare that Christ is the Son of God, born of the Virgin Mary, fully God and fully man, and therefore, incarnate deity. He came to reconcile us to God, not God to us, as Smyth so beautifully said, for [God] "did never hate us, nor was our enemy, but reconcileth us unto God (Art. 32)." In his life and sacrificial death, Christ revealed the God of love and infinite grace. *The confessions are one in declaring that in the person of Jesus Christ, his life, teachings, death, and resurrection, there was historically mediated the fullest and most complete revelation of God.* Therefore, he is the Mediator of the New Covenant and the fulfillment of the Law and the Prophets. It is Christ, not Moses that is God's last Word to man, for to him all authority is given in heaven and on earth (Matt. 28:18).[346]

---

344 Galatians 1:9-11 (NIV).
345 Galatians 1:12 (NKJV).
346 Emphasis added. Estep, *Why Baptists?*, 24.

Baptists, then, are clearly aligned with the New Testament and with the Apostle Paul in seeing Christ as the only and final truth. Even the great covenant traditions of Judaism are, for Paul, never to eclipse this greater revelation of God incarnate. The idea of going back to Moses and the law after the revealing of Christ is anathema. Moses was not able to provide the freedom that comes with the truth of Christ, the New Man. The law could only foreshadow and prefigure such great life-giving gifts which were to come. Paul bluntly upbraids the Galatians for toying with a retrograde tradition of human works: "You foolish Galatians! Who has bewitched you? Before your very eyes Jesus Christ was clearly portrayed as crucified. I would like to learn just one thing from you: Did you receive the Spirit by the works of the law, or by believing what you heard? Are you so foolish? After beginning by means of the Spirit, are you now trying to finish by means of the flesh?"[347] The theme of Galatians, then, is freedom. Freedom from human traditions that promote works-righteousness and freedom from the hopeless task of self-justification. The Spirit, Who gives life through spiritual rebirth, is given by grace through faith.

Works of the law, though the law is given by God Himself, were never meant to justify anyone. This was the major mistake of the man-made tradition of Judaism. Instead, says Paul, "Scripture foresaw that God would justify the Gentiles by faith, and announced the gospel in advance to Abraham: 'All nations will be blessed through you.' So those who rely on faith are blessed along with Abraham, the man of faith."[348] Faith was always the only path to God's favor, and the freedom He offers from sin and death, and thus Paul asserts, "The law is not based on faith."[349] He declares, "For all who rely on the works of the law are under a curse, as it is written: 'Cursed is everyone who does not continue to do everything written in the Book of the Law.' Clearly no one who relies on the law is justified before God, because 'the righteous will live by faith.'"[350] He then clinches his argument to the Galatians with a summarization of the good news: "Christ redeemed us from the curse of the law by becoming a curse for us, for it is written: 'Cursed is everyone who is hung on a pole.' He

---

347 Galatians 3:1-3 (NIV).
348 Galatians 3:8-9 (NIV).
349 Galatians 3:12 (NIV).
350 Galatians 3:10-11 (NIV).

redeemed us in order that the blessing given to Abraham might come to the Gentiles through Christ Jesus, so that by faith we might receive the promise of the Spirit."[351] "And where the Spirit of the Lord is, there is freedom."[352] And Life. But where straining for self-justification through human works is, there is bondage. And death.

This prodigious misapprehension, the attempt to establish one's own righteousness, is uncovered by Paul in his letter to the Romans. Regretfully, Paul writes, his own tradition, the Jewish religion, tended toward this spiritual dead end: "Brethren, my heart's desire and prayer to God for Israel is that they may be saved. For I bear them witness that they have a zeal for God, but not according to knowledge. For they being ignorant of God's righteousness, and seeking to establish their own righteousness, have not submitted to the righteousness of God. For Christ is the end of the law for righteousness to *everyone who believes.*"[353] Apparently, zeal alone isn't everything. The self-righteous pursuit described here by Paul appears to be a deadening, unimaginative zeal focused on the tiny powers of the self. It cannot lift its eyes to see the gifts the great King of all creation has to offer. In essence, self-exalting zeal is blinded to reality. As Paul writes, "It is fine to be zealous, provided the purpose is good."[354] But belief in Christ, who really is good, puts the endeavor to be righteous by one's own efforts to an end. To receive by faith the righteousness of God, Christ Himself, is to be on the solid ground of the truth, of the good news. And thus, the law is fulfilled by Christ on behalf of the believer. The one who has faith is free from his own works. He is also free from his own efforts to be happy or fulfilled by use of the merely temporary things of this world. He has been given the Spirit, God Himself, and a life which is readied for the eternal realm, the Father's house where Jesus, our wonderful mediator, prepares each a place. This is the promise of true freedom, which is only for the born-again, who not only see the Kingdom of God but personally enter into its wonderful reality. This is the freedom to live in the life and the light of God. To be what each of us was meant to be.

---

351 Galatians 3:13-14 (NIV).
352 2 Corinthians 3:17 (NIV).
353 Emphasis added. Romans 10:1-4 (NASB).
354 Galatians 4:18 (NIV).

The antithesis of God's promise in Christ is the deceitfulness and wickedness of those who want to win souls for themselves and their own grim and vulgar (worldly) purposes. The systems of the world and their "leaders" are, by definition, these malignant kinds of soul-winners. Paul describes them: "Those people are zealous to win you over, but for no good. What they want is to alienate you from us, so that you may have zeal *for them*."[355] In Paul's view, this was the program of the Judaizers. He describes them as those "who came in by stealth to spy out our liberty which we have in Christ Jesus, that they might bring us into bondage."[356] Any replacement for Christ operates in this way. Whether religious or secular, popery, caliphate, or utopian progressive, the goal is to sway men and women to commit to something that is less than Christ and which always leads to a great regression where human freedom is concerned. God's plan is infinitely better. Paul writes, "But when the fullness of the time had come, God sent forth His Son, born of a woman, born under the law, to redeem those who were under the law, that we might receive the adoption as sons. And because you are sons, God has sent forth the Spirit of His Son into your hearts, crying out, 'Abba, Father!' Therefore you are no longer a slave but a son, and if a son, then an heir of God through Christ."[357] So we are not just units in a futuristic system or denizens of a 'religious' nation, but heirs and sons of God Himself, whom we may, by Christ's sacrifice, call our Father. No wonder Paul exhorts his fellow believers to: "Stand fast therefore in the liberty by which Christ has made us free, and do not be entangled again with a yoke of bondage."[358]

So we can see that Paul knew first-hand how zeal for a religious system or ideology can turn the zealot from a mere proselytizer to a monstrous persecutor. The divine principle of freedom in Christ by faith is the foundation for the Baptist call for religious freedom and for the nobility of human freedom in the face of state power. But this divine freedom represents something even deeper: the freedom not only from bodily slavery or punishment, but freedom for our souls. Freedom from the slavery and darkness of sin. Freedom from the tyranny of the self and its insistence that

---

355 Emphasis added. Galatians 4:17 (NIV).
356 Galatians 2:4 (NKJV).
357 Galatians 4:4-7 (NKJV).
358 Galatians 5:1 (NKJV).

the whole universe, and all that is in it, bend to our own will and purposes, to our pompous personal agendas, our own insolent insecurities, in service of our own exaltation. Freedom, therefore, from the lie that I can be like God. What a heavy weight this mantle we undertake to wrap ourselves with becomes. We were never meant to be almighty judges. Yet we crave this power in our puffed-up inner man. What freedom to find ourselves simply children of our good Father! How appropriate and fitting it is simply to trust in Him and thank Him for His goodness and mercy. What a mighty and undeserved gift He gives His children, that when we see Him, Jesus our Savior, as He is, that we shall be like Him! It is too much. We, like Peter, on impulse cry out, "Go away from me Lord, because I am a sinner," and yet the generosity and bounty of God's grace and love are manifest in these gifts. This lowly and humble attitude is what true freedom is—allowing God to be our God in all His grace and greatness.

Perhaps freedom, then, is one of the keys to unveiling the distinctive value of Baptist principles. These are biblical precepts that Baptists are not easily persuaded to relinquish: that Scripture is the word of God Himself, and we thus need not bow to the counsel or bidding of any mere man where ultimate truth is concerned. And the ultimate truth is that salvation is received only through Christ, baptism being the symbol and image of His finished work and resurrection victory. Thus, we need not yield to the rites of any religious or ideological authority to intercede on our behalf, since the church, and therefore every believer, has already been established by God as a "spiritual house" and "a holy priesthood."[359] Scripture has already spoken and declares Jesus as the One Mediator. New Testament Baptism tells the story that God's chosen One has already interceded on my behalf, and I place *all my trust* in Him. It points to Christ as the only way, never to the water itself as a way to salvation. Freedom from ritual, with its never-ending religious observances and workings, is secured in the wonderful liberty to rest in Christ's completed work, which has God's full approval. This is the reason Paul asks, incredulously, why the Galatians, after knowing God and this freedom He offers, would "turn again to the weak and beggarly elements, to which you desire again to be in bondage."[360]

---

359 1 Peter 2:5.
360 Galatians 4:9 (NKJV).

Within the framework of Christian liberty, we can see, then, that baptism is not like circumcision.[361] It is the symbol of the freedom, which abides only in Christ, from all that is involved in trying to please God in my own power or in any fleshly observances which might be demanded by fleshly wisdom. Thus, baptism is the celebration of freedom already received by faith, not the initiation into any sort of burdensome religious contract. How very illuminating it is to find, in the long story of church history, so many groups of Christians making of it the latter. Human nature is often zealous for religious rites, which are controlled, and controlling, on a merely human level. The threat of being outside the church (the institution having been equated with salvation) has been the impetus to cast water upon the infant, who knows nothing about what is happening to him. This is the very antithesis of Paul's gospel of freedom. He is succinct in his rejection of the religious rites approach: "The only thing that counts is faith expressing itself through love."[362] Thus, the Baptist receives with joy those who, of their own volition, desire to express their faith by public baptism, freely uniting with the people of God.

Those who freely enter into salvation by faith, then, are marked in baptism by identification with Christ, who bought their salvation. This freedom, given by God, is the mark of the saints in the church, each saint a liberated, Spirit-indwelt man or woman in Christ, as Paul writes, "For you, brethren, have been called to liberty."[363] The church, this body of believers, then, has the right to rule itself. Baptists have always believed in congregational government. No outside or inside hierarchy is to impose itself upon the simple fellowship of believers. This frees the church from authoritarians of any stripe, be they secular powers and

---

361 Galatians 5: 2-6 (NIV): "Mark my words! I, Paul, tell you that if you let yourselves be circumcised, Christ will be of no value to you at all. Again I declare to every man who lets himself be circumcised that he is obligated to obey the whole law. You who are trying to be justified by the law have been alienated from Christ; you have fallen away from grace. For through the Spirit we eagerly await by faith the righteousness for which we hope. For in Christ Jesus neither circumcision nor uncircumcision has any value. The only thing that counts is faith expressing itself through love."

362 Galatians 5:6 (NIV).

363 Galatians 5:13 (NKJV).

politicians, self-appointed hierophantic hierarchies, theological dandies, prigs, and pedants, or pharisaical sacerdotal functionaries. This principle is reinforced by the first key Baptist precept: that formidable and foundational fortress named Scriptural authority, of which Jesus himself and all the apostles are the great exemplars. That watchword, *scripture alone*, has the ring of liberty for Baptist ears, liberating God's people from all human oppression in spiritual matters, and heralding the ultimate authority of its Author in *all* matters. Jesus asked, 'Have you not read the Scriptures?' Peter declared that in Jesus 'we have the prophetic word confirmed, which you do well to heed as a light that shines in a dark place.' And thus, Paul warned, 'Do not go beyond what is written.' Baptists, then, have ever been ready to stake all on an unwavering allegiance to this inscripturated authority: the word of the greatest of all Potentates, He who is Alpha and Omega, the Beginning and the End.